The Fighting Fourth

A Personal Narrative of the History of 4 Kumaon

The Fighting Fourth

A Personal Narrative of the History of 4 Kumaon

Brigadier Jasbir Singh, SM

OCCAM

www.bluone.ink

Title – The Fighting Fourth: A Personal Narrative of the History of 4 Kumaon
Author – Jasbir Singh
ISBN – 978-81-949547-5-0
Edition – I

Published by –
BluOne India LLP

Publisher's Address –
306, Tower-I, Assotech Business Cresterra,
Plot No. 22, Sector 135, Noida.

Website – www.bluone.ink
Email – publisher@bluone.ink

Printed in India at Thomson Press (India) Ltd.

OCCAM

To

my dear wife, Sabrina

CONTENTS

Author's Note

On finding a number of interesting features linked to the history of the Fighting Fourth, I decided to write a book but kept putting it off until now. This book contains a personal narrative of the long history of the highly decorated and fine old infantry battalion—4th Battalion, The Kumaon Regiment, or 4 Kumaon. The Battalion is a vast treasure-trove of history that I feel needs to be carefully probed and retold.

Many years ago, while sitting with my father by the crackling fireplace at the family farm, he had surprised me by stating, 'You know, Jasbir, I think we are the only father-son duo in the unit's history to have been both decorated for gallantry! Also, there is so much of the unit's history that needs to be properly probed and recorded. It is your time now, and you must do it.'

That is the time I was motivated to write this book. But it got inordinately delayed as I went about my life as a soldier and commanded the 3 Kumaon (Rifles). Finally, after my retirement from the Service, I have found time to write the book.

Brigadier Jasbir Singh, SM
'Three Feathers Farm'
Village Devipur, District Nainital
Uttarakhand
August 2021

A Brief History of the Fighting Fourth

'Fighting Fourth' or 4th Battalion, The Kumaon Regiment (4 Kumaon) was raised by Salabat Khan Bahadur, Nawab of Ellichpur (now called Achalpur, Maharashtra, India), in 1788. The Nawab raised a force of 1,500 cavalry and a regiment of infantry (two battalions) to maintain order in Berar and to protect the northern borders of the princely state of Hyderabad. 4 Kumaon is the sole surviving infantry unit of this force raised by Nawab Salabat Khan Bahadur. Through the ages, the Battalion has borne the following designations:

Salabat Khan Bahadur,
Nawab of Ellichpur

1788 – 1st Battalion Salabat Khan Regiment

1804 – 1st Battalion Ellichpur Brigade Nizam's Contingent

1826 – 7th Regiment of Infantry, Nizam's Army

1853 – 5th Infantry, Hyderabad Contingent

1903 – 98th Infantry

1921 – 4th Battalion, 19th Indian Infantry Group

1922 – 4th Battalion, 19th Hyderabad Regiment

1945 – 4th Battalion, 19th Kumaon Regiment

1945 – 4th Battalion, The Kumaon Regiment

Ever since the Battalion's raising in 1788, it has fought with distinction and gloriously etched its name in the pages of history, with honour and pride. In early times it took part in local operations around Ellichpur and Berar, followed by the Maratha War 1803, Pindari War 1817, operations against Bhils and Arabs in 1853, Rohilla War in 1854 and capture of Jhansi in 1857–58. The first Commandant of the Battalion, Major Drew, was killed in action while fighting Pindaris in Central India. In 1900, the unit was selected to join the China Expeditionary Force and it sailed to Hong Kong (China) to quell the Boxer Rebellion. On its return to India in 1902, it was permitted to bear the inscription 'China 1900' on its colours for distinguished service in China.

5th Infantry, Hyderabad Contingent (1853–1902); 98th Infantry (1903–1921); 4th Battalion, 19th Hyderabad Regiment (1922–1947); 4th Battalion, The Kumaon Regiment (1947–date)

At the outbreak of the Great War or World War I, the Battalion sailed from Bombay (now Mumbai) to Mombasa as a part of Indian Expeditionary Force 'B'. This was in October 1915. It fought in the Battle of Tanga and went on to operate very successfully against German-led forces, for the next 26 months, in the Lake Victoria District. After these operations, the Battalion returned to India in 1917. The following year, the Battalion went abroad for the third time to join the East Persia Cordon. It also took part in the Third Afghan War in 1919.

In 1923, 4th Battalion, 19th Hyderabad Regiment was among the first few units selected for 'Indianization', Indians being commissioned as officers for the first time. The first King's Commissioned Indian Officer (KCIO) to join the unit, on 17 October 1924, was 2nd Lieutenant Har Bishen Singh Brar. Thereafter, a number of Indian officers joined the unit including Satyawant Mallanna Shrinagesh and Kodandera Subayya Thimayya, who both rose to become Chief of Army Staff (COAS) of the Indian Army. Some of the other senior Indian officers who joined the Battalion in the 1920s and 1930s were K. Daulat Sen; K. R. Nagar; Mohammed Isfakul Majid (later, a Major General in the

Pakistan Army); Muhammad Azam Khan (later, a Lieutenant General in the Pakistan Army and Governor of East Pakistan, which after the Liberation War in 1971 was to become Bangladesh); Niranjan Singh Gill (veteran of Indian National Army or INA, Colonel and Ambassador of India); Brigadier Apji Randhir Singh (only Indian Gentleman Cadet to be awarded Gold Medal and multiple 'Sports Blues' at Royal Military College, Sandhurst, UK); Major General K. Bhagwati Singh (IC-1, the first officer to be commissioned from Indian Military Academy, Dehradun); Brigadier Balbir Singh, MC (IC-60, fought in the bitter battles in Malaya, 1941, with 'B' Company); Brigadier Pritam Singh, MC (known as 'Saviour of Poonch');[1] and Lieutenant General M. M. Khanna, MVC (commanded the unit during operations in Kashmir, 1947–48, till he was seriously wounded in battle).[2] The Battalion went abroad for the fourth time in 1926. It went to Iraq and returned to India in 1928.

World War II saw the Battalion engaged in ferocious action in the jungles of Malaya and Burma. The men fought heroically under extremely trying conditions and earned battle honours for their determined actions in the ferocious battles in North Malaya and at Slim River. 4th Battalion, 19th Hyderabad Regiment suffered heavily and seven officers, seven junior commissioned officers (JCOs) and 251 other ranks (OR) were killed while two officers, eight JCOs and 358 OR were wounded. The unit was granted battle honours of 'North Malaya' and 'Slim River'. Thereafter, the unit fought in the Battle of Singapore, which was lost to Japanese forces with heavy casualties to the Battalion. After the battle, the Battalion was interned in Japanese prisoner-of-war camps in Singapore, where it lost many officers and men due to sickness and terrible atrocities committed on the prisoners by the Japanese forces.

On 15 August 1941, 8th Battalion, 19th Hyderabad Regiment was raised at Agra, under Lieutenant Colonel E. M. Koch to meet the increasing manpower demands of World War II. After intensive training in the jungles of Central India, under Lieutenant Colonel F. W. Gibb,

[1] Balbir, Pritam and Lieutenant G. S. Parab gallantly escaped a Japanese POW camp in Singapore and reached India after being recaptured twice on the way back, over a period of six months in enemy territory and were awarded the Military Cross (MC).

[2] He was saved by a Kashmiri civilian named Zuma Mohammed, who was later awarded Vir Chakra, the first Indian civilian to be so honoured.

the unit proceeded to the Arakan Area in Burma. Here, withdrawing Japanese forces were being tackled in bitter battles. When Gibb was wounded during enemy shelling, Lieutenant Colonel K. S. Thimayya assumed command of 8/19 Hyderabad Regiment. Thimayya won a great victory in the Battle of Kangaw. For his gallant services during the battle, Thimayya was decorated with Distinguished Service Order (DSO) and went on to be the only Indian officer to command a brigade in World War II. The unit was awarded Battle Honour 'Kangaw'. After the war ended in 1945, 19th Hyderabad Regiment was renamed as 19th Kumaon Regiment, for a short while. However, in 1945 the title was changed to The Kumaon Regiment and the figure '19' was dropped. The newly named regiment was provided the 'lion crest' taken from the coat of arms of Sir Henry Russell, erstwhile Resident of Hyderabad State.

As 4th Battalion, 19th Hyderabad Regiment had suffered debilitating casualties during the severe battles in Malaya and Singapore, it was decided to boost its strength by merging trained manpower from 'war raised' units of 19 Hyderabad Regiment which were to be disbanded.

Thus, the 'Eighth'[3] (8th Battalion, 19th Hyderabad Regiment/8th Battalion, 19th Kumaon Regiment or 8 Kumaon) was disbanded and almost its entire manpower, including the war history and Battle Honour 'Kangaw'[4] became a part of 'Fourth', which also received manpower from the 'Ninth'—similarly disbanded as it was another 'war raised' unit.

Shortly after Independence, newly formed Pakistan tried to seize Jammu and Kashmir (J&K) by surreptitiously sending hordes of armed tribal raiders who were strengthened with Pakistan Army personnel who were ostensibly on leave. The whole web of deceit had British complicity and far-flung areas such as Gilgit and Skardu also fell as Muslim

[3] After the Chinese Aggression of 1962, the need was felt for more troops and thus some additional infantry battalions were raised. In 1963, a new battalion was raised for the Kumaon Regiment, but by some strange quirk of fate it was given the designation of 8 Kumaon, which was same as the unit that had earlier been disbanded and ceased to exist!

[4] 4 Kumaon used to celebrate 'Kangaw Day' as a Battle Honour Day on 7 February each year till 1974, when it began to celebrate the more recent battle honour of 'Srinagar' on 3 November to honour Major Somnath Sharma's 'PVC Action' at Badgam (Srinagar airfield). As per existing orders, a battle honour may be celebrated by any unit of the regiment. Thus, today Battle Honour 'Kangaw' is honourably celebrated by 8 Kumaon.

The Kumaon Regiment 'lion crest' was taken from the coat of arms of Sir Henry Russell, erstwhile Resident of Hyderabad State. The first 'Crest of Kumaon Regiment' presented to 4 Kumaon by Lt Col Balbir Singh, MC, Commandant, Kumaon Regimental Centre, Ranikhet, is presently displayed in the Officers' Mess, 4 Kumaon.

troops deserted the State Force garrisons. To tackle this burgeoning threat, the Battalion was airlifted to Kashmir in October 1947, where it made history at Badgam and subsequent battles in Kashmir valley. During the next fourteen months of tough campaigning, 4 Kumaon inflicted 1,478 casualties on the belligerent enemy. The unit lost one officer, two JCOs and 55 OR during these operations, while one officer, three JCOs and 88 OR were seriously wounded in the bitter actions.

Lt Col (later Lt Gen.) M. M. Khanna, MVC

Maj. Somnath Sharma, PVC

The unit was awarded Battle Honour 'Srinagar' and 57 awards for bravery, including one Param Vir Chakra (PVC), three Maha Vir Chakras (MVCs), 13 Vir Chakras (VrCs), one Bar to VrC and other awards. The gallant actions of the unit saved Kashmir Valley for the Indian Union and changed the course of history in the region. Major Somnath Sharma was posthumously awarded India's first PVC, the highest award for gallantry. Lieutenant Colonel (later Lieutenant General) M. M. Khanna, Naik Nar Singh and Sepoy Diwan Singh won the MVC. Interestingly, Pakistan's first Nishan-e-Haider, the country's highest award for gallantry, was awarded posthumously to Captain Raja Muhammad Sarwar Bhatti, who lost his life – with his company suffering heavy casualties – while trying unsuccessfully to wrest Pt 9108 from 'D' Company, 4 Kumaon commanded by Major Nirvair Singh. It was the same company that had earlier fought a successful, defensive battle at Badgam on 3 November 1947 with Company

Commander, Major Somnath Sharma, posthumously being awarded India's first PVC.

Lt Col (later Brig.) T. B. Kapur, Commanding Officer, 4 Kumaon, at Gaza

In 1959–60 the unit served with United Nations Emergency Force at Gaza, United Arab Republic, under Lieutenant Colonel (later Brigadier) Teg Bahadur Kapur, and earned a name for itself, due to its praiseworthy conduct. On its return to India, 4 Kumaon became the first unit to be presented with regimental colours by Dr Rajendra Prasad, President of India, at Ranikhet on 8 April 1961. Soon there was increasing tension with China along the northern borders, and thus 'D' Company under Major Nasim Arthur Salick, VrC, with Lieutenant D. S. Sandhanwalia, was sent to the Himalayan borders at Munshiari and Shialekh. Thereafter, the unit moved to Tangdhar Sector, J&K, where on promotion, Salick assumed command of the unit.

Just before the India–Pakistan War, 1965, began 4 Kumaon faced the scourge of infiltrators unleashed by Pakistan and lost 11 men killed of 'A' Company who had been guarding a bridge at Kralpura near Trehgam in J&K. Then the unit went on the offensive and attacked in Tangdhar Sector of J&K, capturing a sheer and well-defended hill feature known as Pt 9018 (renamed as 'Kumaon Hill'). 4 Kumaon captured entire Bugina Bulge[5] and destroyed a vital bridge over Kishenganga River at Jura. The destruction of Jura Bridge took place as the result of an audacious and historic trans-border raid. The unique raid was conducted in battalion strength and the troops were launched on an unsuspecting enemy over extremely difficult and unchartered, high-altitude terrain of the Shamshabari Ridge. The enemy forces literally ran away to save their lives when they were struck by the unit that

[5] Today, Pakistan has numerous terrorist camps in Pakistan Occupied Kashmir or POK and it resorts to regular infiltration of terrorists into India. The infiltration is mainly conducted through the areas that were captured (Area Bugina Bulge) and then returned by India.

had suddenly appeared through the swirling mists and from a totally unexpected direction. Not wanting to suffer more casualties, the Jura Bridge was destroyed by fire of a 106 mm recoilless (RCL) gun at the 7th round. The heavy gun and its ammunition had been brought from Haji Pir Pass (1 Para) by jeep and then carried up manually from Tangdhar Valley.

Despite the fact that areas held by the enemy were captured after great travails and many casualties suffered, sadly, after the bitter and successful battle, the astonished troops were ordered to vacate the captured areas (now called Pakistan Occupied Kashmir or POK) and withdraw after returning the captured areas to a belligerent Pakistan. The Battalion won Battle Honour 'Sanjoi–Mirpur' for its tremendous actions. The troops won five VrCs and two Sena Medals (SMs) for gallantry during these operations.

In 1969, the unit proceeded from Kapurthala to the Counter-Insurgency and Jungle Warfare School, Vairengte, Mizoram, for counter-insurgency training. Thereafter, 4 Kumaon was inducted into Nagaland and it conducted intensive operations against the hostile Naga Army. In September 1971, the Battalion was moved from Nagaland for operations against Pakistan Army in East Pakistan. The outlawed Federal Government of Nagaland (NFG) declared a ceasefire, thus allowing some units to move out of Nagaland and proceed for operations to East Pakistan (now Bangladesh).

The India–Pakistan War, 1971, broke out on 3 December and the unit undertook successful, offensive operations in Sylhet Sector of East Pakistan. For outstanding operations during the 1971 War, the Battalion was awarded Battle Honour 'Shamshernagar', along with three VrCs, one SM and other awards. It was a major achievement as the unit had won a battle honour in all the three wars since Independence: 'Srinagar' after 1947–48 operations, 'Sanjoi–Mirpur' after the 1965 War and 'Shamshernagar' after 1971 War.

On its return to Nagaland after the 1971 War, the unit carried out intensive operations and broke the back of the Naga insurgency movement for independence from the Republic of India. 4 Kumaon was awarded the coveted trophy for 'Best Battalion'. It was decorated for the large number of Naga hostiles it had either killed or captured, out of 23 infantry battalions in the formation. After the long tenure in the jungles of Nagaland, the unit had a tenure in Digiana, Jammu, and then it moved to the high-altitude areas of Tangdhar (J&K), for the second time. In 1979, after 10 years of continuous service in difficult field areas, including a war in East Pakistan, savage counter-insurgency operations in the deep jungles of Nagaland and two tenures in J&K, the Military Special train carrying 4 Kumaon finally steamed into Dehra Dun Railway Station. It had been a long and action filled decade since the unit was seen off at Kapurthala railway station by Lieutenant General Premindra Singh Bhagat, VC, General Officer Commanding the Corps HQ at Jalandhar, in 1969.

Six officers who have either served in the unit or commanded the unit, have been 'Colonel of the Regiment' (19th Hyderabad Regiment and Kumaon Regiment). These officers are Major General Sydney Buxton Pope, CB, DSO; General K. S. Thimayya, DSO; Lieutenant General Kanwar Bahadur Singh, MBE; Lieutenant General P. N. Kathpalia, PVSM, AVSM; Lieutenant General Madan Mohan Lakhera PVSM, AVSM; Major General Surendra Shah, PVSM, AVSM, VrC and Lieutenant General Satyevir Yadav, PVSM, AVSM.

The unit has continued to forge ahead in all fields. In April 1984, 4 Kumaon was the pioneer unit among Indian forces to occupy the dizzy heights of Bilafond La, on Siachen Glacier and defeat determined enemy attacks that were launched from their base at Ali Brangza (POK).

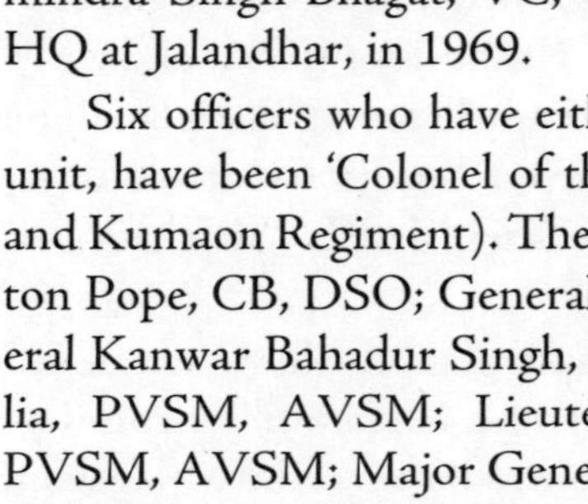

The Bicentenary Logo

After its tenure as the pioneer unit on Siachen Glacier, 4 Kumaon moved to Ranikhet for the second time. After the restful tenure at Ranikhet, the unit moved once again to Jammu where it celebrated its bi-centenary in February 1988[6].

General Krishnaswamy Sundarji, COAS, was the Reviewing Officer at the Bicentenary Ceremonial Parade.

---

[6] After the bicentenary in February 1988, the author was posted to Indian Peace Keeping Force (IPKF) in Sri Lanka as GSO-1 (Operations) of IPKF. He later commanded 3 Kumaon (Rifles). Thus, this book ends around the year 1988.

Reorganization of Hyderabad Contingent

Sikander Jah, the sixth Nizam of Hyderabad (1803–1829).

In 1803, Mir Akbar Ali Khan (Sikander Jah, Asaf Jah III) ascended the throne of Hyderabad on the death of his father Mir Nizam Ali Khan (Nizam-ul-Mulk, Asaf Jah II). Sikander Jah extended vigorous cooperation to his British allies against the common enemy—the Marathas. Consequently, on the conclusion of the Second Anglo-Maratha War (1803–4), the entire province of Berar was made over to the Nizam by the British as reward for his assistance and loyalty. The British would soon launch a concerted multi-directional attack against the Pindaris, who were notorious freebooters and terrorized large tracts around Berar and central India. The troops furnished by the Nizam for the Pindari War (1817–18),[1] were in accordance with the Treaty of 1800[2] and amounted to 5,000 infantry. Of these, two battalions, of 900 troops each, were from

[1] After the regular Maratha forces had been broken up in the campaigns of 1803–5, the Pindaris made their headquarters in Malwa, under the tacit protection of the rulers of Gwalior and Indore. The Pindari War (1817–18) which was nothing other than the Third Anglo-Maratha War was the invasion of the Malwa in pursuit of the Pindaris by the British governor-general, Lord Hastings.

[2] Nizam-ul-Mulk, Asaf Jah II, the fifth Nizam of Hyderabad, entered into the Treaty on 12 October 1800 with the East India Company, extending British rule to Hyderabad State. The administration would now be indirectly controlled by the British Resident posted at the Nizam's court.

the 'Salabat Khan Regiment'[3] and the remainder were from the Nizam's own establishment of regular troops. They consisted of six battalions of infantry. Four of these units were stationed in Berar itself, while two were in Hyderabad. These units were commanded by European officers, who possessed the local or acting rank of Major (that came without seniority or pay).

In 1806, several units in Berar were under the personal command of one nobleman named Raja Mahipat Ram.[4] These units were the remnants of Monsieur Raymond's[5] force. The troops were dressed in French uniforms and were disciplined and exercised with French words of command. Naturally, the men were attached to the French cause and their dispositions were encouraged by Raja Mahipat Ram. So much so that, when an English officer by the name of Draper was desirous of introducing English drill exercises and words of command, the sepoys peremptorily refused to comply with the order. The officer was obliged to concede to prevent a general mutiny by the troops. At the time, the person who really commanded the force and had considerable influence was Colonel Don Clementi di Avila. He was a Spaniard, who was faithfully attached to Raja Mahipat Ram and quite hostile to the British cause. There were also many Europeans and soldiers of mixed races that were distributed among the units in Berar and were mostly under the control of Clementi.

For his part, Monsieur Raymond was popular and when he died, the Nizam had an elegant tomb built near Asman Garh Palace on top of a hillock at Musa Ram Bagh (Musa Ram being a corrupted form of Monsieur Raymond), Malakpet, in east Hyderabad. This is about 3 km from the present-day Chaderghat Bridge, then known as the Oliphant Bridge. Until about 1940, people would visit Raymond's tomb on the anniversary of his death (25 March), taking incense and other offerings with them. The Nizam would send to his tomb a box of cheroots and a bottle of beer. His grave had become a shrine.

---

[3] The 1st Battalion Salabat Khan Regiment which Nawab Salabat Khan of Ellichpur raised in 1788 is the progenitor of 4 Kumaon.

[4] The Nizam had appointed his own Subedar over Berar in consultation with the British Resident at Hyderabad. Raja Mahipat Ram was the first Subedar.

[5] A French general in the Nizam's military, Michel Joachim Marie Raymond (25 September 1755 – 25 March 1798) was popularly known as Monsieur Raymond and became a close friend of the fifth Nizam, Asaf Jah II.

Reorganization

Sir Henry Russell, the Resident of Hyderabad[6] was concerned about the future behaviour of these troops, and in a letter dated 10 December 1806 he put forward proposals for the dismissal of some of the officers then in the various units, including Clementi himself. It was a general scheme for the reorganization of units. However, it was not until 1812 when one or two serious mutinies broke out amongst the two regiments stationed at Hyderabad, that the Resident set about vigorously initiating reforms and reorganization. So, the men in the two mutinous regiments who had remained faithful were drafted into a corps which was being raised by a certain Captain Larride. These two regiments subsequently formed the famous Russell's Brigade[7] and were afterwards known as the 1st and the 2nd Infantry, Hyderabad Contingent.

The attention of government was now directed to the reorganization of the Nizam's regular infantry stationed in Berar. These troops were placed under the Political Agent who was given a staff officer to assist him in his military duties.

The Resident of Hyderabad was anxious for reform and was desirous that the entire force should be reorganized, brought up to strength, and properly equipped. But as this would take much time and as many difficulties stood in the way, it was decided to introduce the reforms gradually and to limit them to the four battalions which composed the first and the second brigades. The remaining battalions were to be left under native officers of the local government.

The battalions which were the best disciplined, were first equipped with the latest weapons and supplied with ammunition for their guns and small arms from the Company's arsenal. In September 1814 an order was issued which is said to be the first regarding the new organization of these regiments. As per this order, the force was equally divided into two units. The units had heavy organizations and each one had two

---

[6] The lion in the present crest of Kumaon Regiment has been taken from Sir Henry Russells' Coat of Arms.

[7] Established by Sir Henry Russell, Resident of Hyderabad in 1813 for the princely state. It fought in the Third Anglo-Maratha War (Pindari War) and later during World War 1 under a different designation.

British officers, two British non-commissioned officers (NCOs), 20 Indian officers and about 1,000 men. In addition, there were about ten attached personnel. Each unit had the following establishment:

Regular personnel:

Commandant	[British Captain/Major/Civilian]
Adjutant	1 [British Lieutenant]
Sergeant-Major	1 [British NCO]
Quarter-Master Sergeant	1 [British NCO]
Subedars	10
Jemadars	10
Havildars	56
Naiks	68
Drummers and Pipers	20
Buglers	8
Pakalies (general duty soldiers)	10
Sepoys	800
Armourer	1
Blacksmith	1
Bellowsboy	1

Attached personnel (approximately 10):

Carpenter	1
Chuckler	1
First Dresser	1
Second Dresser	1
Dhobies (washermen)	3
Hajjams (barbers)	3

The result of these reforms as regards the infantry was that four of the battalions were reorganized and formed into brigades as follows:

1st Brigade [two battalions]

2nd Brigade [two battalions]

These four battalions were afterwards clubbed together and known as the 1st Berar Infantry. The battalions were re-numbered as 3rd, 4th, 5th and 6th Battalions of Nizam's Infantry in 1826. Eventually in 1854, when the Hyderabad Contingent was formed, the 3rd and 4th Battalions became the Hyderabad Contingent, while the 5th and 6th Battalions were disbanded. In 1817 the immediate superintendence of the troops in Berar was taken out of the hands of the Political Agent and the cavalry and infantry were placed under the command of two officers of the Company's service, who were specially selected for this important duty by the Governor-General. But the general control of the whole army still remained in the hands of the Political Agent.

During this period bodies of troops either took their names from the brigade in which they served or the areas where they were located, beyond which they rarely moved except to go on active service. Major Robert Pitman, a distinguished officer of the Company's service (who had earlier proceeded on a dangerous mission to Kabul), was appointed to the general command of the Nizam's infantry in Berar. On 14 June 1817 the Resident of Hyderabad submitted to Sir Thomas Hislop, Commander-in-Chief of the Madras Army, the following report regarding the composition of the four battalions in Berar:

> *The strength of the four battalions is shown in the attached return. Major Pitman of the Company's service has arrived in Hyderabad to take command of them but has not yet had time to join. I have not seen these corps myself but they are well spoken of by those who have frequently been on service and have always done their duty. They are commanded by European officers and are disciplined, armed, and clothed and equipped like our own troops.*

As already stated, the general control of the troops in Berar had been given to the Political Agent, who at the time was Captain Thomas Sydenham, with Lieutenant Parker of the Madras Cavalry as Brigade Major to assist him in his military duties while Pitman was placed in immediate command of the troops. The instructions to these officers were embodied in a letter to Sydenham dated 1 September 1817 as follows:

> *The Governor-General in Council having been pleased to sanction the appointment of Major Pitman of the Bengal establishment to the general command of the Nizam's Infantry in Berar. I have directed him to proceed to Aurangabad with you and have the honour to enclose a copy of the instructions with which I have furnished him. My instructions to Major Pitman and Captain Davis prescribe the general course that is to be observed on such points as are likely to occur in the discharge of your respective duties.*
>
> *I am persuaded that a mutual spirit of conciliation and common zeal for the interests of the public service will prevent any inconvenient collision of authority, and if a question should arise which has not been sufficiently provided for, it must be made the subject of a reference to the Resident.*
>
> *With regard to the rank of the different officers employed under Major Pitman and Captain Davis, those who bear commissions from either His Majesty or the Honourable Company are to have precedence over those who do not hold such commissions. But, as it is due to the senior officers of the Nizam's service to consult their professional feeling as far as possible, it is desirable that, in concert with Major Pitman and Captain Davis, care should be taken to avoid employing them on the same detachment with any of the juniors amongst those officers who, by this rule, would take command of them.*

From the appointment of Major Pitman to the command of the troops in Berar, great advantages were expected. But owing to the close approach of the Pindari Wars, no reforms of any importance could be carried out and only preparations for the impending operations were undertaken.

It must not be imagined that the troops in Berar were living a life of ease in their cantonment, as in 1814 we find that the battalion of the Nizam's Regular Infantry stationed at Jaipur Katbi was employed in guarding the passes against the Pindaris. Again, in March 1817, a regiment of regular infantry, with Reformed Horse and a few pieces of ordnance, moved from Aurangabad under command of Major Elliott against the bandits who were called Naiks, and were infesting the districts of Central Berar. This force, after a siege of twenty-six hours, captured Warur, one of the strongest forts of Laxman Naik, their leader and his principal place of residence. Saorgaon and Dukipur, two formidable forts belonging to him, were also taken, as well as twelve smaller forts.

Unit Action During the Pindari War

In 1804, the 'Salabat Khan Regiment' had been reorganized and renamed as 'Ellichpur Brigade, Nizam's Contingent'. The Brigade had two infantry units and a cavalry unit. One of the infantry units was called 1st Battalion, Ellichpur Brigade, which is today 4th Battalion, The Kumaon Regiment (or 4 Kumaon), with more than 230 years of unbroken service. The cavalry unit is called Deccan Horse or 9 Horse.

Between 1811 and 1815, Ellichpur Brigade was launched twice in operations against the Pindaris, who were robbers and freebooters infesting the Deccan and its neighbouring areas in large bands. The Brigade was commanded by an Englishman named Major Drew. He had a fine reputation of being a just and balanced commander. Importantly, the soldiers of Ellichpur Brigade were regularly paid their salary, which was a rarity in those early times. However, the credit of maintaining well-trained and contented soldiers of the Brigade goes entirely to the far thinking and industrious ruler of Ellichpur (today's Achalpur, located south-west of Nagpur), Nawab Salabat Khan Bahadur.

Raiders of the Malwa

The Pindaris were irregular horsemen, plunderers or foragers attached to the Maratha and Mughal armies, primarily as guides. They were allowed to ride with the Mughal armies and plunder outlying villages, in lieu of being paid a salary for their work as guides. The Pindaris also followed the Maratha bands that raided Mughal territory from the late seventeenth-century onwards. With the collapse of the Mughal Empire in the eighteenth-century, their Pindari camp followers organized themselves in groups and attached to one of the leading Maratha chiefs, whose reach spread all the way to north India.

After the regular forces of Marathas had been broken up by the British in the Second Maratha War of 1803–5, the Pindaris made their headquarters in Malwa, under the tacit protection of the rulers of Gwalior and Indore. But as those chiefs themselves grew weak at the end of the century, the Pindaris became largely a 'law unto themselves' and began to conduct raids from hideouts in central India.

Though a majority of Pindari leaders were Muslims, they recruited brigands of all classes and religions. The ancestors of the Pindaris had probably come from Bijapur in the Deccan. They were augmented by some Pathans and Rohillas who were already present in central India. The Pindaris served as auxiliaries in the army of Aurangzeb, the Mughal emperor. They were freebooters looking for easy gain, and mounted raiders who plundered and burnt down villages. Pindaris acquired a reputation of great cruelty and they were universally feared by common folk all over the towns and villages of central India.

Every year, the Pindaris assembled in the month of November to set forth over British-held territory in search of plunder. They selected their target areas in advance and then launched their raids. In one such raid on the Masulipatam coast, they plundered 339 villages, killed or wounded 682 persons, tortured 3,600 others, and carried off much valuable property. In 1808–9, they plundered Gujarat and in 1812 it was

Atrocities committed by Pindari freebooters

the turn of Mirzapur. By 1814 their numbers had grown between 25,000 and 30,000 horsemen. More than half of them were well-armed and the Pindari forces were ever increasing in their numbers. The terrible cruelty that Pindaris vented on the poor villagers, who had not fled in fear, was most primitive and beastly.

In a dispatch to the government, Sir Henry Russell, British Resident in Hyderabad, mentioned:

> *... two regular battalions belonging to Salabat Khan are very respectable Corps. They are commanded by an Englishman of the name of Drew, who has a few other Englishmen employed as officers under him. The men are dressed like our sepoys, armed with our muskets and what is of much greater importance than anything else, they are regularly paid.*

Soon, the vile practices of the Pindaris became intolerable and in 1816 the British organized a widespread campaign for their destruction which resulted in the Pindari War (1817–18). The Pindaris were targeted by a massive force of about 120,000 men that had converged from far-flung areas like Bengal, Madras, the Deccan and even Gujarat. The overall operations were conducted under the supreme command of the

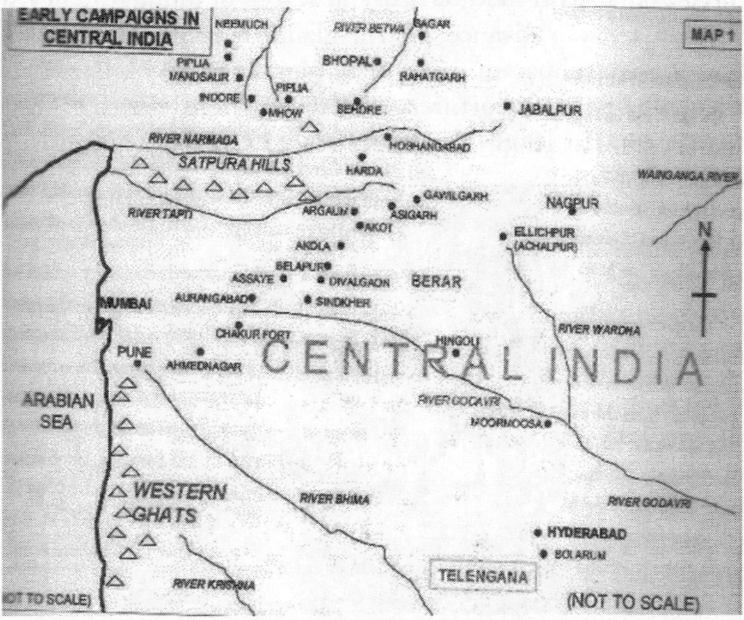

Sketch map of central India

governor general, Lord William Hastings. Considering the limited resources of transportation, coordination and communications available during those early times, the operation was truly a massive effort. The Pindaris' protectors in Gwalior were the first ones to be overcome and they signed a peace treaty with the British in 1817. Their other allies against the British also took up arms and were separately defeated, one after the other.[1] The main Pindari forces offered little resistance and most of their leaders tamely surrendered and their followers quietly dispersed to their homes.

Battle of Moormoosa

At the end of August 1814, orders were received for troops of Ellichpur Brigade to carry out operations against Pindaris in Telangana. Both the battalions of Nawab Salabat Khan were readied for operations and under Major Drew a force was ordered to tackle the Pindari brigands that had been reported to be lurking in the hills near Moormoosa, Telangana. Moormoosa is a small town located north of Hyderabad and along River Godavari. As ordered, a strong detachment moved out of Ellichpur under Major Drew to tackle the Pindari brigands. In those days, move of troops was a slow process and the snaking columns generally moved during the hours of daylight. Troops marched in loose formations and British officers rode on horseback alongside the columns, to maintain order, discipline and ensure the right marching speed. Well before it was dark, the column of troops would halt for the night near a village. Sentries were posted, cooking fires were lit and food was prepared both for the evening meal and next day as well. While the meal was being cooked, small parties were sent out to sneak into the nearby villages and gain information about any Pindari brigands in the area.

The monsoon rains had earlier come down on the region and so it was a cool night. While the troops were halted and resting, Drew confirmed from villagers that the large Pindari force was lurking among the rocky outcrops and hills near Moormoosa. The low hills had plenty of

[1] As part of the preparations for launching his campaign against the Pindaris, Lord Hastings concluded the Treaty of Gwalior with Daulat Rao Sindhia on 5 November 1817. Under this both parties to the treaty would deploy their forces from the Pindaris, with Sindhia deploying 5,000 horsemen against the Pindaris and desist from helping them in any way.

cover because of the abundance of dry grass and bushes on the slopes and valleys. In addition, large boulders of dark volcanic rock were strewn over the gentle slopes. The boulders and tall grass provided ample cover and great opportunities for concealment and ambush. Horses of the Pindaris had been sheltered in a shallow re-entrant, where there was a lot of rich, green grass on either side of a shallow water course. There were a few tribal villages in the valleys and the Pindaris regularly obtained information and rations from the simple village folk.

On that fateful August morning, the column of Ellichpur Brigade began its move early, after the morning meal had been cooked and eaten. The evening meal would be cooked and consumed when the troops returned to camp after the day's fighting was over. The move forward was led by a few scouts who advanced on foot well ahead of the column, from one set of rocks and trees to another. These scouts knew their job well and when they did not see any enemy, they waved forward the main body of troops. Major Drew and two British officers on horseback cantered up the slope to gain the high ground. They knew that once on the hilltop they would be able to observe the slopes that descended to the other side of the rise, and then move the soldiers in preparation for a skirmish with the Pindari force.

The forewarned Pindaris had anticipated such a move, for as described earlier they had left their horses in a nearby ravine under the care of a few of their own, who were not medically fit enough for the day's combat action. The main Pindari force was now cleverly hidden in patches of tall, dry grass and behind the piles of volcanic boulders. From their ambush positions behind the rocks, the Pindaris watched the attacker's column slowly advance up the grassy slope. They were momentarily taken aback when they saw three horsemen in British uniforms break from the column and canter up the slope towards their hidden positions. A British officer, sporting a grey beard and wearing a white, helmet-shaped hat with a large white ostrich feather, led the group. He wore a long, blue coat over grey breeches and well-polished riding boots made of black leather. Watching the leading horseman, the concealed Pindaris had little doubt that he was the officer in command of the column. His stately posture on the brown horse and the manner in which he waved his arms authoritatively and barked orders to his men, sent shivers of fear through the hidden Pindari bandits. Unknown to the

Pindaris, this stately rider was Major Drew, Commandant of 1st Battalion, Ellichpur Brigade, that was rapidly closing in with the Pindaris' position. Two officers mounted on black stallions overtook Major Drew and cantered uphill towards the hilltop. As if on a given signal some agile Pindaris sprang from their concealed positions behind the boulders and bushes, to bring down both the riders. The leading rider tumbled from his mount. The startled horse neighed loudly and galloped downhill with the stirrups of its saddle swinging and clanging loudly as they clashed with one another and the saddle horn. While falling to the ground the officer had contorted his body. He quickly drew his sword and slashed at his assailants, all in one smooth motion. The nearest Pindari's throat was slit from ear to ear, while the other one deftly leapt away. Meanwhile, some more Pindaris had jumped at the second officer. His shiny black horse was mercilessly impaled with a spear and the officer tumbled to the ground. As he yelled something at the top of his voice, he too was brought down to the ground by the Pindaris.

Hearing sounds of the nearby scuffle Major Drew had pulled his horse to a stop and was looking about him. Just then, a bare-bodied Pindari wearing a dirty white turban and rolled dhoti (loin cloth), suddenly leapt out of the tall grass and lunged at Drew from the back. He was dangerously swinging a drawn sword and instantly Drew knew its strike would be fatal. He rapidly turned in his saddle, pulled a pistol from his belt and shot the assailant dead. As his senses were temporarily dulled by the loud pistol shot, Drew failed to notice that another Pindari had risen from behind a couple of boulders, a few feet to his immediate left. With an agile leap, this athletic Pindari lunged forward and stepped on Drew's left stirrup and also swiftly grabbed the horse's reins. Before Drew could swing

Major Drew, the first recorded Commandant of 4 Kumaon, was attacked and killed by Pindaris during the Battle of Moormoosa, in 1814.

around and attempt to reload his pistol, the frightened horse jerked suddenly to the right, unseated and sent him sprawling to the rough ground on his back. The riderless horse neighed loudly and galloped forward. The Pindari sprang upon the fallen officer and in a fluid motion he drew a sharp dagger from the twirled piece of cloth that was tied around his waist. Sitting astride Drew, the Pindari repeatedly thrust his sharp dagger into the officer's chest. The Pindari then jerked his head up to withdraw the dagger and thrust it down for a final time. Major Drew was killed by the repeated dagger thrusts in his stomach and chest.

As Drew lay dead on the dry grass, the troops increased their pace and rapidly advanced up the slope to hurl themselves at the Pindaris, who confronted them on the hill. A spirited close quarter skirmish took place on the grassy slope and there was a liberal use of daggers, swords and muskets. Muskets with the soldiers barked repeatedly and having had enough of a fight, the Pindaris turned and fled downhill. Suddenly, the Pindaris who had clashed with the advancing troops yelled to the others to flee as well from the hill. The remaining Pindaris too broke contact and fled. It was clear the Pindaris had lost the skirmish and did not have the stomach for any more fighting. They left the hill and ran away towards the re-entrant where their mounts were waiting. Speedily mounting their horses, the brigands galloped off towards the valley, with a few of them turning to take pot shots at those soldiers who had tried to follow the fleeing bandits. Soon the battlefield was quiet and the bodies of a few dead Pindaris lay scattered among the volcanic boulders. With the Pindaris' flight, the battle was over even before it had started in real earnest. The brief skirmish had been a total rout for the Pindaris, but there was also sadness for the British-led force as they had lost their leader and two other officers.

The sun was shining brightly as unit followers trudged up the slope to carry down the wounded soldiers. Bodies of Major Drew and the two officers were carried down the hill after they had been lashed onto strong branches that had been cut from some trees. At the bottom of the hill, the dead bodies were placed in an ox-drawn cart and taken back to Ellichpur. The first Commandant of the Battalion was buried with full military honours outside the north wall of Ellichpur. Later, a marble slab was also erected in his memory. The inscription on the white marble slab read:

Here lies Major Drew, who for many years commanded a brigade in the service of Salabat Khan Bahadur, Nawab of Ellichpur.

Today, neither Major Drew's gravestone nor the marble slab can be identified in the vast expanse of close construction that has come up in the heavily built-up area where the north wall of Ellichpur is believed to have once stood.

The battle against Pindaris at Moormoosa, in 1814, is the first known combat action fought by the infantry battalion now called 4th Battalion, The Kumaon Regiment (4 Kumaon). In the centuries that followed, countless actions have been fought across the world and the unit's brave officers and men have established some distinguished traditions of valour. Today, the brave soldiers of this fine outfit make their compatriots in Kumaon Regiment and Indian Army proud with their brave deeds. The traditions of chivalry and valour were well begun by Major Drew and his brave band of men, among the rocky outcrops of Moormoosa on that fateful day in August 1814.

Boxer Rebellion in China – 1900

As the nineteenth century drew to a close, the major Western powers and Japan had forced China's ruling Qing dynasty to accept wide foreign control over the country's economic affairs. In the two Opium Wars (1839–42 and 1856–60) and the Sino-Japanese War (1894–95), it was a losing fight for China with a large number of casualties. There was great loss of national pride and thus in 1900, in what became known as the Boxer Rebellion, a Chinese secret organization called the Society of Righteous and Harmonious Fists led an uprising in northern China against the spread of Western and Japanese influence in the land.

The rebels were referred in the West as Boxers because they performed some physical contortions and exercises. Quite strangely, they believed the exercises they performed would enable them to withstand bullets and destroy foreign property. From June to August 1900, the Boxers besieged the foreign district of Peking (Beijing). Finally, an international force (including the Battalion) moved to China and subdued the Boxer Uprising. By the terms of the Boxer Protocol, which officially ended the Rebellion in 1901, China agreed to pay more than $330 million in reparations.

Heavily armed Boxer rebels, China, 1900

Move of the Battalion to China

The Battalion, then named 5th Infantry, Hyderabad Contingent, was located at Bolarum, from where it often moved out to maintain order in the Nizam of Hyderabad's dominions. 5th Infantry Hyderabad Contingent was commanded by Lieutenant Colonel W. H. Lewin. Lieutenant Colonel W. H. Greany, IMS was the doctor and the rough talking Lieutenant V. W. Tregear the Adjutant of the Battalion. After the unit received orders to join China Expeditionary Force (CEF) and proceed to Hong Kong, feverish preparations were made for the new assignment. As a part of the preparations for duty in China, the unit was issued with new .303 Lee-Metford rifles in place of the old Martini-Henri rifle, which was in use till 1900.

Accordingly, the troops had to carry out considerable firing practice to become proficient in the use of their new weapons. The unit also carefully prepared the stores it was to carry for their expedition to China. The Indian officers were gathered together and given the news that the unit would proceed from Bolarum to Madras by rail and from Madras

Officers of 5th Infantry, Hyderabad Contingent photographed outside the unit's Officers' Mess at Bolarum, before proceeding to China in August 1900
Standing – Junior officers of the Battalion
Seated [L to R] – Lt V.W. Tregear (Adjutant), Lt Col W.H. Greany, IMS, (Medical Officer), Lt Col W.H. Lewin (Commandant), Capt. G.M. Audain and Maj. C.C. Renton (Second-in-Command)

to Hong Kong (China) aboard two ships named RIMS *Dalhousie* and RIMS *India*. They were also given other details of the move. The unit was to move from Bolarum (Hyderabad) by train over the new railway line that had been recently laid to Madras. Since it was the first time the unit would be moving by railway and ship, many administrative details needed to be finalized. All this extensive work was expeditiously completed by Lewin and his staff officers. Tregear, as Adjutant, made out copious details about how the troops would move by rail to Madras and onwards from there by two ships to China. He made out tables for loads to be carried for the journey by rail and ship. He also worked out the routine during the journey and food that was to be cooked and provided to the troops.

On 14 August 1900, the unit loaded up in a train for the first time and proceeded to the port city of Madras. Three horses of the British officers were also loaded in the train along with adequate fodder for duration of their long voyage by ship to China. The unit's first journey by rail was quite a remarkable event for the troops. The men sat huddled near the open windows of their carriages and watched in amazement as the countryside sped by, past the train. The good speed of the train and regular 'clickety-clack' of its wheels fascinated the troops, who were used to slow and silent marches on foot with their British officers riding beside the marching columns on horseback.

When the train carrying 5th Infantry, Hyderabad Contingent reached Madras railway station on 16 August 1900, the troops disembarked from the train and unloaded their stores and the few horses accompanying the unit. The troops pitched tents and established camp in an open field adjacent to the railway station. A few British officers had the mounts saddled and they rode off to Madras harbour to find out more details of the unit's move to China by sea. As per the allotted schedule, the unit was divided in two parts for the voyage to Hong Kong in two ships. The first half of the Battalion was led by the Commandant himself on RIMS *Dalhousie*, while the second part of the unit was led by Major C. C. Renton, 2 IC, on RIMS *India*.

The first half of the unit, under the Commandant, boarded RIMS *Dalhousie* and sailed out of Madras harbour on 18 August 1900. As it was the first time that troops of the unit were venturing across *kala pani*—literally, the 'dark waters'.[1] Prayers and a *havan* were held at the harbour before departure of the two ships. RIMS *India*, the second ship, left Madras on 22 August 1900. Inoculations to protect the troops

RIMS *Dalhousie* left Madras on 18 August 1900, carrying first half of the Battalion

against enteric fever (typhoid) had taken place on board the respective ships. However, these inoculations had a reactionary effect and many of the men had a difficult time, as they developed a high fever after they

RIMS *India* left Madras on 22 August 1900, carrying the second half of the Battalion

[1] Ancient Indian texts mention that people are forbidden from venturing into the deep sea, that is literally translated as *kala pani* or dark waters.

had been given the inoculations.

Both ships sailed from Madras, separated by a period of five days and sailed across the placid waters of Bay of Bengal. The fury of the south-west monsoon winds had passed on to soak the heated landmass of the Indian subcontinent. It was still early for the retreating monsoons to disturb the relative calm of the Bay of Bengal. Both ships had an uneventful voyage to Hong Kong via Singapore, where both had halted to take on drinking water and fresh supplies.

Kowloon Harbour, Hong Kong, China (1900), where the Battalion disembarked from the ships

Separated by about five days, both ships berthed at Kowloon Harbour. It had been a 15-day-long, uneventful voyage for each. While disembarking at Kowloon, the first ship had a minor mishap. On being unloaded, two heavy sacks of precious *atta* (wheat flour) went crashing down the gangway and splashed heavily into the dark waters below. A few motor lorries and numerous heavy-duty horse-drawn carts awaited the arrival of each of the ships. This motor and horse-drawn transport was employed to convey the unit's stores to their camp site, which was located on the low foothills beyond Hong Kong city.

Quelling the Boxer Rebellion – 1900

In 1900, the Boxer movement had spread to the Peking area, where the Boxers killed many Chinese Christians and foreign missionaries, destroyed churches, railroad stations and other properties. On 20 June

1900, the Boxers began a siege of Peking's foreign legation district, where the official quarters of foreign diplomats were located. The following day, the ill-advised Qing Empress Dowager Tzu'u Hzi declared war on all foreign nations who had diplomatic ties with China.

The multinational force organized by Western powers and Japan included the Battalion that had gone to China from India, as a part of CEF to crush the Boxer Rebellion. The Boxers' siege stretched into weeks and the diplomats, families and embassy guards suffered hunger and degrading conditions as they fought to keep the rebels at bay. By some estimates, several hundred foreigners and several thousand Chinese Christians were killed during this turbulent time. On 14 August, after fighting its way through blockades put up by the rebels, the international force of approximately 20,000 troops from eight nations – Austria–Hungary, France, Germany, Italy, Japan, Russia, Britain (including India) and the United States – had arrived in China to take Peking. The German contingent sent to the multinational force had in its ranks a young lieutenant colonel, Count Paul Emil von Lettow-Vorbeck. In the coming First World War (1914–1918), he would command the German and Askari troops in East Africa and the unit would fight bitter actions against the forces led by this German officer. The Rebellion formally ended with the signing of the Boxer Protocol on 7 September 1901. By terms of the Boxer Protocol, forts protecting Peking were to be destroyed, Boxer and Chinese government officials involved in the uprising were to be punished and foreign legations were permitted to station their troops in Peking for their defence. China was prohibited from importing arms for the next two years and it was agreed for China to pay more than $330 million in reparations to the foreign nations who were involved in quelling the Rebellion. The Qing dynasty (established in 1644), had been greatly weakened by the Boxer Rebellion. Then, following an uprising in 1911, the dynasty came to an end and China became a republic in 1912, under Dr Sun Yat-sen.

On the successful completion of its mission in China, an intricate silver piece was prepared for the unit by Chinese craftsmen in 1901. This trophy was aptly named 'China Cup' and dedicated to officers of the Battalion to commemorate the unit's successful tenure in China. Today, this beautiful silver trophy with two ornate dragon handles, adorns the Officers' Mess of the unit. Also, all ranks of the unit were presented with the 'China Medal' and 'China 1900' was inscribed on the unit's colours. On its return from China, the unit's designation was changed from 5th Infantry, Hyderabad Contingent to 98th Infantry in 1903. The inscription 'China 1900' was embroidered on the colours of 98th Infantry.

The elegant 'China Cup' of 4 Kumaon

China Medal – 1900

Battle of Tanga – 1914

East Africa

In 1914, the Great War or World War I began after a political assassination took place in Austria, Europe. The war split the major powers of the world and large-scale fighting broke out in Europe, Middle-East and even in East Africa.[1] The Battalion was drafted into the African Expeditionary Force 'B', and it sailed to East Africa in October 1914. The British had appreciated that local forces were not strong enough to meet the German threat to British East Africa. It was then decided to dispatch Indian Expeditionary Force 'B' from India. This force was to clear the entire region from Mount Kilimanjaro to the coast, and as far south as the German-controlled port city of Tanga (now in present-day Tanzania). Local attacks in the Kilimanjaro area were to be launched by troops already in British East Africa, while the Expeditionary Force 'B' was to carry out larger operations and ultimately defeat the German forces.

In 1903 the Battalion had been redesignated as 98th Infantry and it comprised of two companies of Ahirs, three of Rajputs and three of Hindustani Mohammedans. The unit was located at Sagar, when orders were received on 11 September 1914 to mobilize for service with Expeditionary Force 'B'. The Force was led by Major General Arthur Aitken, who was a soldier more suited in style and appearance to colonial campaigns of the previous century. He had spent 35 years in India

[1] Territories under the control of the British in eastern Africa, namely Kenya, Uganda, Zanzibar and Tanganyika (now Tanzania).

and was certain his troops would 'make mincemeat of the Huns and their Niggers'. He arrogantly refused to accept advice from anyone professing local knowledge or intelligence of the area.

Hurried preparations were carried out in India for the overseas campaign and the Battalion was equipped with Maxim machine guns for the first time. Machine-gun detachments were trained, and sustained firing practices were carried out at Chandmari firing ranges. However, the troops were still using the .303 Lee-Metford Rifles that had been issued just before the unit proceeded to China in August 1900.

When all preparations had been completed, the Battalion entrained at Sagar for Bombay on 7 October 1914, under Lieutenant Colonel T. M. Ward. At Bombay (now called Mumbai), the unit embarked on SS *Nairung* and sailed in a convoy of six ships, on 16 October 1914. After the tenure in China, Major C. C. Renton was doing his second tenure as 2 IC and thus he was well aware of the intricacies of the unit's move by rail and ship. This was to be the unit's third move by rail and ship and the troops were fairly experienced in such moves as a large number of them had travelled to China and back.

The voyage to China and back had literally been a 'dream run', but the cramped quarters and rough sea conditions on the voyage from Bombay to Mombasa caused intense hardship and the troops' morale plummeted to a desperate low. To add to the unit's problems, an unfortunate delay in sailing forced the soldiers to spend sixteen miserable days aboard the transports in crowded conditions at Bombay port. The soldiers suffered in the appalling heat and humidity, till the ships finally sailed on 16 October. Most of the soldiers spent the rest of the voyage either being seasick in their bunks or suffering from dysentery that was brought on by eating the unpalatable food supplied on board the ship, to which they were quite unaccustomed.

When it was suggested to Aitken at Mombasa that he should allow his men ashore to recuperate from ill-effects of the terrible voyage, he had pooh-poohed the idea and added that such an action might alert the Germans! He felt it was safer to take his men straight to their destination and tackle the enemy. In fact, very few in the Expeditionary Force knew anything of their destination, which was the German port of Tanga. During their brief stay at Mombasa, Aitken was offered help by a Lieutenant Colonel B. R. Graham of King's African Rifles to tackle the opposition they were likely to face at Tanga. Aitken obstinately refused the proffered offer of assistance. However, Graham persisted and warned Aitken that the German native troops (Askaris) should not be underestimated, as they were well-trained and physically tough. The General had disregarded the advice, and announced with misplaced bravado that he believed the Askari were untrained natives and he would thrash the lot well before Christmas!

Although move of the expedition to East Africa was supposed to be a secret, the Germans had every possible warning that it was coming. The labels on the crates in Bombay dockyards announced, 'Indian Expeditionary Force "B", Mombasa, East Africa', and headlines in the British and East African press heralded the imminent arrival of this force. In addition, there were plain radio messages between the convoy and Mombasa and letters from German residents in British East Africa to their friends in Tanga. The German commander, Colonel (later Major General) Paul Emile von Lettow-Vorbeck had a lot to thank the British for, for on Aitken's orders the fleet travelled down the African coast in sight of land and thus its progress was easily monitored by the Germans.

On 2 November 1914, the British cruiser HMS *Fox* under Captain Francis Wade Caulfeild brazenly entered Tanga harbour to discuss the status of the town with the German governor, Heinrich Albert Schnee. Earlier, Schnee had arranged a truce with the Royal Navy in order to save Tanga from an anticipated naval bombardment. Aitken's convoy of ships was not far behind Caulfeild, who had brazenly come to tell the Germans that the truce had been scrapped. Schnee was not available, but the local commissioner, Herr Auracher was met and informed personally by Caulfeild about the situation. The meeting took place in Hotel Kaiserhof, Tanga. When Caulfeild asked Auracher if the Tanga harbour was mined, not

British cruiser HMS *Fox* commanded by Capt. F. W. Caulfeild

surprisingly the German had promptly replied that it was full of mines!

Leaving the trusting British naval officer waiting, Auracher had rushed off to send an urgent message to von Lettow-Vorbeck that the British had arrived and seemed interested in Tanga and its harbour. He then donned an army uniform, raised the German flag, and went off to join his military unit. When Aitken's convoy arrived, they had to endure the frustration of waiting because of the supposedly 'mined harbour'. They were finally diverted to land at another location, some distance away from Tanga. There were no mines in Tanga harbour, and Auracher's ruse worked well and provided adequate time for the defence of Tanga.

The Battle of Tanga is also known as the 'Battle of Bees'. Although the Allies launched the attack, the operations went on to establish the burgeoning reputation of the German commander, von Lettow-Vorbeck, by the manner in which he beat back the Allied attempt to capture German East Africa. Tanga was the busiest German seaport on the Indian Ocean, besides being the start point of the important Usambara Railway, which snaked its way inland. The attack on Tanga was to be the first major action of the war in German East Africa. Alerted by the move of British ships and openness of Aitken's intentions, von Lettow-Vorbeck had quickly mustered his forces and reinforced Tanga's local defence contingent.

The Battalion was part of 27 (Bangalore) Infantry Brigade (commanded by Brigadier General Richard Wapshare), which arrived off the coast of Tanga on 3 November 1914. Other units of this 'four-battalion brigade' were 2nd Battalion, Loyal North Lancashire Regiment, 63rd Palamcottah Light Infantry and 101st Grenadiers. As intelligence reports had stated that there were unknown hazards at Tanga, Aitken decided to land at a point farther along the coast, out of sight of the town of Tanga. Because of mistaken reports about mines in Tanga's harbour, the main portion of 27 Infantry Brigade disembarked south-east of Tanga during the early hours of 4 November 1914. The landing force formed a bivouac or firm base, from where the attack was to be launched. Surprise, upon which success of the operation depended, had been lost at the very outset. 27 Infantry Brigade was given orders to attack Tanga at 11 a.m. on 4 November. 98th Infantry moved from the bivouac at 11.20 a.m. As it had been nominated as 'brigade reserve', the troops sloshed in the water-filled swamps, behind 2nd Battalion, Loyal North Lancashire Regiment,[2] at a distance of about 200 metres. 63rd Palamcottah Light Infantry led the attack on the right side and it was followed by 101st Grenadiers. Quite incomprehensibly, no reconnaissance had been conducted before the 27 Infantry Brigade attack was launched.

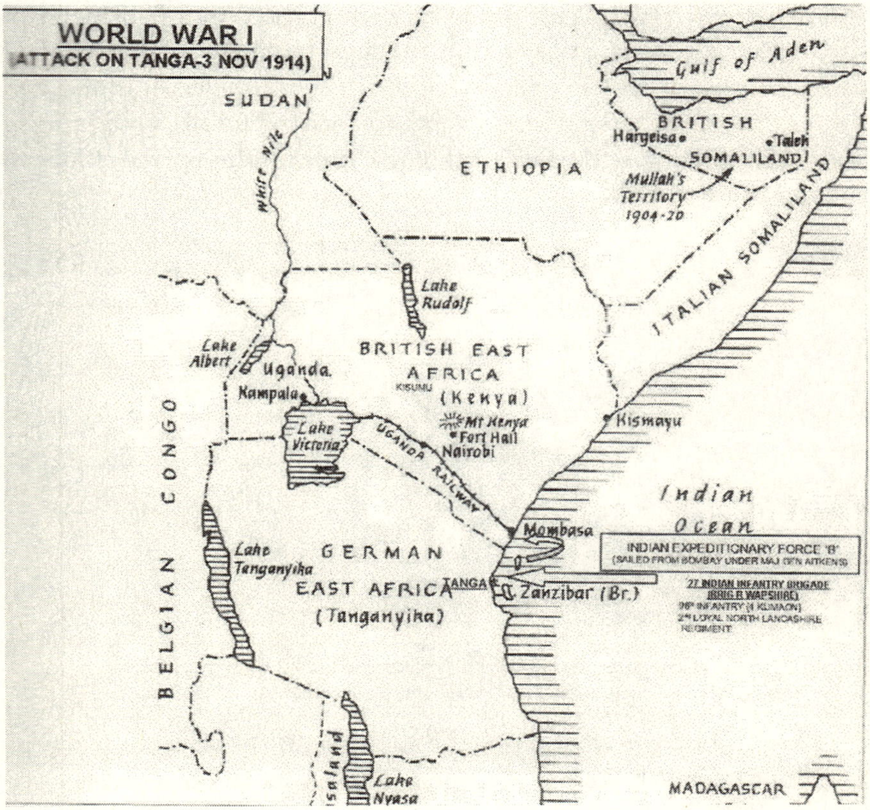

Map of East Africa

The area selected for landing was in fact the worst possible place to land. Situated amidst dense mangrove swamps, it was full of leeches, poisonous water snakes and swarms of hostile mosquitoes. The hapless

---

[2] In August 1914, 2nd Battalion, Loyal North Lancashire Regiment had moved from Bangalore in India to East Africa with the India Expeditionary Force 'B'. In May 1916, the unit was moved to South Africa to recuperate from mass ill-health it suffered in the African jungles and swamps.

troops were plunged into this swamp very soon after their sickening experiences during the miserable sea voyage from India. By the time the Indian troops were fully ashore, the Germans had had nearly 48 hours in which to make their preparations for an effective defensive battle. As soon as Aitken ordered the advance on Tanga, a number of things began to go wrong. The terrain was difficult, with slushy mangrove swamps and dense undergrowth providing little observation and poor fields of fire. The men perspired heavily in the high humidity as they sloshed through ankle-deep water and made their way through dark foliage in the swamps. The Brigade attack moved forward at an excruciatingly slow pace, which gave the Germans ample time for their preparations to counter the attackers.

Thick mangrove swamps through which units of 27 Infantry Brigade launched their attack on 3 November 1914

Due to heavy vegetation in the marshland, the advancing troops could not see much around their line of advance. To get a better view, Captain B. H. Hall of 98th Infantry, climbed an ant-hill to look around him. Hall was immediately gunned down by a German sniper who was deployed in a well concealed position in the surrounding, tall baobab trees. Thus, Hall was shot dead with an accurately fired sniper bullet through his head. At about 2 p.m., the enemy was contacted and heavy firing broke out all over the swamps. The Loyal North Lancashires who were ahead of 98th Infantry, were halted in their tracks by accurate German machine-gun fire and suffered heavy casualties in the swamps. In darkening wilderness, suddenly the distinct sound of a German bugle call was heard and the Askari soldiers rushed to attack 63rd Palamcottah Light Infantry, the right forward battalion. That unit had simply turned and fled through the slush, leaving twelve personnel (both officers and soldiers) killed on the spot.

Although outnumbered by eight to one, von Lettow-Vorbeck was not without hope. He later remarked on the clumsiness with which the British and Indian troops had been led into battle. The Germans had a strong defensive position, linked by field telephones and fronted by barbed wire obstacles. There were snipers hidden in the large baobab trees and many machine-gun nests had been set up at close intervals on the ground. Though 98th Infantry was a spirited unit with commendable training, the advance through this terrain was a formidable challenge for even the best troops. The hot and humid weather conditions made it quite unbearable for the troops.

By this time many of the soldiers were in a state of collapse from excruciating heat exhaustion and thirst, having already consumed the contents of their water bottles and canvas *chhaguls* (water carriers). By

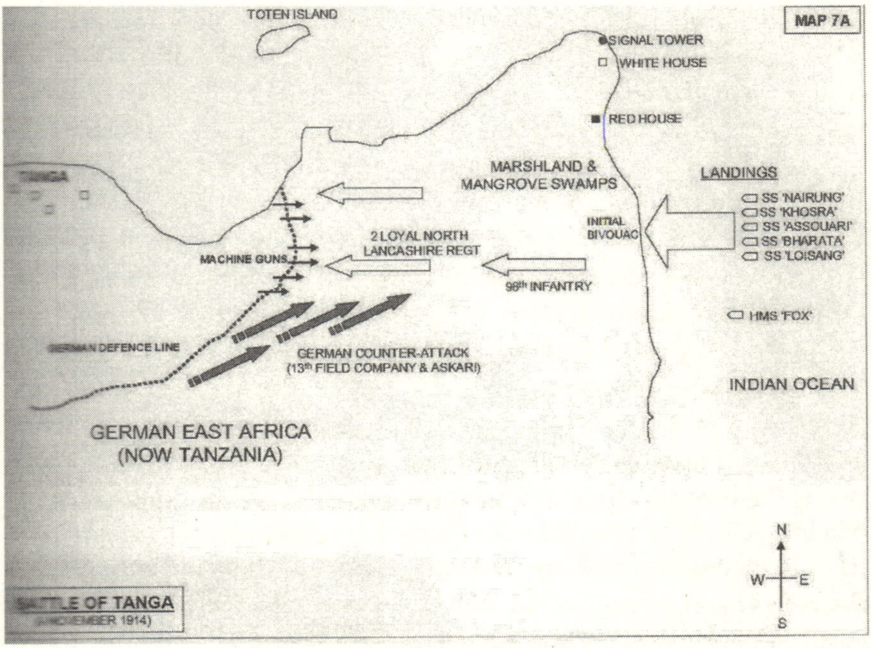

Map, Battle of Tanga, December 1914

Askari troopers launch a blistering counter-attack on the assaulting 27 Infantry Brigade, during Battle of Tanga on 3 November 1914

about 3 p.m., the fighting had taken the form of bitter jungle skirmishing. At 4.30 p.m., the Battalion was ordered to move ahead from its reserve position and reinforce the sluggish attack. No. 1, 2 and 3 Double Companies sloshed their way through the dark, water-filled swamps. At this very time, No. 3 Double Company unknowingly began to drift to the south, thereby creating a gap between itself and the other two advancing companies.

No. 3 Double Company continued to drift to the south and soon clashed with German parties who had surreptitiously been working their way north, to get around the attackers. Close range machine-gun and rifle fire rang out in the stifling swamps. Although, it was not realized at the time, No. 3 Double Company's unplanned drift to the south had unwittingly saved the attackers from being outmanoeuvred and totally surprised by the enemy's outflanking parties. Thus, a crushing defeat with heavy casualties had been unwittingly averted. Soon, even the Brigade attack was not making progress due to heavy casualties and accurate fire coming from unseen enemy parties who had moved around the attackers' flanks. Meanwhile, Loyal North Lancashires had earlier unfurled a large Union Jack on Tanga Hospital. The hospital comprised a main building and four, large outhouses, which were all thatch roofed structures. The hospital complex was located well to the east of Tanga town, on a raised piece of ground at the very edge of the forbidding swamps. Though the Lancashires had left some of their serious casualties at the hospital, they could not advance any further due to accurate machine-gun fire. Since No. 3 Double Company of 98th Infantry was fixed in its position by heavy enemy fire and could not advance further, the reserve company (No. 4 Double Company) had to be moved up. It engaged the enemy to allow No. 3 Double Company to extricate itself.

At about the same time, it was decided to call off the Brigade attack and Wapshare ordered a general retirement at 5.30 p.m. Thus, the reserve company took up positions about 300 metres to the rear and covered the withdrawal of the forward companies. It was soon dark, when at about 10.15 p.m. further orders were received for all troops to fall back on the coastal bivouac and establish an outpost on the coast. Reading the battle closely and on seeing the attackers begin to flounder, the wily German commander ordered his 13th Field Company and Askari troopers to launch a vicious counter-attack on the Lancashires and 98th Infantry.

Although the Germans and their Askari troops were numerically outgunned, von Lettow-Vorbeck made a bold move and initially launched his counter-attack with about 1,000 troopers. The Askari had been trained in the Prussian tradition and were as good as the German troops. When von Lettow-Vorbeck saw the Allied troops were beginning to flounder under pressure, like a prudent commander he took a further gamble and threw in whatever troops he possessed. The thirsty and exhausted Allied soldiers suffered heavily and rapidly withdrew to the area from where they had commenced the attacks in the morning.

Askari troopers move on the double to get into position before launching the counter-attack on 27 Infantry Brigade

In hindsight, the manner in which von Lettow-Vorbeck mustered his troops and launched the counter-attack in fast approaching darkness, is indeed laudable and highlights his tactical, military genius. The coordination by von Lettow-Vorbeck was indeed praiseworthy, as there were no 'radio sets' available to convey battle commands for counter-attack. Interestingly, all orders were conveyed by fleet-footed Askari soldiers carrying bits of paper on which orders had been hurriedly scrawled, while loud bugle calls alerted the attackers to be prepared to receive the Askari runners.

Tanga Hospital complex at the time of Allied attack (November 1914)

Machine-gun fire ripped through the darkening mangrove swamps, as parties of German and Askari troops silently moved around the open flank of the attackers. The floundering attackers were soon receiving fire from the flank and also the rear. This caused great confusion and added to casualties being suffered by the Allied force. In those days, casualty evacuation was a rather rudimentary affair and wounded men were generally left where they had fallen, to be picked up later by either follow-up troops or 'camp followers'. The Germans and their Askari troopers kept up their counter-attack and pushed the erstwhile attackers all the way to the shoreline. The firing kept on raging all through the night and desultory rifle shots could even be heard around the beach bivouac during the early hours of the next morning.

However, while they had withdrawn through the swamps, the attackers were to face an even greater enemy than the wily Germans and their Askari troops. Deep in hollow logs and hanging from the trees almost across the battlefield, were large beehives containing vicious type of African bees. These particular bees were a large and aggressive type of the flying insect. Infuriated by the noise and sweeping hail of bullets, the enraged bees emerged in huge, dark clouds from their hives and descended on the hapless troops. These swarms of wild African bees began to mercilessly sting the thirsty and tired troops, who were by now withdrawing through the darkening swamps. Panic had spread at once and troops began fleeing towards safety of the sea. As they fled, the Allied troops were pursued by the angered bees which stung them repeatedly! Though some bees stayed in the swamps to sting the counter-attacking German and Askari troopers, the main bee attacks were directed at soldiers of the attacking Allied force who had earlier been advancing through the swamps. One Engineer was stung about 300 times, while another British soldier who was unconscious after heavy bleeding from a deep battle wound surprisingly regained his consciousness after being repeatedly stung by the bees. He screamed to his comrades to urgently remove the angry bees that were stinging his face and neck!

On board the HQ ship the sudden appearance of hundreds of troops on the beach, waving their hands above their heads and leaping into the sea to ward off the bees, was a humorous yet astonishing sight to see. 'You don't suppose they're being driven back?' a bright young staff officer had asked in astonishment. On the beach one British officer could hardly understand the 'cowardly behaviour' of the troops, and remarked, 'I would never have believed that grown-up men of any race could have been reduced to such utter shamelessness'. Furious and panicky, Aitken ordered an immediate naval bombardment, which had to be urgently stopped when the only hits recorded fell on Tanga Hospital, that was crammed with dead and wounded soldiers from the Lancashire Battalion. Some shells even fell into the retreating attackers, causing further panic and casualties. The battle had turned into the worst kind of nightmare leaving the tired troops of 27 Infantry Brigade quite stunned.

Failure of the Brigade attack was a major disappointment for all ranks. It had been a distressing and costly failure, and the Battalion had suffered 73 casualties. The battle-weary troops were thoroughly disoriented and demoralized. During the night some wounded personnel were evacuated from where they had fallen in the dark and desolate swamp and given medical aid. Unsuccessful attempts were made to locate the four soldiers and one 'camp follower' who had gone missing during the attack. The disappearance of these five personnel has remained a mystery for more than a hundred years, ever since that fateful day of the attack on Tanga in 1914.

It has never been known whether the missing personnel were taken prisoner by Germans during close fighting in the dark mangroves or they were lost in the coastal swamps and perished. However, there is also a remote possibility that men somehow managed to reach habitation and survived. In the area of Tanga, there is a population of people of Indian origin (labourers from Bihar and their families), who had earlier been brought from India by the British to construct the railway line that snaked its way inland from Mombasa (Uganda Railway). Later, these labourers and their families settled in the area. The Indians who made the railway had suffered great hardships from rampant tropical diseases and attacks by vicious wild animals, especially lions. Today,

Uganda Railway under attack, in 1915

some of the local Indians residing in East Africa could well include descendants of the five missing soldiers of 98th Infantry and many others of 27 Indian Infantry Brigade, who were lost during the attack on Tanga on 4 November 1914! This will remain yet another lingering mystery that has surrounded the Battalion, for more than a century, as the Expeditionary Force had a large figure of 250 soldiers who had gone missing during the attack on Tanga.

Major General Jacob Louis van Deventer, CB, who had succeeded Lieutenant General Arthur Reginald Hoskins, CMG, Distinguished Service Order (DSO), in May 1917 as Commander of the Allied Forces (earlier, Hoskins had succeeded General Jan Smuts on 20 January 1917), in his final dispatch has said, 'There were occasions when atrocities were committed on our wounded, and the treatment of our prisoners—especially the Indians, was at times infamous ...' However, in all fairness it must be said that the actual fighting of the East African Campaign was on the whole, clean—and sometimes even chivalrous. The war in East Africa has been always considered somewhat courtly and gentlemanly. After the Battle of Tanga, the British met the Germans under a white flag. Over a bottle of brandy, they compared notes and opinions of the battle, in addition to taking care of the wounded!

After the battle, the Germans got a well-deserved respite and withdrew further inland. The ill-fated attack had cost the Expeditionary Force 1,550 casualties (800 dead, 500 wounded and 250 missing). In turn, the Germans suffered 148 casualties (67 killed and 81 wounded). Colonel Paul von Lettow-Vorbeck gained much booty from the supplies left behind by the attackers in their hasty retreat, including machine guns, rifles and 600,000 rounds of ammunition. By mid-day on 5 November 1914, the unit received orders to re-embark in the ships, which hurriedly left for Mombasa. Casualties suffered by 98th Infantry during the Battle of Tanga were as follows:

Killed: Captain B. H. Hall, Subedar Jaipal Singh and 35 OR

Wounded: Captain G. D. Wright, Captain A. E. Grisewood, IMS and 38 OR.

Missing: Four OR and one Camp Follower

Soon after the British ships laden with troops had hurriedly left Tanga area, von Lettow-Vorbeck was able to equip new regiments with captured British rifles and machine guns. Also, he had enough food, coats, blankets, motorcycles, telegraph equipment and supplies, to last him for a year. Though the Expeditionary Force 'B' moved to Mombasa, there was little respite for Aitken for his rather unprofessional conduct. Lord Kitchener, Secretary for War, refused to see him on his recall to Britain and he was reduced in rank to Colonel and retired on half pension. Aitken achieved further infamy by being named among the 'eight generals who have been the worst commanders in the British Army, in all time'. At Mombasa, the Customs officials refused to let the Expeditionary Force disembark unless they paid five per cent ad valorem tax.

A rare photograph of Indian battle casualties during the attack on Tanga (4 November 1914). Interestingly, this photo was snapped by the German defenders of Tanga immediately after the attack, more than a century ago. By their dress it appears the two individuals seen in the photograph are probably 'camp followers', who had followed the attackers in the swamps around Tanga.

However, unsheathed bayonets of the angry troops quickly convinced the Customs officials to waive the tax and permit the troops to land.

Thus ended the Battle of Tanga, which is mainly remembered for ineffective leadership by the British higher command and the attacker's ill-luck to encounter the deadly African bees. However, considerable bravery was displayed by the Allied troops amidst great hardships and suffering, initially during their voyage from India and then in the swamps around Tanga. Also noteworthy was the stellar performance of von Lettow-Vorbeck and his German and Askari troops.

One of the three World War I cemeteries at Tanga

Operations 1915 – 1919

German patrols frequently threatened the Uganda Railway that wound its way inland from Mombasa, from their nearby posts near Lake Victoria. Thus, it was decided to raid these offending German positions and put an end to the threat to this vital railway line. On 6 June 1915, the enemy post at 'Guriki Hill' was successfully raided by a double company of 98th Infantry under Lieutenant Douglas Raymond Montford. Plans were also made to raid another offending enemy post on the bank of Lake Victoria, at Lubembe.

During the early hours of 3 December 1915, 'E' Company of 98th Infantry under Montford, with 2nd Lieutenant Hansard as the 2 IC, rowed out in three longboats from Kurungu to raid the German post at Lubembe, located on the shores of Lake Victoria. The post comprised of a number of hutments which housed about 20 German and 40 Askari soldiers. The boats moved silently through the dark, choppy waters of the lake, and in the early morning light they approached the beach near the enemy camp. Without a sound, some soldiers lowered themselves into the cold water and guided the boats forward to the narrow beach at the waters' edge. Here the three boats beached gently on the gravelly sand with a low, grating sound. Remainder of the troops stepped ashore and silently cocked their Lee Enfield rifles of .303-inch calibre. The soldiers crouched low and moved towards the dark hutments with sleeping enemy soldiers. However, an alert enemy sentry deployed outside the hutments saw the crouched figures of raiders silently advancing from the beach. Alerted, he shouted at the raiders to halt and simultaneously fired off a round from his 7.92 mm Mauser rifle. In the silence of the night, the loud sound of the single shot reverberated across the beach and hutments of the enemy post, waking the defenders. At the sound of the rifle shot, the advancing raiders had quickly fired back. The raiders straightened from their crouched positions and stormed the German post, amidst volleys of rapidly fired rifle shots.

Today, the placid waters of Lake Victoria gently wash the gravel and sand beach at Lubembe. This is the very spot where the 'raiding party' of 98th Infantry had landed from three longboats, during the early hours of 3 December 1915.

As at Guriki Hill, the surprised enemy defenders hurriedly vacated their post and fled into the surrounding bushland for safety. However, before speedy departure of the raiders, the German sentries had reacted with nervous shouts, followed by the heavy stutter of rifle and machine-gun fire. Some raiders were killed, as they stepped onto the shore. Also, a number of the unit's soldiers, including Montford,[1] were hit by the enemy's bullets and flung to the ground. The enemy had fired from their Mauser rifles as they hurriedly abandoned the hutments and ran into the bush beyond the camp. A number of bodies of dead German and Askari soldiers with weapons[2] were found at the perimeter defences of the post. As the sun rose in the sky, the vacated enemy post was searched by the raiders. A large quantity of ammunition, equipment and military stores were recovered from the post. The wounded raiders were quickly given rudimentary first aid and carried to the waiting boats. Tall plumes of white smoke rose in the sky as the abandoned German post, captured equipment and stores were set ablaze by Montford's men, as they stepped into the three boats and departed from Lubembe's narrow beach.

After the raid, as the raiders were embarking in the boats, they suddenly heard the rapid stutter of a machine-gun. The bursts of automatic

[1] Montford had been wounded thrice during the operations in East Africa when he was posted to Egyptian Expeditionary Force (58th Infantry). Sadly, this gallant young man was killed on the last day of World War I (1918).

[2] Today, some of these German weapons are displayed in the Officers' Mess of 4 Kumaon.

fire were coming from an unseen enemy machine-gun detachment that had returned from the nearby bush area. Enemy bullets swept the lake's surface and made the water splash on the troops as they climbed into the boats. Soon the first boat had moved into the lake, while the second and third boats were still casting off. The enemy was seen filtering back from the bush to the water's edge in large numbers. They seemed determined to cause maximum casualties on the withdrawing raiders. Some of the men in the boats, including Hansard, were wounded by the accurate bursts of German machine-gun fire. Most casualties were suffered by troops in the second boat that was echeloned towards the approaching Germans.

Encouraged by the results of their fire, enemy parties began to splash into the water looking for an easy kill. Although Hansard's boat had only one rower remaining in a fit condition, despite his wounds he himself gallantly grabbed an oar and put back to assist the personnel in the third boat. Not caring for the machine-gun bullets which were thudding into the wooden hull of the boat, young Hansard unsteadily rose to his feet and affixed a rope to the bows of the damaged third boat that was floundering in the water. Loudly shouting encouragements to the lone rower in his boat, Hansard leaned forward and grabbed an oar. He dug into the water despite his wounded condition and managed to tow the third boat deeper into the lake. The boat was towed away from the clutches of the German soldiers, who were by now waist deep in the water and rapidly approaching the boat. Meanwhile, raiders in the first boat (that was deeper in the lake) turned and began to provide accurate fire support with their rifles.

Raids Around Lake Victoria (Africa)

The rifle fire caused some casualties to the enemy troops who were wading in the water, in the most determined manner. However, the accurate rifle fire from the boats deterred the enemy from moving further towards the second boat and third boat. The German troops had been left floundering in Lake Victoria's waters.

Slowly, the three boats limped back across the placid waters of Lake Victoria to Kurungu, where the wounded were carried ashore, for medical treatment. As the troops were disembarking from the boats, a wounded soldier raised a clenched fist in the air above his head and he was heard shouting loudly, 'Hansard sahib ki jai!' Others too joined in this chant, and soon it filled the air around the beach at Kurungu. A great cheer spread across the waterfront.

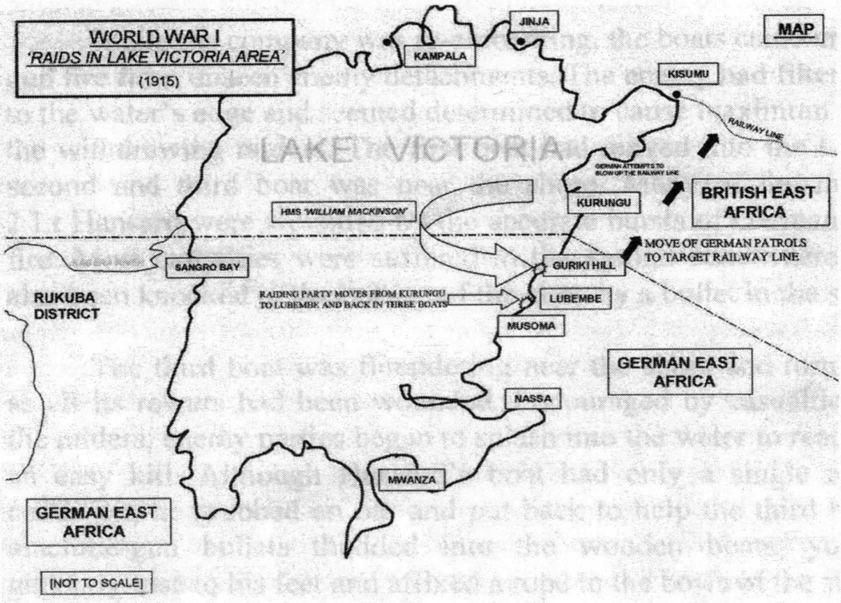

Map for raids along Lake Victoria

The embarrassed and shyly smiling, young officer slowly climbed down from his boat and whipped off his cap. Hansard acknowledged the men's cheers with a raised arm followed by an uncovered and bowed head. Cheering by the troops was truly a unique and befitting gesture to recognize young Hansard's brave act that had saved the lives of many of his men.

Sadly, there is no photographic record available of Hansard and his plucky raiders. These men received neither an official recognition nor any gallantry awards for their gallant actions. There is also no record of what became of Hansard, after World War 1 had ended. In all probability, this brave, young officer was boarded out of military service due to the wounds he had sustained during the raid, in 1915. However, remembrances of the gallant actions of young Hansard and his brave band live on in the annals of 4 Kumaon's history, where the memory of the brave deeds stands tall and is remembered to this day.

Thereafter, the 98th Infantry launched offensive operations against the German forces around Lake Victoria and advanced against strong opposition, along the Mwanza–Tabora (in present-day Tanzania) front. The Battalion won acclaim for the impressive operations that followed and the great gallantry displayed by troops. Indian soldiers had repeatedly proved their mettle in battle and displayed great fighting spirit and gallantry against heavy odds. The bravery of Indian troops was considered even more impressive as the bitter fighting was taking place in distant lands that were far removed from the soldier's hearth and homes in India. One of the unit's Company Commanders, Major J. P. Mitford[3] won the DSO in the heavy fighting during the unit's spirited advance to Tabora.

Commemorative brass medallion presented to the family of all personnel who were killed in action. This medallion was presented to family of one Sepoy Mohar Singh, killed during raid on Lubembe, on 3 December 1915.

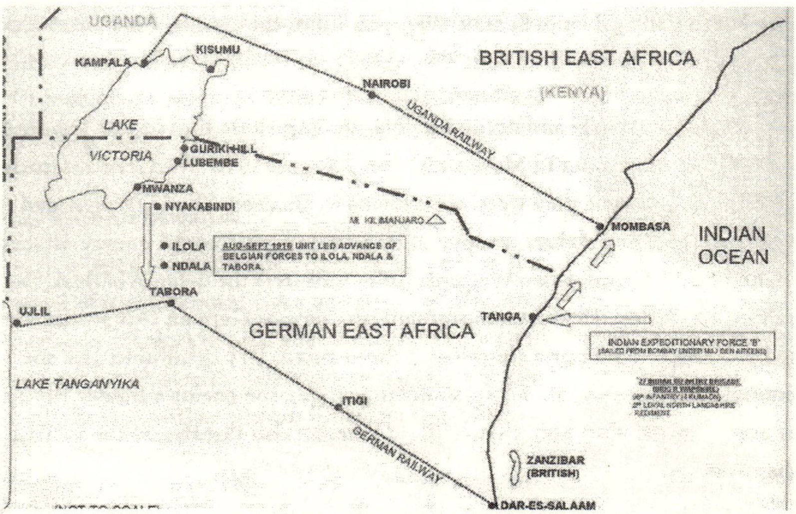

Operations on the Mwanza–Tabora front

[3] Major J. P. Mitford, DSO and Bar, is one of the highest decorated personnel from the Battalion.

Having successfully completed its operations in the Tabora area, on 1 November 1916 the Battalion was reorganized under the new 'four coy system' and ordered to move to Egypt for operations in Mesopotamia. But the order was cancelled due to the large number of casualties that had been suffered by the unit during the heavy fighting in East Africa. Thus, on 13 December 1916 the Battalion was relieved by Gwalior Rifles and given orders to return to India.

After its heart wrenching operations in the swamps around Tanga with leeches and poisonous water snakes and fighting the German and Askari troopers of Count Paul von Lettow-Vorbeck, the unit had a taste of the debilitating African killer bees and other hardships during their unique war experience of 26 months in East Africa. The unit returned to India along with other units of Indian Expeditionary Force 'B'. The unit embarked at Mombasa on 5 January 1917 in SS *Aragon*, and it arrived at Bombay harbour on 14 January 1917.

The return voyage to India on SS *Aragon* (5–14 August 1917) was more pleasant than the outward journey from Bombay, due to lessons learnt by the troops on the way out to Mombasa. Once they were back in India, the unit disembarked at Bombay and moved to its next duty station at Ferozepur by a Special Train. At Ferozepur, 98th Infantry under Lieutenant Colonel V. F. W. Tregear carried out intensive training based on the lessons that had been learnt in the swamps around Tanga, the vast Lake Victoria with enemy posts on its shores and the dry and waterless tracts around Mwanza and Tabora.

SS *Aragon* carried the Battalion from Mombasa to Bombay, India, after World War I

Lt Col V. F. W. Tregear

The new commanding officer, Tregear, was a hard task-master. In 1918, he trained the unit well and executed it with an iron hand. The new recruits were made to train hard to fulfil future commitments. All ranks undertook detailed firing lessons on the new weapons which the unit had been issued with, such as the Lewis machine-gun and short Lee Enfield rifle. The training was indeed useful as for the next three years the Battalion would undertake frequent moves and send out company-sized and smaller detachments for various field service duties.

On 30 September 1917, 'C' Coy under Captain W. R. Selby moved out for field service on the Nushki–Saindak Road. The road runs south of Afghanistan, and connects Quetta (now in Pakistan) with Siestan in Persia (now named Iran). Ten days later, 'D' Coy under Major J. P. Mitford, DSO, took up defence in Dalbindin area. On 27 June 1918, a special company under Lieutenant A. S. Miller proceeded down the Nushki–Saindak Road to join the East Persia Cordon at Khwash. At the same time another special company under Captain D. R. Montford was sent as part of reinforcements to 58th Infantry, which was on active with Egyptian Expeditionary Force.

Montford had performed gallantly during operations in East Africa, where he was wounded numerous times. The gallant officer was killed in an action with 58th Infantry that was a part of the Egyptian Expeditionary Force, during the closing days of World War I. During the end of 1918, the Maree tribe caused considerable trouble and a punitive expedition had to be launched. Lieutenant Colonel D. R. Adye, Commandant, took control of Sibi Area, while Lieutenant Adams and 78 men occupied a defensive position to guard the Sibi–Quetta Railway. During end of 1918 and early 1919, severe influenza epidemics swept the region. This was a new affliction and one Indian officer and 100 soldiers of the Battalion died of influenza.

In May 1919, the Third Afghan War broke out and regular Afghan forces supported by guns and cavalry appeared on the Persian border. From Persia, a powerful column was sent by the British, which included the Battalion. Heavy fighting took place near the border, in which the Afghans suffered heavily. The unit snipers were effectively deployed in thickets and broken ground and they took a heavy toll on the marauding Afghans. Mitford personally led many raiding parties with great gallantry and won a Bar to his DSO.

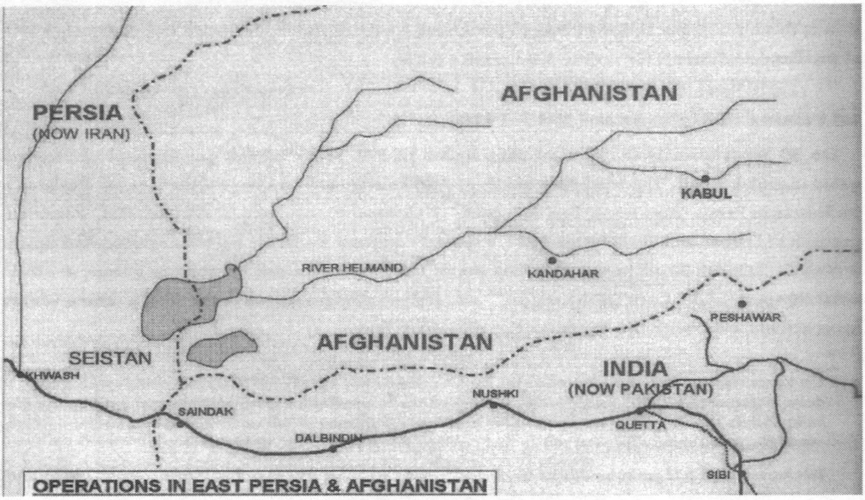

Map for operations in East Persia and Afghanistan

On completion of its operations during the Third Afghan War, 98th Infantry moved back to India for a well-deserved rest after the long operational service. The troops were awarded the following medals for services during the years 1914 to 1919:

1914–1918 Medal

British General Service Medal

Victory Medal

Indian General Service Medal 1908, with clasp Afghanistan 1919

The Glorious Years 1926–1939

In 1922 there was large-scale reorganization of the Indian Army and many units were redesignated. Among them, the Battalion was redesignated from 98th Infantry as 4th Battalion, 19th Hyderabad Regiment or 4/19 Hyderabad Regiment. The Battalion was also given a new crest. And then, it was time to move again.

Crest of 4th Battalion, 19th Hyderabad Regiment instituted in 1922

Crest of 98th Infantry

Field Service in Iraq – 1926

After serving in India for nearly six years, on Thursday, 28 March 1927, the unit (4/19 Hyderabad Regiment) sailed from Karachi to Basra in SS *Versova*. From Basra the unit moved on to Baghdad and settled in Arakhanna Barracks. Lieutenant Colonel J. A. Britton was the Commandant and the Battalion's main task was to guard important civil and military installations in the area and continue with its training. On 1

The unit travelled from Karachi to Basra, Iraq, aboard SS *Versova*

April 1927, the Battalion left Arakhanna Barracks, Baghdad, in a convoy of Leyland lorries for the Table Mountain, where it established a camp and carried out further training. The Table Mountain camp's location was about 68 miles (about 109 km) away from the unit's barracks in Baghdad. On its arrival at the new site, the unit pitched its tents and established a camp. The troops were glad to be permitted to lay out their gear in the sun as the men's kit had been dampened by a sudden rain shower while moving to Table Mountain camp.

While they were at Table Mountain camp, every day the troops conducted unit level training and rifle firing at the 'Long Range'. The unit level training was followed by collective training. In addition to supervising the daily training schedule, the officers often went out to shoot

Firing in progress at Table Mountain Long Range, Iraq, early June 1927
Lt K. Daulat Sen is second firer from right

the teeming wildlife. The lively shoots included hunts for wild boar, grouse and black partridges. It was a happy time for everyone and after a month and half of collective training, the Battalion returned to Baghdad on 17 May 1927.

On 28 May 1927, Lieutenant K. Daulat Sen was detailed to proceed to Baghdad and receive a newly posted young officer named 2nd Lieutenant K. S. Thimayya. His first impression of the newly arrived officer was— '.... Indeed, a very nice lad'. While in Baghdad, the unit performed very well in sports and won the hockey championship. There was great rejoicing in the unit. The Battalion marched in a procession, carrying the hockey trophy aloft with great pride. The unit *safaiwalas* led the procession, jubilantly beating tin cans and singing their melodious Indian village songs! Some local Arabs also joined in the celebrations, as the joyous procession passed their homes. On 4 December 1927, Britton departed on a year's leave to the United Kingdom and a British officer named Major C. G. Bacon took over as the temporary Commandant. Mercifully, he had a short tenure with the unit, which was racked with tensions as he always wanted to do '...everything in a hurry and all at once'.

With the unit's tenure in Iraq having ended successfully on 5 February 1928, the unit moved to Basra and loaded its stores in a vessel named SS *Vasna* for the return voyage to India. The journey was pleasant and every evening the unit brass band played melodious tunes on the main deck of the ship. These times were made all the more pleasant as a cool breeze blew from the sea and large waves noisily lashed the ship.

After a pleasant voyage, the unit arrived at Bombay via Karachi on 11 February 1928. After quickly unloading its gear from the ship, the unit left for Allahabad by a special train at 1830 hours on the same day. At Allahabad, Lieutenant Colonel H. V. Lewis, DSO, MC, arrived from 1/18 Royal Garhwal Rifles and took over as Commandant of the Battalion.

The Battalion was stationed at Allahabad, from where numerous parties of troops and officers paid regular visits to nearby Benares, where the Hyderabad Regiment Training Centre was located, under the command of Lieutenant Colonel A. Latham, DSO (of 1st Kumaon Rifles). In 1932, 'Indianization' of the Battalion progressed further and many British officers were replaced by Kings Commissioned Indian Officers

2 Lt (later General) K. S. Thimayya, on joining unit, 28 May 1927

Young Thimayya's room in Baghdad

Captain K. Daulat Sen

(KCIOs). At Allahabad, the KCIOs present in the unit were Captain K. Daulat Sen, Captain Jai Singh, Captain S. M. Shrinagesh, Lieutenant Niranjan Singh Gill, Lieutenant M. I. Majid, Lieutenant G. R. Nagar, Lieutenant K. S. Thimmaya, Lieutenant M. Azam Khan, Lieutenant K. Bahadur Singh, Lieutenant Balwant Singh and 2nd Lieutenant Apji Randhir Singh.

While at Allahabad, Daulat Sen (the most senior Indian officer) suggested to Major E. L. Ricketts (2 IC) that since there was a sizeable number of Indian officers in the Battalion, Indian dishes should be cooked in the Officers' Mess along with European dishes. Also, Sen told his 2 IC that all Indian officers had desired that the unit band should have some Indian music in its repertoire. They felt that Indian tunes should also be played from time to time. However, the innocent and well-intentioned suggestions were taken amiss by the 2 IC, who turned against Daulat Sen. Things went from 'bad to worse' and it was felt by the British officers that the 'Daulat Sen incident' had a mutinous content. The higher authorities were apprised of the incident and an inquiry was instituted against Daulat Sen 'for un-officer like behaviour',[1] and this senior Indian officer had to sadly leave the Army. The British seemed to have felt the rising surge of nationalistic feelings that existed among the Indian officers. Thus, there was a spree of lectures conducted for the Indian officers of 4/19 Hyderabad Regiment, on their expected behaviour! This unusually sharp reaction of the

[1] The papers of this unfortunate incident are preserved in the Battalion.

4/19 Hyderabad Regiment on parade in Baghdad, Iraq, 1927

British proved they had been 'deeply rattled' by the 'Daulat Sen incident' and they wanted to make urgent corrections before the feelings of Indian officers snowballed into an unacceptable revolt.

Some officers and ladies during the voyage (5–11 February 1928) from Basra to Bombay on board SS *Vasna*

On completion of its tenure at Allahabad, the unit moved to Hindubagh (Fort Sandeman) in Waziristan in 1931 and then to Quetta in 1934. At Hindubagh the unit made a nice-looking crest with big, white stones on a hill behind the unit camp. A great earthquake struck Quetta during the early hours of 31 May 1935, causing great destruction and a grave loss of life. The unit helped greatly in the large-scale relief work

(Sitting L to R) Lts Azam Khan, G. R. Nagar, M. S. Wadalia, Capt. K. Daulat Sen and (standing) Lt K. S. Thimayya, at Fort Sandeman. This group of young officers would jocularly call themselves as members of the 'Sandeman Club'

A large unit crest was made with white stones and bricks on a hill behind the unit camp at Hindubagh, June 1932

and received a letter of commendation from the Viceroy, Lord Willingdon. Lance Naik Mata Din did commendable rescue work and saved an

L Nk (later Subedar) Mata Din, GC, IOM; he was awarded Indian Order of Merit in Burma in 1944

individual who had been buried deep in the rubble. Mata Din was awarded the high gallantry award of Military Cross (MC), which was soon upgraded to the newly incorporated and highest award for an act of bravery, not in face of the enemy—the George Cross (GC).

From Quetta the unit proceeded to Secunderabad in 1936, where new colours were received by Lieutenants Dilsukh Maan and K. Bhagwati Singh from Lieutenant General Sir J. E. S. Brind, KCB, KBE, CMG, DSO, GOC-in-C, Southern Command on 4 December 1937, during a glittering parade. It was the first time that colours were received by Indian officers. At Secunderabad the unit had ample time to conduct training, parades and sports.

The Battalion arriving at Quetta station in 1934

Officers of 4/19 Hyderabad Regiment at Quetta, 1934:
Standing (L to R): Lt. K. S. Thimayya, Lt. Azam Khan, Capt. S. M. Shrinagesh, Lt. Balwant Singh, Lt. A. Randhir Singh and Lt. K. Bahadur Singh
Sitting (L to R): Capt. S. Jai Singh, Capt. D. Q. H. Agnew, Maj. A. B. R. Leech, Maj. W. H. Hall, Maj. Colsey, Capt. A. D. Brown and Capt. C. E. Kennedy

Capt. Dilsukh Maan is seen receiving King's Colours from Lt. Gen. J. E. S. Brind (GOC-in-C Southern Command) at Secunderabad on 4 December 1937. On his left, Capt. K. Bhagwati Singh is kneeling to receive the battalion colours.

Move to Singapore

In August 1937, due to the deteriorating international situation, the Battalion was mobilized and placed on three days' notice to proceed to an undisclosed location. There was great excitement in the unit and troops on leave were recalled. But the move was cancelled at the last moment. The unit was then being commanded by Lieutenant Colonel (later Major General) Wilfred L. Lloyd, MC (he commanded the unit from July 1936 to July 1939).[2] Among those officers who sailed with the unit were Lieutenant Colonel D. Stuart (CO), Major J. B. Macdonald (2 IC), Major A. D. Brown (later CO and killed in action), Captain S. M. Shrinagesh (Adjutant and Chief of Army Staff in 1955), Captain M. I. Majid (later Major General in Pakistan Army), Captain Niranjan Singh Gill (later Colonel in INA and India's Ambassador to Panama and Mexico), Captain K. S. Thimmaya (later General and Chief of Army Staff in 1957), Captain M. Azam Khan (Quarter Master, later Lieutenant General in Pakistan Army and Governor of East Pakistan), Captain Apji Randhir Singh (later Brigadier), Captain K. Bhagwati Singh (IC-1 and later Major General), Captain Balbir Singh (later Brigadier, awarded Military Cross), Lieutenant M. M. Khanna (later Lieutenant General, awarded Maha Vir Chakra), Captain M. G. Jilani (later Major General in Pakistan Army), Lieutenant Pritam Singh (later Brigadier and 'Saviour of Poonch'), Lieutenant Balwant Singh (bayoneted to death in jungles of Borneo), Lieutenant Gulzara Singh (killed during Battle of Slim River) Captain V. W. Harris (killed at Chemor), and Lieutenant S. M. Bal. The officers who joined later were Lieutenant Colonel E. L. Wilson-Haffenden (later CO and wounded in action), Captain G. R. Parab [later Colonel, awarded Military Cross), Captain S. V. Phadnavis (died in POW camp at Singapore), Lieutenant L. C. Lind (killed during Battle of Singapore; awarded Military Cross), Lieutenant G. K. Mehta and Lieutenant K. D. Vasudeva (both officers were killed during Battle of Slim River) and Lieutenant A. E. Darling (killed

[2] By the end of the World War II, Wilfred L. Lloyd had become Major General and was a most highly decorated officer with CBE, DSO and Bar, MC, and Croix-de-Guerre. He was only 47 years old, when on 22 January 1944 he was unfortunately knocked down by a speeding lorry and killed near Cairo, Egypt. Lloyd's medals were presented to 4 Kumaon for safekeeping and display by his son Lieutenant Commander Peter Lloyd, Royal Navy, in 1988.

in Malaya).

The tenure at Singapore was to be a 'peace-time posting'; thus, while at Secunderabad teams of officers and VCOs had conducted a selection of stores that were in the best of condition, to be taken by the unit to Singapore.

In August 1939, the unit received its mobilization and movement orders for a third time. This time the unit finally moved from Secunderabad to Madras by train. Lieutenant Colonel Douglas Stuart, OBE, had replaced Lieutenant Colonel W. L. Lloyd, DSO, MC as CO of 4/19 Hyderabad Regiment. At Madras the unit linked up with other units of 12 Indian Infantry Brigade under Brigadier Archibald Charles Melvill Paris. 5/2 Punjab and 2 Argyll & Sutherland Highlanders were the other two infantry battalions of 12 Indian Infantry Brigade.

The unit boarded the 10,000-tonne vessel named SS *Tilawa,* and after customary prayers at Madras the unit sailed as a part of 'Force EMU'. On its arrival at Singapore, the Battalion was quarantined for three days on a small island just off Singapore, named Pulau Blakang Mati. Thereafter, the Battalion moved into some tents that had been

Officers and VCOs of 4/19 Hyderabad Regiment in field dress, when they sailed to Singapore in August 1939
Sitting (L to R): Capt. M. I. Majid, Capt. S. M. Shrinagesh, VCO, Maj. J. B. McDonal, (2 IC), Lt. Col. D. Stewart, (CO) Sub. Maj., 'A' Coy Commander, VCO, Capt. Niranjan Singh Gill.
Middle Row (L to R): Lt. Azam Khan, Lt. V. W. Harris, Capt. K. S. Thimayya, Lt. K. Bahadur Singh, Lt. Balbir Singh, Lt. Apji Randhir Singh, Lt. Balwant Singh, Lt. Pritam Singh, Lt. K. Bhagwati Singh, Lt. K. D. Vasudeva, Lt. G. K. Mehta, Lt. K. D. Law.
Rear Row (L to R): Lt. Juneja, Lt G. S. Bal, Lt. Dilsukh Maan, 2 Lt. M. M. Khanna, Lt. M. G. Jilani, VCO, Lt. S. M. Hussain, Jem. Kabul Singh.

pitched on the grounds of Tanglin Gardens, till new unit accommodation of wooden hutments had been constructed at Tyresal Park.

SS *Tilawa* transported 4/19 Hyderabad Regiment from Madras to Singapore, August 1939

World War II 1939–1945

Actions Against Advancing Japanese Forces in Malaya

The Japanese landings in Thailand and north Malaya rudely jolted the Allies into action, as they had expected the enemy to directly attack Singapore, which had been strengthened with battleships, additional troops (Australian Division) and numerous large calibre sea-facing guns. 12 Infantry Brigade (commanded by Brigadier Archibald Charles Melvill Paris) was ordered to immediately proceed to north Malaya and hold the advancing Japanese forces from hastily prepared defensive positions. The Japanese advance had to be halted at all costs, to allow the forward troops to regroup and safely withdraw to defensive positions in depth. On the Brigade's arrival at Krai by train from Singapore, during the early hours of 9 December 1941, the unit moved to Ketereh in vehicles, and hastily occupied a defensive position.

After landing from the sea, a part of the Japanese invasion force advanced on bicycles that were laden with their supplies and ammunition. It was easy for these troops to advance rapidly along narrow jungle-tracks as they were not supported by an unwieldy logistics back-up. The advance of 'bicycle troops' was not slowed down by the move of heavier logistics elements, for they carried all their sustenance with them on the bicycles. The Allies tried to slow the Japanese advance by demolishing bridges and larger culverts, but the enemy was quick to make improvised footbridges and resume their rapid advance. The enemy infantry would usually bypass the obstacles that had been prepared by the Allies with so much effort to cause delay. However, the Japanese follow-up vehicles had to halt till a proper crossing had been created.

Japanese 'Bicycle Troops' advance in Malaya, carrying their kit, rations and ammunition on the bicycles

Many reports were being received of Japanese landings and it was even reported there was heavy fighting taking place around Kota Bahru. Under severe enemy pressure, elements of 8 Indian Infantry Brigade, that had been contesting the Japanese landings, kept falling back. The Brigade was withdrawn to a position some four miles south of Kota Baharu. The new deployment had 2/12 Frontier Force Regiment on the right, 1/13 Frontier Force Rifles on the left and 3/17 Dogra was at the rear. However, the withdrawal of forward units did not go as planned as the enemy had already got across the road linking Kota Baharu and Kubang Kriang. 2/12 Frontier Force Regiment fought its way to Kubang Kriang village, where there was already heavy fighting taking place.

By about 11 a.m., the enemy had captured the village and most of the Allied troops withdrew rapidly towards Peringhat, which was located four miles further south. Here, they were joined by two companies of 2/10 Baluch, which had been withdrawn from beaches to the south, and the position was temporarily stabilized. 4/19 Hyderabad Regiment (Command Reserve) had arrived in the area and it was ordered to move into a position at Ketereh, twelve miles south of Kota Bharu. By 7.30 p.m., the Battalion was in defensive position with good fields of fire across the jungle and paddy fields. There was also a three-gun battery of 4.5-inch howitzers that had been deployed under the unit's operational command. However, because of the rapid withdrawal there had been no time for reconnaissance to effectively employ these artillery guns.

All night long the forward troops kept falling back in disarray and strong rumours abounded regarding the ferocity of Japanese attacks and the atrocities they had perpetrated on civilians and soldiers alike. Commanders kept a firm grip on their troops due to the heightened state of uncertainty, but fortunately no enemy appeared during the first night. Next morning a readjustment of defences was carried out. However, the men remained nervous and expected the Japanese forward elements to show up at any time. The weather was cool as there had been intermittent showers during the night. By nightfall, the 8th Indian Infantry Brigade had withdrawn through 4/19 Hyderabad Regiment, which was comparatively concentrated in favourable terrain, instead of being spread out over great distances with few landmarks for communications.

It was a dark night with light drizzle, when first contact was made with the advancing elements of 'Takumi Force', at about 9 p.m. on 10 December 1941. Many of the Japanese troops were lightly clad and equipped, and it was difficult to tell friend from foe and differentiate Japanese soldiers from Malay or Chinese villagers. The situation quickly became confused as about 60 Japanese soldiers armed with light machine guns (LMGs) and rifles emerged from the dark jungle and engaged 'A' Company and 'B' Company. The Japanese supported their attack with the fire of medium mortars.

Thus, the first shots by the Battalion in World War II were fired by 'A' Company. The exploding enemy mortar bombs made a lot of noise, but the Japanese fire was rather erratic and did not cause much damage. During the night, 'A' Company asked for artillery support and 80 rounds were fired by the howitzer battery. Heavy small arms firing could be heard from 'A' and 'B' Company areas, till the early hours of the morning. Troops were jittery in the darkness and each company reported it was either being outflanked or attacked. At dawn on 11 December, the defensive positions were readjusted and 'A' Company was moved behind 'D' Company. The first encounter with the Japanese was encouraging, as the Battalion had managed to hold the position with only a few casualties. After gauging the opposition, the enemy suddenly broke contact and withdrew to regroup their forces.

Rearguard Action at Machang

On 11 December, 8 Indian Infantry Brigade was ordered to withdraw to Machang and move across the bridge over Kelantan River. The Battalion was ordered to fight a rearguard action and allow 8 Indian Infantry Brigade to break contact with the enemy. The complex move was carried out smoothly except for an enemy 'jitter party' that infiltrated the temporary position of 3/17 Dogra. The Japanese opened fire on the Dogras, resulting in delay and considerable firing to drive out the intruding enemy. Despite the firing, the withdrawing brigade had almost successfully crossed the bridge over Kelantan River and moved south of Machang. Only a company of 1/10 Baluch and 'B' Company of 4/19 Hyderabad Regiment were left to cross the bridge, when the enemy had attacked the Baluchis. The bridge had been prepared for demolition, and on hearing firing in their close vicinity an alarmed Sapper depressed the handle of his Exploder Dynamo Set and blew the bridge.

The 'fog of war' had led to a precarious situation, wherein a company of 1/10 Baluch Regiment and 'B' Company of the Battalion were left stranded on the enemy side of Kelanten River. In the absence of any other option, both companies wisely took up hasty defences and occupied a weak bridge-head position. The surrounding thick jungle and poor visibility around the bridge-head had made this position across the river extremely precarious.

In the dark of the night, Lieutenant Colonel E. L. Wilson-Haffenden, CO, Major A. D. Brown, 2 IC and Captain M. G. Jilani, Adjutant, bravely went back across Kelantan River in a boat to inspect the bridge-head positions and to instill confidence in the men who had been left on the enemy side of the river. It was a difficult decision for the CO to take the key officers on this dangerous mission. However, it speaks highly of his concern for the troops, for him to venture back across the river in the night. The enemy engaged the boat carrying CO's party with small arms and also used the fire of heavy mortars. The mortar bombs exploded in the river and sent tall geysers of water into the air, but the explosions missed the boat. The CO's party successfully entered the bridge-head and on seeing the officers in their midst, the men cheered and their morale skyrocketed. The CO's party went around the defences and cheered up both the Hyderabads and Baluchs.

As they came across the river, the CO's party had been met by Captain Balbir Singh and a small 'protection party' from 'B' Company. The officer led them around his company where the troops were huddled in shallow trenches, guarding the narrow bridge-head position along with the company of 1/10 Baluch Regiment. It was an action filled night and the enemy made several unsuccessful attempts to assault the bridge-head. The troops fought tooth and nail and did not permit the Japanese to get near their isolated defences. The bitter fight went on all night, with remainder of the Brigade providing the required fire support from across the river.

During early hours of the next morning, firing broke out from three sides leading to a difficult tactical situation. The enemy fired a number of star-shells to illuminate the defences before launching determined attacks. To make matters worse, the company's wireless communications with the Battalion HQ had broken down. The fire of one enemy mortar was very accurate indeed and the Battalion suffered 13 casualties (seven killed and six wounded). But the troops successfully beat back the determined and repeated Japanese attempts to capture the shallow bridge-head. The action at Machang will always be remembered as a gallant fight amidst the chaos of a general withdrawal. During the next morning, 12 December, all the troops stranded across Kelantan River were moved to the home bank. It was a difficult operation as the men had to be moved across the river in boats, under the cover of heavy artillery and mortar concentrations. Wounded troops were helped to the boats and taken across, while the bodies of soldiers killed during the night were left in the abandoned bridge-head on the far bank. As the boats were crossing Kelantan River, the enemy continued to bring down heavy fire on the withdrawing troops. The Japanese had suffered heavy casualties during the night and they did not make any attempts to follow-up the withdrawal to the other bank of the river.

Withdrawal Down the Malayan Peninsula

Administrative tasks like washing of clothes and cooking a hot meal were being done when a massive Japanese air raid struck Krai. It was the unit's first experience of an air raid. Men dived for cover as bombs screamed into Krai and exploded with shattering bangs. One bomb exploded in the Battalion area and luckily only one sepoy was wounded with bomb shrapnel. After the air raid, the shaken troops would often look up at the sky, as they completed the remaining administrative tasks. The unit spent the night of 14 December at Krai. Next morning, orders were received to occupy the south bank of Nal River at Sungei Nal as the advancing Japanese had reportedly broken through the Allied defence line and were reported to be speedily advancing to the south. Thus, the Battalion was tasked to prevent the enemy from making either a river crossing or allow any move down the river in boats. Very attentively looking for the advancing enemy, the Battalion held a large frontage of about 6 miles (about 9.5 km) along Nal River, for the next two nights.

At this time, Japanese reconnaissance aircraft constantly flew overhead and there was a marked increase in their patrolling activity. On 17 December, 4/19 Hyderabad Regiment was relieved at the Nal River position by 2/10 Baluch Regiment, and the Battalion marched back to Krai. The Battalion entrained at 8 p.m. and finally steamed out of Kalantan Area. The unit vehicles and a 'rear party' of one Viceroy's Commissioned Officer (VCO) and 30 men, was left behind at Krai. The 'rear party' followed by road in the unit's vehicles. The unit reached Tanjong Malim by the next afternoon and detrained. After a refreshing cup of tea, provided by local hospital staff, the troops put up bivouacs for the night. On 19 December, orders were received to again move by train to Kuala Kangsar. The 'rear party' rejoined the Battalion briefly and they were moved on to Kuala Kangsar as well. The CO proceeded to Advance HQ of 3 Indian Corps, for a briefing.

After the briefing, CO rejoined the Battalion at Kuala Kangsar where the unit had deployed its sentries and spent the night in local school buildings. On 21 December, the Battalion was ordered by Archie Paris, to be prepared to occupy a position either at Chenderoh Damak on Grik Road or astride the Taiping Road. However, the Japanese were again reported to have broken through the Allied defences. Thus, late in the afternoon fresh orders were received to occupy the south bank of Perak River, on the right flank of 5/14 Punjab and to also guard the Alexandria Bridge.

It was already dusk by the time troops moved into the new position. Once again, the position was occupied with little reconnaissance and in the dark. The unit was made responsible for a frontage of more than 6,000 yards (about 5.4 km). The poor visibility due to thick jungles and rubber plantations on all sides added to the woes of the rifle companies. On the next day, the unit was ordered to extend its frontage by another

1,500 yards (about 1.3 km), making the position even more precarious than the one they had held at Sungei Nal.

Maps were practically useless as the rubber plantation roads and tracks bore no resemblance to those marked on the maps. Along the Perak river-bank it was not possible to lay telephone cable from Battalion HQ to 'A', 'B' and 'C' Companies due to their large distances from the Battalion HQ. Since there was a problem of passing orders, rudimentary communications were maintained by using dispatch riders (DR), who nervously traversed the extremely poor jungle-tracks on motorcycles and bicycles. It was a risky job as there was a constant threat of Japanese patrols striking through the thick jungles. Due to the extended frontage, Brown, as 2 IC, was made in-charge of 'A' and 'D' Companies while CO personally looked after the remaining unit deployment.

On the morning of 23 December, heavy enemy air raids struck Perak Area and a number of the unit's trucks were destroyed. The 2 Argyll & Sutherland Highlanders suffered most and its troops sustained 20 casualties. Along with the air raid, the enemy rapidly infiltrated through the thick jungle. The Japanese build-up along the Kroh–Kuala Kangsar Road was so quick that 11 Infantry Division, which was located a short distance ahead, was forced to fall back. Consequently, 12 Brigade was ordered to withdraw at midnight. With the enemy's break-out, the overall situation had once again degenerated rapidly.

Due to the darkness and poor communications, it was a major effort for the Battalion to concentrate from their far-flung positions. Next morning, 4/19 Hyderabad Regiment moved in a vehicle convoy to the new brigade position at Chemor. Although, concentration during the dark night and subsequent move had been difficult, all the commanders performed admirably well and the unit reached Chemor on time, as per the allotted schedule of move.

During the repeated withdrawals, only rudimentary logistics support was available to the troops. Hot meals had become a rarity and whenever there was an opportunity, troops cooked *khichadi* (pre-mixed rice and lentils) in individual mess tins or in 'section pots'. Normally, half of the cooked meal was eaten immediately by most men, while other half was stashed away in the troops' personal packs, to be consumed as the next meal. Thus, the hot meals were greatly relished by the troops.

Whenever it was possible, the wounded soldiers were speedily evacuated and well looked after by the dedicated medical staff, but there was little time or dry wood to perform last rites and cremate the men who died. The bodies of soldiers who had been killed were quickly consigned to shallow graves, as the troops were often ordered to commence the withdrawal at short notice. On numerous occasions, dead bodies of soldiers had to be left where they had fallen, as the unit hurriedly pulled back to a new position, under heavy Japanese pressure. Sadly, it was hoped that the dead would later be given a decent farewell by Malay villagers. However, troops were growing weary of the frequent night moves, occupation of extended frontages without reconnaissance and constant enemy pressure.

Despite exhaustive efforts made by officers and the VCOs to care for the men, the mounting administrative problems were beginning to tell on the soldier's morale. Commanders understood this worrisome problem, but there was precious little they could do because of the unfavourable battle situation that was unfolding. The unit's determined actions and orderly withdrawals under enemy pressure are a testimonial of the Battalion's good training and splendid fighting spirit. It is creditable that the Battalion kept on fighting as a cohesive fighting force during the bitter actions that were fought while withdrawing through the Malayan jungles. The actions on the island of Singapore followed by the dreadful years in Japanese prisoner of war (POW) camps are a telling record of the extremely difficult times the Battalion went through during World War II.

'The Ruddy Plan Has Backfired'

While at Singapore, before moving north to contest the enemy landings, 4/19 Hyderabad Regiment was involved in numerous training manoeuvres as a preparation for operations in the jungles of Malaya. Although it was felt by the British High Command that the Japanese would attack from the sea,

Japanese troops land from the sea

Lieutenant Colonel D. Stuart, CO did not agree with assessment of higher HQs and engaged in continuous training for operations in Malaya (now Malaysia). Stuart was finally proved correct as the unit clashed with rapidly advancing Japanese forces that had landed in North Malaya/Thailand and advanced to the south through difficult terrain that was covered with thick jungles. The unit was in action from 10 December 1941 onwards, when it had first clashed with Japanese troops (Takumi Force) at Ketereh, 12 miles (about 19.3 km) south of Kota Baharu, Malaya. After the first fierce action with Ahirs of 'A' Company, there were a series of fighting withdrawals which left the troops tired and thoroughly demoralized.

There was little administrative support for the units of 12 Indian Infantry Brigade (5/2 Punjab Regiment, 2 Argyll & Sutherland Highlanders and 4/19 Hyderabad Regiment) and other Allied forces. The dead bodies of Hindu soldiers killed in action had been hurriedly buried in shallow graves before the unit withdrew under enemy pressure to its next battle position. There had been neither time, nor dry firewood to cremate the dead. Troops had been growing weary of the frequent night withdrawals, occupation of extended defences without any reconnaissance and the constant Japanese pressure in the thick Malayan jungles.

Action at Chemor

On the morning of 23 December 1941, heavy enemy air raids struck Perak and many of the unit's vehicles were destroyed. The enemy took advantage of this distraction and rapidly infiltrated through the thick jungle. The Japanese build-up along the Kroh–Kuala Kangsar Road was so quick that 11 Indian Infantry Division, which was located ahead of the unit, had to rapidly fall back. Consequently, 12 Infantry Brigade (including the unit) was ordered to withdraw at midnight. Due to darkness and poor communications, it had been difficult to quickly concentrate the unit from its far-flung company positions. Next morning, the unit was moved in vehicles to the new brigade position at Chemor.

For a change, the defensive position at Chemor was occupied after some reconnaissance had been conducted. 5/2 Punjab was deployed ahead, while 4/19 Hyderabad and 2 Argyll & Sutherland Highlanders were deployed in depth. However, soon the enemy began crossing Perak River and was engaged with artillery fire. As Japanese pressure began to mount, intelligence reports were received that a major attack was expected on 26 December. Thus, an ambitious plan was formulated at the Brigade HQ to lure the enemy into a trap and cause major destruction of the invading Japanese forces. Members of staff at 12 Indian Infantry Brigade HQ were rather upbeat for it was felt that after many dismal days of withdrawals, finally an outstanding victory would soon take place. The plan was that on being attacked, 5/2 Punjab Regiment was to withdraw quickly to a designated line. The enemy would then be annihilated with the use of timed artillery barrages. To assist the Punjabis and to channelize the enemy, 'D' Company of 4/19 Hyderabad Regiment was to deploy on a hill feature that was called 'Limestone Rock'. Necessary instructions about the impending operation were passed to companies of 4/19 Hyderabad Regiment by Jilani, the Adjutant. Once the trap had been sprung, the unit was to prevent the enemy

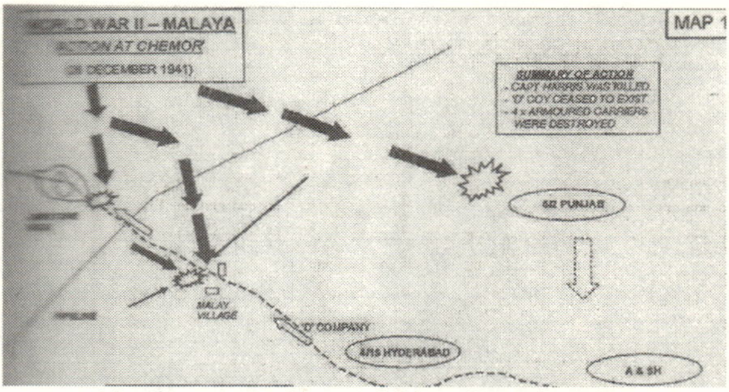

Map for action at Chemor, Malaya, December 1941

Vehicle convoy moves 4/19 Hyderabad Regiment south to Chemor

from escaping, by engaging with rapid LMG and 3-inch mortar fire. Zero Hour was loosely fixed at 9.15 a.m. on 26 December 1941, although it depended on when the Japanese commenced their attack on 5/2 Punjab.

As per the plan, at 7.30 a.m. 'D' Company under Captain V. W. Harris set out for Limestone Rock. Harris was a soft spoken and physically tough young officer. As was expected, the Japanese attack on 5/2 Punjab Regiment commenced on time, but the situation soon got out of hand. By approximately 8.45 a.m., the enemy had pushed 5/2 Punjab Regiment well beyond the designated limit of withdrawal, with the Japanese infantry following closely behind, and in contact with the Punjabis. Thus, the planned artillery barrages were not fired, as the enemy had moved well beyond the designated 'killing ground' and kept mingling with the withdrawing Punjabis. It was as if the enemy had got to know of the Allied plan! Heavy firing was also heard from the direction of Limestone Rock, where 'D' Company of 4/19 Hyderabad had gone to make sure the advancing Japanese moved into the designated 'killing ground'. It soon became apparent that events had taken a turn for the worse and something had gone awfully wrong with the plan! Thus, the operation was wisely called off by HQ 11 Infantry Division.

Since the operation had been called off, Wilson-Haffenden, CO, realized Captain V. W. Harris and 'D' Company had to be urgently recalled, before the troops got involved in a major engagement with the enemy and suffered heavy casualties. But there was no way to inform 'D' Company, since they were not in wireless communication with rest of the unit. Therefore, two bicycle-mounted DRs were urgently sent to convey to the company that the operation had been called off and they were to immediately return to the unit. However, the DRs soon returned without being able to locate the company.

Capt. M. G. Jilani, Adjutant

Realizing that 'D' Company had to be stopped before they ventured any further, Jemadar Ram Swarup, Battalion Intelligence VCO, was sent for the task with a section of troops from Battalion HQ. But before reaching 'D' Company's expected location, the group under Jemadar Ram Swarup came under heavy fire from two well-placed Japanese LMGs and was forced to turn back. Worried by the developments, CO and his staff felt that the enemy had probably trapped 'D' Company. As the situation was now desperate, Lieutenant Lind (an affable young officer with a tremendous sense of humour) was summoned by Jilani and told, 'The ruddy plan has backfired, and the operation has been called off. Lt Lind, you will move out immediately with four armoured carriers and return with "D" Company.' After clarifying a few doubts, Lind had set out immediately with the four armoured carriers.

Soon after leaving Battalion HQ, Lind and the armoured carriers came under accurate enemy fire from Malay Village. The men dismounted and cleared the village by lobbing hand grenades and spraying the area with bursts of LMG fire. The party then resumed their advance. When they reached a pipeline, the carriers were again subjected to intense automatic fire and could not advance further. Returning the fire, the carriers managed to pull back to the village. However, the enemy had reoccupied the village and Lind's party came under fire from two directions.

In addition, the enemy engaged the carriers with armour piercing rounds that were fired from a heavy machine-gun (HMG). All the carriers were riddled with bullets and 12 of Lind's party of 16 men had become casualties in the shootout. The bold rescue attempt had failed and all four armoured carriers were badly damaged due to the HMG bullets and had to be abandoned. Lind and four survivors reached back on foot, after further clashes with enemy on the way back. Lind reported to Jilani that he had been unable to contact Harris. He also reported the disastrous tidings that all four armoured carriers had been lost in clashes with the enemy.

Apparently, a disaster had occurred with 'D' Company, but nothing was known at the time of the tragic events. Much later, three survivors had somehow reached Singapore and told the unit all about 'D' Company's final actions. When 'D' Company moved out and headed towards Limestone Rock, Harris had been with the leading section along with Jemadar Pritam Singh, the leading platoon commander. The other two platoons had followed at a distance of about 50 yards. 'D' Company had gone some distance from the 'pipeline' when the scouts saw enemy soldiers moving on the right side. Harris had halted the men, but he did not engage the enemy as he did not want to jeopardize the overall plan.

They watched, as the Japanese troops advanced. The enemy group was in large numbers and craftily some were dressed as local Malays, to deceive the defenders. Suddenly, the Japanese had spotted 'D' Company and opened fire on the leading platoon. A fierce firefight ensued and the enemy was forced to retreat after leaving behind some casualties. Harris was seen shouting orders and moving among his men, and firing from his pistol at the enemy. During this action, Harris was wounded in the leg and Pritam Singh and some others were killed by the initial volleys fired by the Japanese.

The enemy moved around the right flank and managed to cut off the company from the 'pipeline'. In this later action, a number of men were killed and others were wounded and taken prisoner. Harris gallantly joined the others and counter-attacked the Japanese. Heavy close quarter fighting raged and Harris was hit in the throat by an automatic burst of fire. The brave officer had slumped to the ground and died instantly. Subedar Daya Ram, a platoon commander, was seriously wounded and placed on a stretcher by his troops. The remaining two platoons had then tried to move around the left flank, but they ran into some more Japanese soldiers. Knowing there could be no further withdrawal, the troops had then stood together in a rock-solid manner and fought to the bitter end. At about 11.30 a.m. on 26 December 1941, the jungle finally fell silent as 'D' Company ceased to exist. A few wounded survivors were taken prisoner by the Japanese, only to be later brutally bayoneted to death.

The three soldiers who were taken prisoner when 'D' Company had fallen, were sent under a white flag and Japanese escort with fixed bayonets, to ask an isolated platoon of 5/2 Punjab Regiment to surrender. While they were hailing the Punjabis, providentially some Allied artillery shells exploded nearby and the Japanese party scattered. Seizing the moment, the three survivors darted forward into the 5/2 Punjab Regiment platoon location and warned them of the enemy's moves. However, the unit was to suffer further crippling losses, including the loss of their CO and 'B' Company, during their next action at the Battle of Slim River.

Later, after trying times in Japanese held areas, the three soldiers had reached Singapore and narrated the grim fate that had earlier befallen 'D' Company at Limestone Rock. This is the moving story of a bitter action fought by 4/19 Hyderabad Regiment (today called 4 Kumaon) in the jungles around Chemor. Soon, the unit would again suffer very heavy casualties in the Battle of Slim River, Battle of Singapore and the long internment in wretched POW camps on Singapore Island, for nearly three years, till end of the War. Yet, despite the Allied defeat in Malaya and Singapore with the unit's heavy losses, the troop's great gallantry was recognized with the award of Battle Honours 'Slim River' and 'North Malaya'. These two honours are truly special as they honour the unit even after its terrible losses, for the gallant actions in overall adverse battle situations. The bravery and supreme sacrifices of over two hundred brave soldiers who never returned from the deep Malayan jungles, are well remembered by all ranks of 4 Kumaon.

After the Battle of Slim River, 4/19 Hyderabad Regiment withdrew from the Malayan peninsula to Singapore Island. Here the unit faced the attacking Japanese forces in various vicious battles in north Singapore (Area Kranji), Bukit Timah and finally Singapore City, at the southern end of the island. After Singapore fell to the Japanese forces of General Tomoyuki Yamashita on 14 February 1942, the unit spent the next three years in dreary POW camps facing the brutality of their Japanese captors.

Blood and Guts at Slim River

After the disastrous actions at Chemor, the unit withdrew further to the south. There was nearly continuous enemy air activity, with a single reconnaissance aircraft scouting the Allied defensive positions. The reconnaissance aircraft was followed by a fleet of bomber aircraft, which were escorted by fighter aircraft. On 3 January 1942, as the unit was moving into its defences, an LMG deployed in anti-aircraft (AA) role opened fire on a low flying Japanese reconnaissance aircraft. An hour later, 'A' Company was heavily bombed by four enemy bombers, escorted by six fighter aircraft. Though numerous bombs exploded in close proximity of the trenches, only one OR was caught in the open and killed.

At 3 p.m., Lieutenant Colonel E. L. Wilson-Haffenden, CO, went forward to visit 'A' Company and inspect the damage caused by the air attack. While he was returning from the company, there was suddenly another air raid and CO was wounded with bomb shrapnel in the arm. He had been passing two Carriers and an Ambulance Car parked on the roadside, when a bomb exploded nearby. Wilson-Haffenden was evacuated in the evening and A. D. Brown took over as the officiating CO of the unit on 3 January. It was to be the briefest command tenure, sadly ending in Brown's untimely death during the coming battle.

In happier times – Capt. Balbir Singh with No. 6 Platoon, 'B' Company at Secunderabad in 1938, after winning the Inter Platoon Hockey Tournament. Sitting on Balbir's immediate left is Hav. Kabul Singh. He had been recently promoted to Jemadar. He was killed while fighting gallantly during Battle of Slim River, and was awarded a posthumous Military Cross for gallantry. Most of the personnel in this photograph were killed during the Battle of Slim River, on 7 January 1942.

Battle of Slim River

After the air raids, it was reported the enemy had begun attacking areas north of Bidor. It was appreciated that if the Japanese managed to break through, the artillery guns and transport fleet of 12 Infantry Brigade would be unable to reach the main road to Trolak. The artillery guns and transport fleet were vital to offer any sustained resistance to the advancing enemy. Therefore, during the afternoon of 3 January, the Brigade withdrew further and occupied a new position north of Trolak. It was planned for the Brigade to occupy a 'one up' defensive position with 4/19 Hyderabad deployed at the 'outpost position', ahead of the other two units. The Battalion reached Mile 60 during the night and immediately began to prepare the new defensive position. 'A' and 'C' Companies were deployed ahead, while 'B' Company was retained in depth. 'A' Company guarded the railway line which ran parallel to the road. The company was deployed along a high embankment which was on one side off the railway line. 'C' Company covered the main road from positions atop some steep cuttings, which could not be directly assaulted by armour. The only defences against enemy tanks that the unit possessed were three anti-tank guns, some concrete blocks, tar barrels and desert wire!

To stop the advance of enemy tanks, a small bridge on the railway line had been demolished using explosive charges. However, there was no convenient culvert on the road that could be destroyed and neither was there sufficient time nor any explosives available to blow a large impassable crater on the road. The Battalion's defences were in the midst of unusually thick jungle. Adjacent to the jungle was a rubber estate, with a number of byroads leading out from the main road. 5/2 Punjab and 2 Argyll & Sutherland Highlanders were deployed in depth and had some anti-tank mines. 28 Infantry Brigade was deployed to the rear of 12 Infantry Brigade. It held to a road bridge near Mile 76.

On the morning of 5 January 1942, a visibly flustered Tamil plantation worker came through the lines and reported that Japanese troops with nearly 100 heavy vehicles and tanks were only about three miles away. The troops immediately readied their weapons and went on an alert. During the afternoon about a company of Japanese soldiers was observed moving cautiously down the railway track. The well camouflaged troops of 'A' Company allowed the enemy to advance till they were practically on the defensive wire obstacles and then they suddenly opened fire. Automatic fire raked the surprised enemy, who tried to jump down on either side of the elevated railway embankment. The LMGs did a commendable job and tore large gaps in the enemy's ranks and caused heavy casualties. The remaining enemy fled into the surrounding jungle, where they were successfully engaged with high explosive bombs of the 2-inch mortar with 'A' Company. The enemy suffered heavy casualties and over 150 dead bodies of Japanese soldiers were strewn on either side of the railway line.

Japanese tank column on the move

The elated Ahirs of 'A' Company knew that many more Japanese soldiers had been killed and wounded in the surrounding jungle due to the exploding mortar bombs. The Japanese halted their advance and withdrew north, the way they had come. 'A' Company waited expectantly all night for a renewed assault, but there were no further attacks. The company's second clash with the Japanese had again been a successful one.

On the next morning patrols were sent into the jungle on the flanks to search the area, but no enemy was encountered. The patrols found immense carnage caused by their accurately fired mortar bombs. Numerous dead bodies of Japanese troops with weapons strewn around were found among the dense trees and bushes. After a tense day, at around midnight, the Japanese returned in strength to avenge their earlier losses. Clashes commenced with patrols and listening posts that had been deployed ahead in the direction of the main road and railway track. At about 3 a.m. on 7 January the enemy contacted the unit's defences in strength and also brought down an intense barrage of artillery fire. Troops in the trenches could distinctly hear the rumble and clanking sounds of advancing enemy armour. In brilliant moonlight the Japanese moved down the main road with about 10 light tanks. The leading light tanks were followed by about 20 armoured cars and a few medium tanks. Lastly, enemy infantry advanced close behind the medium tanks. The Battle of Slim River soon began in earnest with a well-coordinated attack on the Allied defences.

The Japanese had been surprised on the previous day by strong reactions from 'A' Company, and had suffered heavy casualties and withdrawn. Expecting stiff opposition, the Japanese now launched an Infantry Division supported by armour against 4/19 Hyderabad and rest of 12 Infantry Brigade. 'C' Company and then 'B' Company heard tank noises and reported advancing enemy armour. This was the unit's first experience of facing enemy tanks. The only anti-tank weapons they possessed were improvised Molotov cocktails. The tanks were supported by enemy infantry, as this enemy force moved around the company areas to isolate the forward defensive positions. Shells from tank main guns and their machine-gun fire blasted the defences and provided accurate fire support for Japanese infantry that soon began to attack the Allied defences. After providing initial fire support the Japanese tanks also joined in the assaults. The defenders fought on to desperately hold off the Japanese assaulting tanks. There were many instances of hand-to-hand fighting with the enemy soldiers who were accompanying the tanks.

The anti-tank gunners could fire only two rounds at the assaulting tanks. In the smoke-filled darkness, both these rounds either missed their targets or were ineffective to halt the tanks. The enemy armour roared through the defensive positions causing enormous destruction and confusion in their wake. The battered defenders rallied in small groups and continued to engage the onrushing Japanese troops. Telephone lines were cut and the isolated company groups fought on despite the total lack of communications with their neighbouring sub-unit or the Battalion HQ. Enemy tanks that had broken through the Battalion's defences succeeded in cutting up 5/2 Punjab and 2 Argyll & Sutherland Highlanders, who were both deployed in the rear. With unrelenting pressure and heavy casualties suffered by both sides, the battle soon degenerated into a tactical nightmare and utter confused prevailed. In the inky darkness, there was complete bedlam. The darkness was punctuated by the flashes of blinding light from exploding artillery and mortar shells. Added to the flashes of intense white light, there were sharp bangs of tank guns, battle-cries and loud shouts of both the Japanese and Indian soldiers.

On seeing the deteriorating tactical situation, Archie Paris ordered the Battalion to withdraw from the outpost position and deploy to the rear of the other two battalions. This order entailed an extremely difficult tactical manoeuvre. Officiating CO, Major A. D. Brown passed orders for 'A' Company under 2nd Lieutenant Edmund Loughlin, to withdraw down the railway line. 'B' Company, located in depth was to await the arrival of 'C' Company that was to move back along the main road. Thereafter, both sub-units were to withdraw together. In hindsight, it is clear that such orders for withdrawal at a time when the troops are desperately fighting the enemy, can only aggravate a delicate tactical situation, cause heavy casualties and finally lead to disaster and defeat. This is exactly what happened at Slim River. In these circumstances a safe withdrawal would only have been possible after the attackers were halted and contact with the onrushing enemy had been broken.

Telephone cables were severed by the enemy tanks and communications had been cut. As the worsening tactical situation became critical there was little time to waste. Captain Gopal Krishan Mehta, OC, 'B' Company took a party forward to personally convey the orders for withdrawal to 'C' Company. This is the last time Mehta was ever seen.

Meanwhile, 'C' Company was under massive attack after being cut off by enemy infantry and tanks. Desperate hand-to-hand fighting could not save 'C' Company from being overrun and the sub-unit soon ceased to exist. The brave Kumaonis of 'C' Company, along with their Company Commander 2nd Lieutenant Darling were never seen again. Some stragglers who eventually re-joined the unit at Singapore recounted that Mehta had been captured by the Japanese near 'C' Company's position, tied to a tree and brutally bayoneted to death.

Capt. G.K. Mehta

Soon 'B' Company also came under heavy attack. In the absence of Mehta, Lieutenant Lind had hurriedly assumed command of the sub-unit. He tried to extricate the company, but with heavy fighting raging all round them only two platoons managed to fight their way out of the beleaguered position. Two platoons and HQ of 'B' Company (about 65 men) withdrew along the west side of the metalled road, where some jungle-tracks existed. Jemadar Kabul Singh, one of the platoon commanders had fought the enemy bravely and he had been wounded in the fighting. He was being carried back by five stretcher-bearers. Kabul Singh realized that he could not be carried for long and bravely insisted on walking the remaining distance of about 10 miles (about 16 km). On the way he collapsed from loss of blood and died on the road. He had recently been promoted from Havildar and his conduct all through the operations had been admirable.

Jem. Kabul Singh, MC

Meanwhile, the Japanese had positioned a tank opposite the Battalion HQ. Thus, the HQ personnel had to be pulled back along a detour through thick jungle. Brown, officiating CO, remained in the vicinity of Battalion HQ to warn his men to keep off the road, which were being used by Japanese tanks and armoured cars. Captain M. G. Jilani, Adjutant was sent to report to Brigade HQ and explain the tactical situation, since all communications had been disrupted. As the Brigade was out of communication with other battalions as well, the Brigade Commander sent Jilani to contact 5/2 Punjab and also reconnoitre the road through nearby rubber estates. Jilani found the road occupied by Japanese armour and soon returned and reported the precarious situation to Archie Paris, the Brigade Commander.

Meanwhile, 'A' Company under Loughlin had commenced its withdrawal along the railway track. It came under the fire of heavy calibre weapons, from an armoured train or from some tanks moving down the railway track. The company moved to its right and slipped into the dark rubber estates. By following a rubber estate road, the men reached Slim River and worked their way to the Railway Bridge. But to their horror and great dismay, 'A' Company found the bridge had been demolished. Thus, the men quickly lowered themselves into the swirling, muddy waters and began to swim to the far bank, just as the Japanese were nearing the river. In their haste, some Ahirs drowned in the waters while crossing Slim River. Brown and a few Battalion HQ personnel had made contact with 'D' Company of 2 Argyll & Sutherland Highlanders. This company had been reduced to about 30 men and was moving on the west side of the road. Shortly, Lind also arrived with two platoons of 'B' Company. Through a large gap in 5/2 Punjab defences, the Japanese poured in and got astride the road. The enemy cut off the withdrawal of Brown's group. To assist CO's group, 'B' Company sent a platoon to a small, dominating knoll. On seeing the platoon occupy the knoll, the enemy closed in and cut them off from the rest of 'B' Company. A fierce fight commenced and Lind took up positions with the two platoons and began to engage the enemy.

The battle-weary men of 'B' Company held off the onrushing Japanese troops with their accurate fire. Above the din of battle Lind shouted to A.D. Brown to bring the few men of Battalion HQ and 2 Argyll & Sutherland Highlanders around to the other side of the road, while he held off the enemy. Lind and his men began to engage the enemy while Brown began to move the troops with him to the right side of the road. But his group came under withering fire from that direction. Lind held his position while the enemy sprayed Brown's party with deadly automatic fire and closed in for the kill. The men fought to the very end when they were finally all overcome. Brown was instantly killed as machine-gun bullets felled the entire group. They had made a gallant stand and caused serious casualties to the enemy, before they were all mowed down. On seeing Brown being killed and the men with him being wiped out, Lind extricated his troops – with difficulty – and made a wide detour to the right. On the way, his party had encountered more

Japanese, but they managed to reach Slim River. Here, Lind and 18 survivors of 'B' Company joined Jilani who had brought back a few survivors of the ill-fated Battalion HQ group.

Japanese troops involved in street fighting at Johore Baharu

A message had been sent to Lieutenant K. D. Vasudeva, Transport Officer, to move the unit transport to the south of Slim River and save the valuable unit vehicles from destruction. Several times earlier, orders for the move of unit vehicles had been changed by staff officers, in contradiction to the orders sent by CO. This had led to inordinate delays and grave administrative problems. Realizing the gravity of the situation, Vasudeva wanted to confirm the order and check the area up to where the enemy had reached, before he moved the unit vehicles. Therefore, starting up a motorcycle, Vasudeva went up the road and crossed a nearby bridge. He was never seen again. It is presumed that Vasudeva was killed by the fire of Japanese tanks. A little later, enemy tanks shot up and destroyed the unit's vehicles and a complete artillery battery of 25-pounder artillery guns which was deployed nearby. Not having any means to stop the Japanese tanks, Captain Gulzara Singh, Quarter Master (QM), collected the unit's drivers and hurriedly issued them with hand grenades. Led by Gulzara Singh the drivers took positions along the road and bravely hurled hand grenades at advancing Japanese tanks. There was complete chaos and bedlam with loud clanging sounds of tank tracks, deep throated roar of tank engines, automatic fire of enemy machine-guns and exploding hand grenades. As was expected, the hand grenades bounced harmlessly off the Japanese tanks and had no detrimental effect. In retaliation, the onrushing tanks directed the fire of the tank machine-guns and main guns at the helplessly brave drivers under Gulzara Singh and caused severe casualties on them. The QM himself was last seen being riddled by a burst of enemy machine-gun fire.

By 7.30 a.m. on 8 January, Japanese armoured columns had penetrated deep into the depth areas. 5/14 Punjab, a reserve Battalion allot-

Japanese troops march through the streets of Singapore

ted to 12 Infantry Brigade, could not halt the tanks and was also overrun. Meanwhile, the armour played havoc with 28 Infantry Brigade that was deployed in depth of 12 Brigade. A troop of anti-tank guns was wiped out before they could fire even a single shot, a Gurkha battalion was overrun and two batteries of 28 Infantry Brigade Artillery were completely destroyed. By 9 a.m., enemy tanks had also destroyed a light AA battery that had tried to block their path. The Japanese columns crossed a bridge near the gun position of 155 Field Regiment. The Gunners gallantly resorted to direct firing of their guns and managed to stop the leading tank, only 30 yards from the guns. However, the tanks were only temporarily halted and they plunged on after destroying the artillery regiment.

Captain G. S. Parab was one of the survivors. He was separated from the Battalion during the fighting. Parab made his way back after some exciting adventures behind Japanese lines, over a period of several days. When the initial tank attacks took place, Parab was just behind Subedar Karam Singh, Jemadar Prithi Chand and Battalion Havildar Major Gopal Singh. As the Japanese tanks raced through the unit followed by waves of infantry, Parab found himself isolated in the jungle. He made his way through the jungle and near Tanjong Malim he joined a party of about 200 officers and men, including Lieutenant Colonel C. C. Deakin, CO of 5/2 Punjab. He learnt from the Punjabis that while moving towards Kuala Lumpur the group had clashed with a strong Japanese column and the Japanese had been dispersed.

Parab made his way south, guided by the rail track. He was unfortunately seized by the Japanese and put to work on a damaged bridge. He managed to escape into the nearby jungle and reached Kuala Lumpur. The Japanese were already in occupation of the city and were busy looting the shops and homes. Parab was elated when he saw a Japanese soldier go into a store, leaving his bicycle unattended outside the shop. He quickly mounted the bicycle and rode off, carefully avoiding Japanese held localities and re-joined the Battalion. The remnants of both 12 Brigade and 28 Brigade were withdrawn across Slim River over the surviving railway bridge which had been expeditiously repaired by Engineers. Along with other troops of 12 Indian Infantry Brigade, the Battalion had borne the brunt of savage fighting as it fell back from the Slim River position. The officers and men had implicitly followed their orders, fought well and gallantly laid down their lives. After the Japanese tanks cut through the formation the overall situation became untenable. Surviving troops of the Battalion had formed isolated pockets of resistance and grimly fought to the very end. After the Battle of Slim River, all that remained of 4/19 Hyderabad Regiment were three officers and 180 men!

'Chal Chal Re Naujawan'

This chapter is about a daring escape from a prisoner-of-war camp in Singapore and the jungle crossings to reach Thailand and Burma.

During their attempts to halt the rapid advance of Japanese forces down the Malayan peninsula the unit had suffered heavy casualties and withdrawn to the island of Singapore. Here, the unit was reinforced and again fought pitched battles against the advancing Japanese forces of General Tomoyuki Yamashita. Finally, the Allies lost at Singapore on 14 February 1942, and the unit became prisoners along with other Indian, British and Australian Forces. Two officers of the Battalion, Captain Balbir Singh and Captain G. S. Parab had been planning their escape to India since the very night of surrender of Allied forces in Singapore. But they had temporarily shelved the idea since everything was topsy-turvy and indiscriminate shooting was taking place in the city. Also, 4/19 Hyderabad Regiment was grossly understaffed due to serious casualties to its officers. Balbir and Parab rightfully felt their presence in the unit was essential to ensure the welfare of their men and thus they stayed on at the prisoner of war (POW) internment centre, Neesoon Camp.

After a while, a company of troops with both Balbir and Parab was transferred to a nearby POW camp, called Fatigue Camp. Here, the prisoners were employed for construction of Tengah Airfield, on priority basis. Both officers realized they could not escape, till a senior officer arrived in the POW camp to give the Japanese the daily morning report. If they escaped, their absence would be immediately known to the Japanese, leading to an early recapture and certain death. Their prayers were quickly answered, for soon they were joined by Major Pharnavis, Captain Dilsukh Maan and Captain Ramaniah, the unit Regimental

Medical Officer (RMO).[1] The arrival of these officers made the escape easier because Pharnavis as the senior officer began to report daily to the Japanese Camp Commandant, instead of Balbir. On learning of their plans for escape, Ramaniah provided them with quinine tablets and other 'life-saving drugs' for their trek to India.

However, their happiness was short-lived for they were told they would be soon moving with the company to Andaman & Nicobar Islands. Since such a move would wreck their escape plans, Balbir discussed about the impending move of the company with a senior officer of the unit (Major Niranjan Singh Gill) who had joined the Indian National Army (the INA) and had a senior appointment in the INA HQ. Gill told Balbir he would try his utmost to have the planned move to the Islands cancelled, but he was quite apprehensive as to the Japanese agreeing to his request. He had added that the escape could be made from the Islands. He said they could review their plans and get a boat or sampan and make for the nearest island. Once they were out of the main Islands, they could somehow reach India. Balbir had told Gill it would be a dangerous plan, since the coast and harbour were all well-guarded by Japanese troops. Even if they managed to procure a boat, they had little knowledge of handling a craft in the open sea.

Meanwhile, Captain Pritam Singh of 3/16 Punjab Regiment (originally of 4/19 Hyderabad Regiment) used to come over from the POW Bidadari Camp. Pritam would visit both Neesoon Camp and Fatigue Camp with the assistance of Major G. R. Nagar (ex 4/19 Hyderabad Regiment). Nagar had joined INA and was on the Administrative Committee of Bidadari Camp. Pritam had heard of the getaway plans and was eager to join the escape attempt. Balbir and Parab thought it over for a few days and finally decided to include Pritam in their plans for escape. Since there was an acute shortage of accommodation and food on Singapore Island, civilians were being allowed to return to their homes on the mainland with permits issued by the Japanese.

It was known to the three officers planning the escape that their recapture would mean brutal torture and certain death. Therefore, in preparation for the escape, all three officers had changed their names,

[1] Later, he became Lieutenant General and DGMS.

posing as clerks from a rubber estate. While on fatigue duty[2] in Singapore City, Balbir and Parab managed to enrol as civilian members of the India Independence League (IIL) and obtained the necessary travel permits. The false names were endorsed on their IIL cards[3] and later even Pritam[4] managed to enrol with the IIL.

Capt. (later Brig.) Balbir Singh

Since the prisoners were becoming physically weaker with each passing day due to dysentery, malaria and other diseases, it was decided to speed up the escape. Lt Balwant Singh (of 5/14 Punjab Regiment and earlier 4/19 Hyderabad Regiment) often expressed a desire to join in the escape bid, but he was refused as it was felt any increase in their numbers would make the escape difficult and they could be easily recaptured.[5] Clothes, rations and money were secretly smuggled into Fatigue Camp. Ramaniah, although short of quinine and other drugs, arranged medicines for the escape. In the meanwhile, Pritam, got himself transferred to Fatigue Camp through 'friends' in Bidadari Camp Administrative Committee.

Capt. (later Col) G. S. Parab

Ten days passed, but no word was received from Gill. Meanwhile, the company received orders to sail to the Andaman & Nicobar Islands the next day. In the afternoon, with a heavy heart, Balbir and Parab lined

---

[2] Fatigue duty is the labour assigned to military men that does not require of armaments.

[3] Balbir's IIL card was prepared in fake name of 'Bhajan Singh'. Officials were told his parents had migrated from India to Malaya, where Balbir was born in 1910. It was also recorded that he worked as clerk, at a rubber estate in Malaya.

[4] Pritam Singh – an officer of 4/19 Hyderabad Regiment who had been transferred to Punjab Regiment – had been badly wounded in an air raid on Singapore, during the fighting in February 1942. He later commanded 1 Kumaon (Para) (now 3rd Battalion, Parachute Regiment) during the 1947–48 operations in Jammu and Kashmir. Under Pritam's command, the unit entered Poonch over Hajipir Pass, and was besieged there for nearly one year. Pritam was promoted to Brigadier at Poonch and he successfully conducted the defensive battle in a professional and gallant manner, till the link-up from Rajauri took place. Exploits of this gallant soldier are now part of the folklore of the region and his yellowed photograph still adorns many a civilian home in Poonch.

[5] Balwant was later transferred to a labour camp in Borneo, where he was sadly bayoneted to death by Japanese guards, for a minor infringement of camp rules. In later years, Balwant's widow would often chastise Balbir for not permitting him to join the 'escape'.

Maj. N.S. Gill

up the troops. Vehicles were loaded and the men awaited final orders to move to Singapore Harbour and sail to the Islands. Both officers felt their plans were doomed to fail even before the escape had been attempted. Just then, a Jeep careened into the Camp at high speed. Gill was half standing in the co-driver's seat. He waved his arms and shouted, 'Balbir, Balbir, your move has been cancelled. You are not to go to Andaman Islands.' Gill's arrival was almost providential and once again the escape was possible.[6] The officers were elated and made the men quickly unload the vehicles and moved them back into the Fatigue Camp huts.

The Escape

Construction work at Tengah Airfield intensified and prisoners were taken daily in trucks to a nearby quarry to break stones and load them in vehicles proceeding to Tengah. Feverish preparations also began for the escape to India. In consultation with other officers, the date for escape was finalized as 4 May 1942. Pharnavis, the senior officer in the Camp, promised to give the escapees a clear headstart by concealing the escape for the first 24 hours. As part of their final preparations for the escape, a hole was surreptitiously cut in the Camp's perimeter fence and it was concealed with boulders and bushes. The three officers disguised themselves as refugees and carried small bundles containing a sheet, blanket, towel and some personal items.

Before dusk on 4 May 1942, the three escaping officers were given

---

[6] Major (later Colonel) Niranjan Singh Gill had studied in RIMC, Dehradun and trained at Royal Military Sandhurst (RMA), Sandhurst, UK. He was among the initial Indian officers to join 4/19 Hyderabad Regiment, and later served at 19 Hyderabad Regiment Training Centre, Benares in 1936. In 1936–37, he was one of the first Indian officers to be posted to Army HQ, New Delhi. After completing course at Staff College, Quetta, he was posted to Malaya. After the fall of Malaya and Singapore, Gill joined INA, as a founder-member with Mohan Singh, Shah Nawaz Khan and Gurdial Singh. Later, he served as India's ambassador to Ethiopia (1955–60), Thailand (1962–64) and Mexico (1964–66). He died in Amritsar in 1992. It was only known after the War that Gill had made very concerted efforts to ensure the Japanese authorities cancelled the company's move to Andaman & Nicobar Islands. A battery of Hong Kong and Singapore Royal Artillery was sent to Port Blair, in place of the sub-unit of 4/19 Hyderabad Regiment. This cancellation greatly facilitated the escape.

a hearty meal that had been prepared from carefully smuggled food supplies. A heartrending parting took place with old comrades, including the JCOs and men. After the farewell, all three officers left the barracks and silently hid themselves close to the perimeter fence. Movement outside barracks after dark was banned and could invite severe punishment, even death. Near the fence, they crouched and waited behind some bushes and in a small fold in the ground. After confirming there were no Japanese guards around, Balbir sprinted to the fence, crawled through the concealed hole after removing the small boulders and bushes. He lay prone and unmoving outside the fence. Looking back, he signalled to the others to follow him. One by one, Parab and then Pritam crawled through the hole in the fence. Avoiding lights and Japanese guards, the trio carefully rose and moved away from the Camp. With a feeling of great relief, they began the long walk to the heavily guarded Singapore Railway Station. The escapees gained confidence as they trudged along the dark and deserted side streets of Singapore. On the way they felt confident enough to board a passing tram that was clanging its bell loudly in the dark. Once they had got on the tram, they happily discovered they were the only passengers on board. The tram's Chinese conductor took them to the huge building of the railway station. Getting off from the tram, they saw the area was well lit, with a number of armed Japanese soldiers moving about in small groups.

Capt. Balbir Singh dashes to the POW camp fence to execute the escape, while Capts G.S. Parab and Pritam Singh are hidden in the undergrowth

At the railway station, the three officers mustered courage and walked confidently to the ticket counter. Here, Balbir purchased train tickets with help of the IIL cards. After purchasing the tickets, the trio felt confident, even though they had to spend the entire next day in the vicinity of the railway station. They tried to walk and converse like weary refugees. Their conversation was in low whispers. They deliberately avoided the numerous detachments of Japanese soldiers and in the evening of 5 May they boarded the train and sat well apart, to avoid detection.

A wood-burning, steam engine hauled the train through the heavily forested and picturesque countryside of Malaya (Malaysia). For the entire next day, the escapees sat quietly in the swaying, railway compartment. They were lost in thought as their great adventure had finally begun. The excitement of escaping from the POW camp blocked out fears of recapture and all anxieties of the torturous journey that lay ahead. The rhythmic, clickety-clack of the train's wheels induced deep slumber and soon the three officers dozed fitfully in the swaying compartment. At about 7 p.m. on 6 May, the train pulled into Alorstar, near the border with Thailand. The escapees picked up their ragged bundles and cautiously alighted from the train. In the dark, without asking for directions, they headed out of the township and were soon safely hidden in the dark jungles that surround Alorstar.

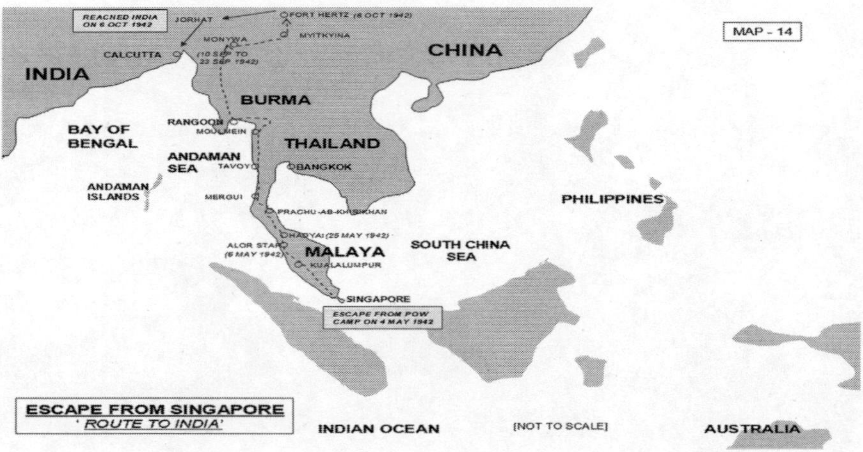

Escape route of Capts Balbir Singh, G.S. Parab
and Pritam Singh from Singapore to India, 1942

Crossing into Thailand

To cross the border into Thailand it was necessary to have valid passports stamped with endorsements by Japanese authorities. Although they did not have the necessary documents, they decided to attempt a surreptitious border crossing. On the next night (7 May), the three escapees moved out of the jungle and approached the border. Hidden in the undergrowth, they observed the crossing place was well-guarded by Japanese patrols. Thai Army guards on the other side of the border were in full cooperation with the Japanese guards. As they did not have required documents, the escapees returned and remained hidden in the thick jungles near the border. They did not attempt a crossing as they were likely to be caught on the other side and handed back to Japanese Military Police. They knew their capture would invite dire consequences, so they hid for a number of days, trying to find a way to surreptitiously cross into Thailand. Swarms of mosquitoes made their lives difficult and there was the constant threat of contracting malaria. As their patience and supplies were running out, on 19 May they made an attempt to get across to Thailand. However, they were caught by Japanese guards and taken to the Border Check Post at Padang Besar. Feigning ignorance about the International Border (IB), they were lucky to be released with only a sound beating by the guards. During their brief stay in custody of Japanese Border Guards, they were rudely searched and their precious anti-malaria quinine tablets were confiscated. This was a serious setback as malaria was rampant and they could not afford to fall ill during the escape. Besides, Ramaniah had procured the precious quinine tablets with considerable difficulty.

Despite a few close calls, they hid conveniently near the IB for more than a fortnight and avoided recapture. Woefully short of food and water, the escapees realized that they had to move on, if they were to continue with their journey and also avoid recapture. There was little hope of obtaining necessary travel documents to legally get across the IB. Thus, they decided to take a calculated risk and anyhow cross into Thailand. During one of their surreptitious trips into Alorstar, the officers came to know of a local farmer who frequently crossed the IB with a loaded bullock cart. He was supposed to know the guards well on both sides of the border. They gingerly approached the farmer, who readily agreed to take them across the IB for cash. Some of the cash had to be paid in advance. They had nagging doubts about the farmer's integrity, but in their desperate condition the escapees had no choice but to take the risk. They pooled their meagre financial resources and paid the farmer to take them across the IB. On the agreed day, the farmer hid them under loose hay in his bullock cart and took them to the IB. They had anxious moments when they heard loud voices of Japanese guards at the border crossing. The three escapees lay unmoving beneath the hay, knowing that there was no chance to escape if the guards decided to search the cart. Luckily, the guards conducted only a random search and prodded the hay a couple of times with the long bayonets fitted on their rifles. The escapees lay unmoving under the hay and their doubts about the farmer's sincerity eased when they heard him joke with first the Japanese and then Thai border guards, as he took the bullock cart safely across the border crossing. Once the cart was well hidden in jungles on the Thai side of the border, the three officers gingerly emerged from the hay and happily jumped to the ground. They profusely thanked the smiling farmer, paid him the remaining cash and quickly melted into the jungle. The three were thrilled to be in Thailand, which was not officially under Japanese occupation.

Once in Thailand, they decided to risk travelling without documents. After trudging for a distance through the jungle they boarded a train at the small town of Hadyai, on 25 May 1942. They sat in different compartments to avoid detection as the train chugged along the narrow Thai peninsula and reached a small town named Prachu-ab-Khirikan, on 27 May. On the way, the train had crossed Bandoh and Chumphon, where they had seen many Japanese soldiers camping on the railway platforms.

Jungle Crossing to Burma

At Prachu-ab-Khirikan, they were sheltered by a benevolent, old Pathan named Khan Zaman. Khan Zaman was married to a Thai girl and lived near the town, where he ran a meat shop. The couple had a playful little daughter, who was fascinated by the strange looking travellers. As they talked of North-West Frontier Province (NWFP) and Punjab in India, they gained Zaman's confidence and he disclosed his colourful past. He had committed a murder in his native NWFP and was wanted by British authorities. Thus, Zaman had fled to Burma and moved to this remote Thai town, as a fugitive. He now earned his livelihood by smuggling cattle from Burma to Thailand and made a profit selling the cheap meat in his shop. He was well versed in smuggling and had many efficient servants. The Pathan told them about hidden jungle trails that crossed inhospitable terrain, into Burma. He, however, warned them that traversing the 175 km or so to Burma by the jungle tracks was extremely difficult, even in good weather conditions. He confided the first day's march would take them to a small village at the edge of the deep jungle. He knew the crafty villagers and said they would surely assist them, if they mentioned his name. However, as monsoon rains were already lashing the area, the Pathan urged them not to follow the jungle route to Burma. He said he knew the area well and insisted it would be a suicidal venture.[7]

Faced with difficult options, the escapees reviewed their future plans. Khan Zaman had offered them the tempting option of staying on at Prachu and working with him. He said they could easily get married and settle down to a good life. Zaman assured them cattle smuggling was a lucrative business. Considering the uncertain times, it was a tempting offer. But, their status as Indian Army officers and burning desire to reach India made them willingly face the risks of travelling to Burma along the jungle route. After they made up their minds, they informed Khan Zaman. With a heavy heart the old Pathan allowed them to leave his home. Zaman's kindly Thai wife gave them food packets for the journey and Zaman sent his servant-boy named 'Kaka' and a young Thai man to guide them on their way.

After leaving Khan Zaman's home, the small group of five individuals walked the whole day over narrow paths. As the sun was going down, they neared a village that lay at the edge of the jungle and in the foothills. Kaka and the Thai man spoke to the village elders in front of

---

[7] Nearly 47 years later, in 1989, Balbir returned to Singapore and retraced his journey along the escape route. He met and thanked most of the people (or their descendants), who had assisted them in the escape. At Prachu-ab-Kirikhan, he was saddened to learn that both Zaman and his Thai wife had passed away. However, he met their daughter and they joyfully recounted the old times. The young daughter (now a middle-aged woman) told Balbir that it had been rumoured that they were captured in the jungle and shot by the Japanese. She was happy to learn that they had reached India safely and she celebrated the event by inviting Balbir to dinner.

a large thatched hut. After an animated discussion, the group was taken upstairs and made comfortable for the night. They were given a hot meal of rice and lentils. When the villagers had left, Kaka chuckled and told them the village elders had been impressed, when told that the three escapees were accomplices of Khan Zaman and well-established, professional cattle-lifters. They were proceeding to Burma over the jungle route to bring back a large herd of stolen cattle. Next morning before leaving the village, the escapees convinced the incredulous villagers they were indeed cattle-lifters. With difficulty, they controlled their laughter at the new-found respect that the profession of cattle lifting had earned for them. After a lengthy farewell, the three escapees followed Kaka and the young Thai into the nearby foothills. Though Kaka had been boasting about his knowledge of the route to Burma, he could not lead them to a proper track. But as he had been living with Khan Zaman and taking his cattle out for grazing, he possessed knowledge of the area. Kaka soon found the entry to the jungle, beyond which lay the route to Burma. Thereafter, Kaka and his companion said hurried goodbyes and happily returned to Prachu and their master Khan Zaman.

Jungle Crossing from Thailand to Burma

Monsoon rains had set in and leeches and mosquitoes turned the trek into a terrible nightmare. The danger of wild animals and merciless dacoits added to their woes. The old Pathan's description of the perilous track could not have been more accurate. Faced with terrible hazards, often the escapees wondered if they had made the right decision to follow the jungle route. However, the anticipation of reaching India, spurred them on and they banished their frequent thoughts of abandoning the trek. So, with sheer determination, the tired and famished officers plodded on in incessant rains and often lost their way in the thick jungle.

At the beginning of their trek a group of inquisitive monkeys followed them, swinging overhead from the tall branches and chattering shrilly. When the escapees walked into the dark and silent primary jungle where the sun's rays never entered, the monkeys turned back. The stench of rotting wood assailed their noses, as they trudged through the jungle. Although they never spoke out aloud, each officer was aware of the grave dangers that lurked ahead. The torrential monsoon downpours made movement difficult and at times they could barely see one another, in the after-rain, heavy mist. They had lost track of time and did not recollect the day or date. However, they marched on and were determined to succeed. To overcome their fears and fatigue, they would loudly sing as they trudged deeper into the silent and deep jungle. Words of the song in Hindustani were, '*Chal, chal re naujawan, door tera gaon, aur thake paon. Rukna tera kaam nahin, chalna teri shaan. Chal, chal re naujawan* ...'. The song spurred them on and they could forget their travails for a while. Having taken the difficult decision to move by the jungle route, they vowed to either reach Burma or perish in the venture!

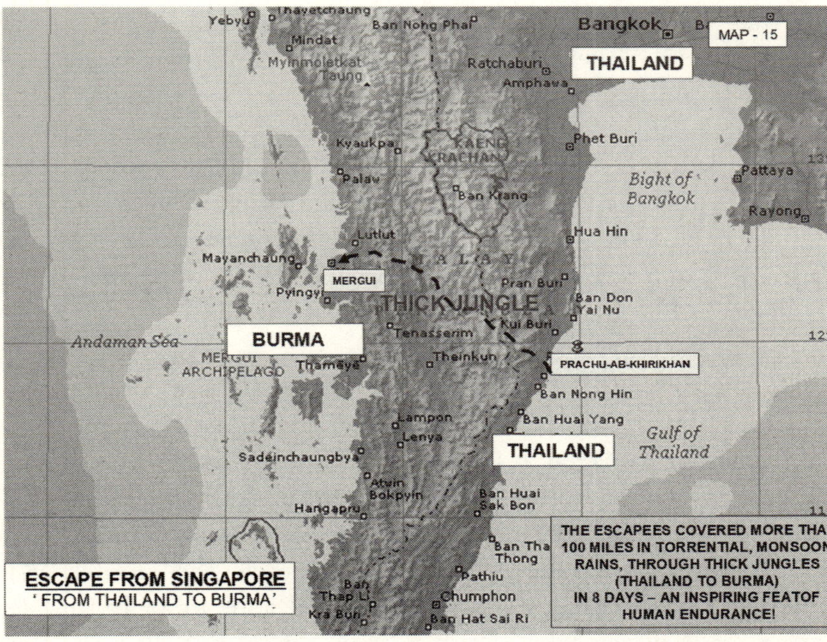

Escape route of Capts Balbir Singh, G.S. Parab and Pritam Singh, 1942; Thailand to Burma section

In this manner they trudged on through the forbidding jungles. When they halted for the night, Balbir would collect firewood and help Parab to cook their only meal of rice and lentils. They carried a portion of the meal and ate it as the next days' midday meal. Pritam would scout around and find a safe spot for the night. He would build a small shelter with sticks and leaves, pulled off the surrounding trees. Invariably, the heavy rains would leave them soaked to the skin and it was difficult to find dry firewood for the cooking fire. As they lay down to sleep in their wet clothes, swarms of ants would often crawl over them and cover their skins with painful bites. Mosquitos too were a constant irritant. On the second day after leaving the village, they were surrounded by mean looking cattle-lifters, just as they began to cook their evening meal. Six or seven men stood around them while another two or three men remained in the dark, with about 20 head of cattle.

The cattle-lifters' clothing was dark coloured and drenched in the rain. They had dirty scarves tied around their heads. The cattle-lifters wielded mean looking *dahs* and large knives. The trio were rudely lined up against some large trees and roughly searched. The cattle-lifters took away their medicines, but later threw them down in disgust as they could not read the labels in English and did not know their usage. With loud words and fingers placed on lips, spelt a solemn warning for the trio to remain quiet. After giving solemn warnings the cattle-lifters departed as silently as they had come. Only the hoof beats and occasional mooing of cattle marked their presence. The escapees were shaken by the incident and knew they were extremely fortunate to have survived. They vowed to be more careful in future and Pritam was positioned as a 'look-out' while Balbir and Parab cooked the meal whenever they stopped for the night.

On the third day after leaving the village, all three officers were swept away by raging torrents while crossing a fast-flowing stream. They somehow managed to survive by desperately clinging on to roots that were protruding from the heavily eroded banks. However, all their belongings were washed away in the turbulent stream. Soaked to the skin and panting from exhaustion, they helped each other to safety, atop the slippery bank. They were tired, terrified and suddenly they felt hopeless, as if all was lost. However, after a good rest they recovered some strength and their spirits rose enough to allow them to resume their onward trek.

After walking for a few hours, the trio observed they were repeatedly passing the same landmarks. They had a strong suspicion they were going around in circles and were lost in the forbidding jungle. In a weary state, as they hacked their way up steep slopes and along overgrown tracks, their fears continued to grow. Soon, they were certain they had been going around in circles and were surely lost. In their exhausted state, the situation again seemed utterly hopeless.

They had long run out of the provisions that Khan Zaman's wife had provided them and soon they were on the verge of collapse. Their starvation caused them to be plagued with hallucinations and they soon began to harbour visions of a sad and lonely end in the deep jungles of Thailand. Morose and disillusioned on the fifth day, as they sat huddled in the dense undergrowth, the most unbelievable thing happened. They heard the unfamiliar sounds of dogs barking and a cock crowing—all indications of habitation! After time spent in the silent jungle, they thought their ears were playing tricks in the exhausted state. They immediately sat very still and listened carefully above the constant hum of jungle insects. Their amazement knew no bounds as they could even hear the excited shouts of children at play. With great joy they knew the sounds were indeed real and not a figment of their weary imagination. It was too good to be true and seemed like a gift from heaven. With renewed energy they followed the sounds and staggered into a small jungle clearing with thatched huts.

Half-naked children shrieked in amazement and ran back as the strangers broke from the jungle. Dogs barked wildly and startled villagers stared in wonder at the three dishevelled figures who staggered into the jungle clearing. The exhausted officers collapsed in the clearing, near the thatched huts. They appeared to have walked in from another world! When they had suitably recovered, the simple folk offered them a sumptuous meal of hot rice, delicious lentils and ripe bananas. Many villagers sat silently on their haunches and watched the famished escapees eat. It was a lavish treat after the frugal meals they had been eating. They warmly thanked their hosts and were taken inside a large thatched hut. Despite the overpowering musty smell, they immediately fell into a deep slumber. The delicious food and good rest suitably revived the officers. That evening, inquisitive children overcame their fears and sat with the escapees. They were fascinated by the officer's beards and some children even ventured to touch their faces. The escapees wanted to stay longer in the welcome surroundings of the jungle village and rest their weary bodies. But, the harsh reality of their status as escaped prisoners forced them to continue with their journey. They did not want the friendly villagers to face the wrath of Japanese for providing food and shelter to escapees. Next morning, they warmly thanked the hospitable villagers and departed.

On 17 June they left Tavoy and proceeded by ferry and bus to Yeh. They reached Yeh in the evening of 18 June and again stayed at the local Gurudwara. They were told there was a railway line from Yeh to Moulmein, but trains were not plying as a bridge had been destroyed during the earlier fighting. On morning of 19 June, they set off from Yeh and walked for about 35 km along the railway track to Lamaing. This part of their journey was difficult, as they had to walk over jagged stones on the railway track. Their torn shoes and painful blisters on the soles of their feet added to the miseries. Hostile people lived near the railway track and they were a constant menace. One village on the railway line was said to be particularly dangerous. They had been warned at Yeh to stay away from the hostile people of this village. They had been warned with stories of the sorry plight of some Tamil refugees, who had been waylaid while they were moving with their baggage. The Tamil refugees had been robbed and murdered by local Rohingya bandits from the hostile village. The trio could feel the hostility when some villagers stared at them as they sat in front of their huts along the railway line. The three officers hastily pushed along the railway line, never looking at the villagers or stopping to talk with them. The villagers were not given any time to organize themselves and harass the escapees. With their rapid speed of walking, they quickly distanced themselves from the village. The trio increased their speed by taking large steps on the stony surface and even broke into a run after they were a couple of miles on the other side of the notorious village.

In great pain from badly bruised feet, they staggered into Lamaing in the dark. They stayed the night at Lamaing and left the next day by train. They had had enough of walking for a while and their relief was unimaginable when they sat in the swaying railway carriage. Through the carriage windows they glimpsed the beautiful, blue-green waters of Andaman Sea and Bay of Bengal. It was a heady feeling to know that the shores of India lay across these cool waters. However, their joy was dampened by realization that a long and tricky journey still lay ahead, across unknown territories that were occupied by enemy forces. They continued by train and reached Moulmein on 24 June. They left Moulmein on 30 June and arrived at Martban by ferry-boat. On the boat they encountered four stragglers from 8 Gurkha Rifles. The Gurkha soldiers were silent and subdued, but glad to be in the company of the three Indian Army officers. They proceeded together by road, ferry and on foot to Pegu via Thaton. They crossed Sittang River by boat, as the bridge had been destroyed in the fighting and all movement across the river was conducted in country boats. They stayed in Pegu for a day or two and moved to Rangoon. The Japanese were in occupation of Burma. The escapees had some exciting adventures as they evaded a series of enemy check-posts. As they walked into Rangoon, a large number of Allied bombers droned towards the city in broad daylight. Soon, Rangoon was rocked by massive explosions and a number of buildings were reduced to rubble. It was a deserted city and only a few locals and Japanese troops were visible. The escapees and Gurkha stragglers stayed in a Gurudwara out of Rangoon. They did not stay long in Rangoon and moved on to Mandalay by train. The Gurkha stragglers were unwilling to go any further and thus, they were left behind at Rangoon. From Mandalay the escapees moved by road to Monywa. They had been told it was easy to reach the frontlines from Monywa and then sneak across to the side of Allied forces. Thus, they were excited as their ordeal seemed to be coming to an end.

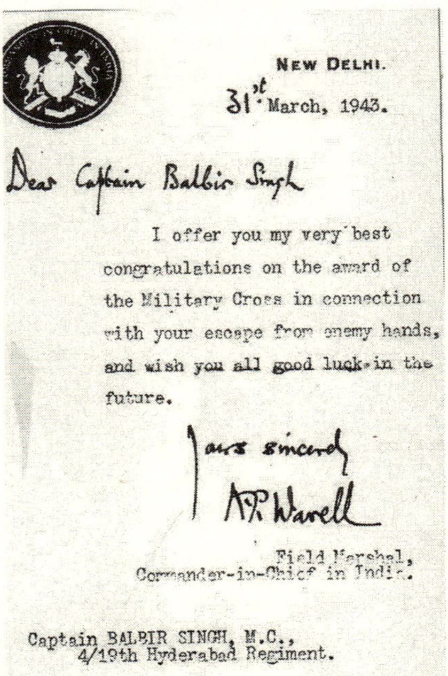

NEW DELHI.

31st March, 1943.

Dear Captain Balbir Singh

I offer you my very best congratulations on the award of the Military Cross in connection with your escape from enemy hands, and wish you all good luck in the future.

Yours sincerely

A.P. Wavell

Field Marshal,
Commander-in-Chief in India.

Captain BALBIR SINGH, M.C.,
4/19th Hyderabad Regiment.

After arrival in India, the three officers were decorated with Military Cross and received a complimentary letter from Field Marshal A.P. Wavell.

Colours of the Fighting Fourth

The origin of the custom of carrying colours goes back to the early days where a leader affixed his family emblem to a pole and it was held aloft during a battle for the dual purpose of indicating the leader's position and also acting as a rallying point, should the occasion arise. With the introduction of regimentation, battalions were allowed to carry flags or colours of a standard specification which were taken into use only after a special ceremony. These colours had the regimental crest inscribed on them as well as numerous battle honours the unit may have won.

Regimental colours are a symbol of the spirit of the regiment. Prior to being taken into use, the colours are consecrated at a religious ceremony, and on them are emblazoned the sacred memory of heroic deeds and distinction of long and honourable service, the battle honours and the regimental badge. The colours are in fact a portable, silken regimental history regarded in veneration and a source of pride to serving and retired soldiers. The colours have been described as:

A moth-eaten rag on a worm-eaten pole,
It does not look likely to stir a man's soul,
'Tis the deeds that were done 'neath the moth-eaten rag,
When the pole was a staff and the rag was a flag.

—Sir Edward Hamley

After their service had been completed, a unit's colours were laid up in a sacred place, thus maintaining an atmosphere of veneration with which they are surrounded. No record exists of the date of the first presentation of colours to the Battalion; however, Colonel Philip Meadows Taylor, an officer of the Nizam's Army has written that colours were carried by battalions of that force as early as 1853 onwards, when the Hyderabad Contingent was formed from the Nizam's Contingent. It is thus possible that both Queen Victoria's Colours and regimental colours were carried by the Battalion. Vintage of the unit's regimental colours can be ascertained by the fact that 'Central India' is inscribed on the old colours of 4 Kumaon.

Colours of 5th Infantry, Hyderabad Contingent

On 14 March 1886, while the Battalion was at Aurangabad, colours were received from Mrs Bell, wife of the Commissioner there. The colours were emblazoned with the designation of 5th Infantry, Hyderabad Contingent and 'Central India' was written below. These colours now rest in the Kumaon Regiment War Museum at Ranikhet.

Colours of 98th Infantry

In 1900, the Battalion proceeded overseas along with the 'China Expeditionary Force'. Because of its distinguished services in China, the unit was permitted to have 'China – 1900' emblazoned on its regimental colours. However, on the unit's return to India from China, in 1903 the unit's designation was changed to that of 98th Infantry. Accordingly, the Battalion was presented with new colours. Thus, 'China – 1900' was inscribed on the new colours presented to 98th Infantry.

Regimental colours of 4/19 Hyderabad Regiment

The unit fought in East Africa during World War I, with the colours of 98th Infantry. In 1922, there were large-scale changes in the Indian Army and 98th Infantry was redesignated as 4/19 Hyderabad Regiment. On 4 December 1937 while stationed at Secunderabad, the Battalion received new King's and regimental colours from Lieutenant General Sir J. E. S. Brind, KCB, KBE, CMG, DSO, General Officer Commanding-in-Chief, Southern Command. It was a colourful ceremony held on the occasion of the Battalion's 150th anniversary. It was the first time that King's Colours and regimental colours were received by Indian officers Lieutenant K. Bhagwati Singh and Lieutenant Dilsukh Maan respectively.

With the departure of the British in August 1947, the King's Colours of the unit were presented to Indian Military Academy (IMA), Dehradun, for safekeeping at Chetwode Hall, IMA. The presentation was done at a joint parade in May 1956. The practice of presenting King/Queen's Colours along with the regimental colours was discontinued, and only President's Colours were presented to the unit.

4/19 Hyderabad Regiment is presented Colours at Secunderabad on 4 December 1937, by Lieutenant General Sir J. E. S. Brind, GOC-in-C, Southern Command

On the Battalion's return from Gaza, it became the first unit of Indian Army to be awarded President's Colours at Ranikhet, on 8 April 1961. The colours were presented by Dr Rajendra Prasad, the first President of India to Captain (later Major General) D. P. S. Raghuvanshi, at Dulikhet Ground, Ranikhet. The old colours of 4/19 Hyderabad Regiment were laid up for safe custody in the Kumaon Regiment War Museum at Ranikhet.

Dr Rajendra Prasad, first President of India, takes the Ceremonial Parade salute after the country's first Presentation of Colours on 3 April 1961

Legend of the Silver Bugles of the Fighting Fourth

On its return from overseas service in Iraq on 11 February 1928, the unit proceeded from Bombay to Allahabad. Here, an important issue was raised by officers during a mess meeting in the Officers' Mess. It was proposed that the unit should procure a set of silver bugles. The proposal was promptly approved by Major E. L. Ricketts, Second-in-Command (2IC) and a set of silver bugles was ordered from a reputed firm of silver-smiths in the United Kingdom (UK). It was directed to the dealers that each bugle of the set should have the unit (4/19 Hyderabad Regiment) crest and a serial number prominently engraved on the bugle horn.

Silver bugles of the Fighting Fourth

The new set of silver bugles was soon received by the unit and promptly incorporated in the Battalion's band, in 1930. Thereafter, the new bugle set was used very effectively during band performances in Waziristan,

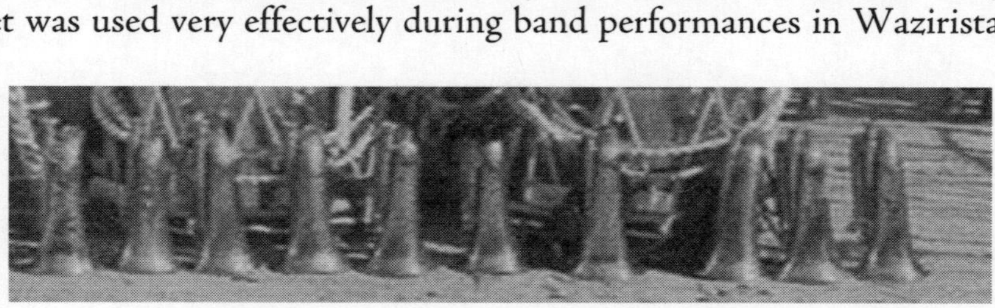

The new set of silver bugles with the unit band in 1930

Quetta and Secunderabad. The silver bugles were also highly appreciated during the grand colour presentation parade at Secunderabad on 4 December 1937 by Army Commander, Southern Command.

Soon, it was time for the unit to proceed abroad again and the set of silver bugles accompanied the Battalion and its band to Singapore. However, World War II broke out and the unit moved from Singapore and took up defences in Area Kuantan (North Malayan peninsula) to oppose Japanese sea landings in that area. Before the unit moved north for operations, the unit band had stacked its instruments in the 'Unit Rear Dump' located at the unit lines in Tanglin Gardens, Singapore. The bandsmen and buglers were distributed to various companies for the operations. Before proceeding north into the Malayan jungles, the silver bugles were covered with khaki cloth, so they would not reflect the sun's rays and disclose the location of our troops to the enemy. Two bugles were given to the buglers in each rifle company. These bugles were to be used to make necessary bugle calls to alert the men and pass messages.

In Malaya the unit unsuccessfully tried to halt the rapidly advancing Japanese forces, but they were repeatedly pushed back with heavy casualties. Finally, it was decided to make a stand at Chemor and defeat the advancing enemy. As per the overall plan, units of 12 Indian Infantry Brigade (5/2 Punjab Regiment, 2 Argyll & Sutherland Highlanders and 4/19 Hyderabad Regiment) were to withdraw and draw in the enemy units. Then, the Japanese were to be destroyed with a pre-ponderance of artillery fire. 'D' Coy of the unit under Captain Harris was sent about 12 km north, to a feature named 'Limestone Rock'. Here the company was to box in the Japanese and prevent them from escaping northwards from the trap.

However, the Japanese avoided the planned destruction; due to their rapid advances they had nearly merged with the defenders and thus the artillery bombardments had to be called off. Despite numerous attempts, 'D' Company of 4/19 Hyderabad Regiment at Limestone Rock, could not be informed that the plan of the operation had been cancelled and they were to immediately return to the Battalion. As a result, 'D' Company got involved in a serious firefight with the enemy and were ultimately wiped out to a man. Amidst the heavy firing, three soldiers of

'D' Company escaped into the jungle. They later managed to reach Singapore and inform the unit about what had happened at Chemor on that fateful day. Meanwhile, after running over 'D' Company, the Japanese had apparently picked up the two silver bugles (Bugles No. 3 and 16) and continued with their advance to Singapore.

Later, while 7th Battalion, The Worcestershire Regiment was advancing in Burma, they had a bitter clash with an enemy detachment. After the engagement, they were amazed to find two dead Japanese soldiers who were each carrying a silver bugle on their person. The silver bugles had numbers 3 and 16 inscribed on them, along-with the crest of 4/19 Hyderabad Regiment. The troops of 7 Worcestershire Regiment retained the two silver bugles and kept them in safe custody for the rest of the war. When the war ended, the Worcesters presented the bugles to the Hyderabad Rifles, Auxiliary Force (India) under a mistaken impression that the two bugles belonged to them. However, the Commanding Officer (CO) of Hyderabad Rifles realized the mistake and sent the bugles to 19th Hyderabad Regimental Centre, Agra.

That is how the two silver bugles returned to 4th Battalion, The Kumaon Regiment in February 1946, after their incredibly long and interesting wartime journey, having been in the severe jungle fighting in Burma and Malaya with both the Battalion and enemy forces. Ever since the two silver bugles were returned to the unit in 1946, they have been given a 'place of pride' in Officers' Mess of 4 Kumaon. The two bugles adorn the walls of the anteroom with pride. They are no longer used for playing tunes with the band or for making bugle calls in the unit.

The Greany Cup and Other Incredible Gifts

The Greany Cup

The Greany Cup

There is a beautiful silver cup displayed in Officers' Mess, 4 Kumaon. The origins of this ornate cup were shrouded in mystery till Brigadier N. A. Salick, AVSM, VrC, obtained some Army Lists (1895–1910), which had been carefully preserved by the Caretaker of the Palace at Cooch Behar. With the help of these antique Army Lists, the mystery of the silver cup was finally solved.

The silver cup is of exquisite craftsmanship, about fourteen inches in height, five inches in width and sits on a well-carved wooden base. The face of the cup bears a faded inscription that reads, 'Presented by Lt Col H. Greany, IMS'. On its reverse, the cup has the 98th Infantry crest. The engravings are worn out with regular polishing over the years and are barely visible.

Although there is no record of Lt Col H. Greany in the Battalion, the old Army Lists reveal that one Hugh Greany, MD, was an officer of the Indian Medical Service (IMS). Details given in the Army Lists are as follows:

Born	28 March 1859
Commissioned into IMS	1 October 1881
Joined 98th Infantry	2 August 1891
Appointed Lt Col	1 October 1901

Lt Col Hugh Greany, IMS

In 1905, Greany is shown as Senior Medical Officer, Ahmednagar, but continues to be on the rolls of 98th Infantry. In the 1910 Army List, he is back on the rolls of 98th Infantry and shown on leave in United Kingdom (UK) for two years along with Major Treager. In another Army List he is shown as having qualified for the 'China Medal – 1900'. He remained in China as Medical Officer of 98th Infantry, till it left for India.

As historical records stop here, it is can be fairly assumed from inscriptions that the exquisitely crafted silver cup displayed in Officers' Mess of 4 Kumaon was presented to the unit by Lt Col Hugh Greany, IMS.

Beret of 3rd Royal Marine Commandos

'We cannot buy anything here, but would like you to accept this, as a token of our great admiration of the bravery and achievement of your Battalion.'
(Typewritten note attached to the beret)

This beret was presented to Lieutenant Colonel K. S. Thimayya, DSO, Commanding Officer 8/19 Hyderabad Regiment by Brigadier C. K. Hardy, Commander, 3rd Royal Marine Commando after Battle of Kangaw.

The First Crest of Kumaon Regiment

After the end of World War II, it was decided by the British to make changes to the designation of an Infantry Regiment of Indian Army, due to the gallantry shown in battle by Kumaoni troops in both the World Wars. Thus, it was decided to shower glory on people of the Kumaon region and rename units of 19th Hyderabad Regiment as Kumaon Regiment.

The first crest of the Kumaon Regiment

It was also decided that the Kumaon Regiment would have a roaring lion holding aloft a cross (taken from the Coat of Arms of Sir Henry Russell, erstwhile Resident of Hyderabad) as its new crest. The new crest was prepared for Kumaon Regimental Centre (KRC), Ranikhet by silver craftsmen at Hazratganj, Lucknow. The first crest of Kumaon Regiment thus prepared was presented to 4 Kumaon by Lieutenant Colonel Balbir Singh, MC, Commandant, KRC.

The Golden Gloves

In 1960, while 4 Kumaon was serving with United Nations Emergency Force (UNEF) in Gaza, there was also a Swedish battalion in UNEF. Serving with the Swedish battalion was one Ingemar Johansson, World Boxing Heavyweight Champion, who signed the gloves and presented them to the unit.

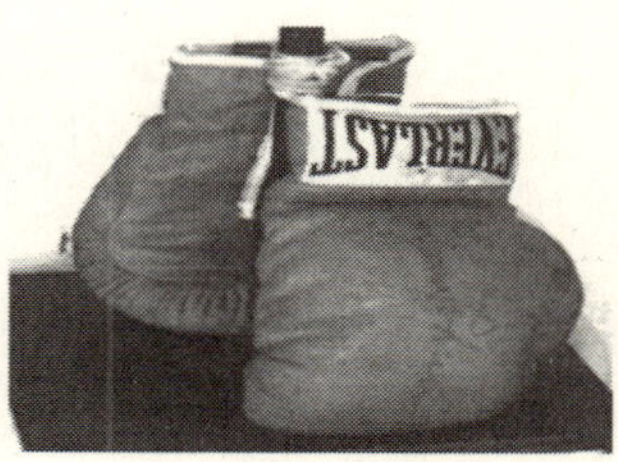

The Bison Head

In December 1935, Lt K. Bahadur Singh went on a shikar expedition to Africa to shoot wildlife. The mounted head of this African bison adorns the Dining Room of the Officers' Mess, 4 Kumaon.

A Superhero in Our Times – Nasim Arthur Salick

It was nearly 3.30 a.m. on 31 May 1948 and strong winds buffeted the thick fir forests around Pt 6873 (code-named 'Master'), in the high mountains of Uri Sector, Jammu and Kashmir (J&K). 'Master' is a massive hill feature and it was heavily bunkered by the enemy. The approaches to the top of the massif were swept by the accurate fire of enemy medium machine guns (MMGs). Slopes of the pyramid-shaped feature were heavily forested and had a steep gradient to the top. Intelligence reports had indicated that 'Master' was held by a regular company of Pakistan Army with about 150 tribal raiders from North-West Frontier Province (NWFP) of newly created Pakistan.

Capture of 'Master' on 31 May 1948

In early morning darkness, the handsome young officer had his back against a fir tree as he nervously clicked open the breech of his revolver to check if the ammunition cylinders were properly loaded. Jemadar Har Singh, Platoon Commander of the leading platoon had seen the young company commander open the breech of his revolver a number of times and loudly snap it shut. He knew

Maj. (later Brig.) N.A. Salick, VrC at Malpa, UP–Tibet border

that Lieutenant Nasim Arthur Salick[1] was preoccupied with thoughts of the impending attack, and deep concerns for his men filled his mind. The troops of 'B' Company, 4 Kumaon lay hidden behind rocks and in folds of the ground. Salick and his men had just climbed a steep foot-track that wound its way to the 'forming-up place' (FUP) that had been selected behind the enemy-held 'Master' feature. At 2 a.m., the company had left the strong bunkers of the recently captured hill named 'Pandu'. 4 Kumaon had been launching a series of successful attacks since 21 January. After intense fighting, one after another the dominating positions of Kopra, Goasher, Nangapar, Maidan Forest, Tragan, Chinal Dori, Chhota Qazinag and Pandu had been wrested from the enemy. 'Master' was the last enemy-held position left to be captured in the area. Major R. S. Basera, 2IC, had accompanied the attackers as 'Master' was expected to be a hard nut to crack. Lately, regular Pakistan Army troops had joined the tribals from NWFP to defend 'Master'. Uniquely, the honour of capturing 'Master' had been given to 'B' Company, commanded by young Salick and accompanied by Basera, 2IC of 4 Kumaon.

All of a sudden, the stillness of the cold night was shattered as artillery shells fired from Indian field guns began to explode in rapid succession on the objective. Shockwaves from the tearing explosions hit the anxious soldier's faces and sounds of the hollow bangs jarred their ear drums. Some young soldiers even plugged their ears to shut out the awful din. The softening-up process had commenced prior to the assault. The attackers were anxious and excited and they wanted to get to grips with the enemy on 'Master'. When the shelling stopped, Salick ordered the men to their feet and the platoon commanders took command of their troops. On a low command, there were urgent swishing sounds as the gaunt faced young Kumaoni lads drew bayonets from the scabbards which were slung from their webbed belts. Then sharp clicks were audible as the bayonets were affixed onto their .303 calibre rifles. Troops were now ready for the assault to commence.

On a hand signal from Salick, the platoons began creeping up the slope stealthily through the early morning mist. Quickly, he was on his

[1] In August 1947, when both India and Pakistan received their Independence from British rule, Lieutenant Nasim Arthur Salick, who was in the Baluch Regiment that went to Pakistan Army, opted to join the Indian Army and was posted to 4 Kumaon. The unit was in Kashmir, fighting hard to drive out the enemy tribal infiltrators and Pakistan Army units.

feet and skilfully manoeuvred his men to within 50 yards of the enemy's trenches, using more hand signals. Suddenly, all hell broke loose and the enemy began to target the attackers with accurate light machine gun (LMG) and MMG fire. In addition to the long automatic bursts being fired, hand grenades began to explode all around the leading section, with shrapnel whining into the distance. The leading platoon lowered their rifles with bayonets pointing towards the enemy and charged the opposition. But because of the heavy enemy machine-gun fire they did not make much headway and had to hit the ground once again and take up lying positions. The other two platoons following in the rear had also come under effective enemy fire of mortars and rifle grenades. The troops and both officers were forced to take cover behind boulders and fir trees. The ding-dong fighting continued till the first rays of dawn began to light up the area. Further attempts were made to assault 'Master', but the attackers did not succeed.

The enemy was well entrenched and the men were exhausted by the long climb to the FUP and nearly two hours of battle. The troops had suffered casualties and they now hugged the rocks and pine trees to avoid the enemy's accurate fire. Enemy MMG and LMG bullets ricocheted off the rocks, sending jagged rock splinters into the troops. It had become an awful predicament for the young company commander. Basera had stepped away from the bullet-swept slope and was keenly observing the raging battle. Having been selected for the honourable task of capturing 'Master', Salick knew he had to succeed at all costs. Without any delay, Salick took Basera's permission to renew the attack after the men had rested and eaten some of the packed food they were carrying. Meanwhile, he positioned snipers to keep the enemy's head down and reorganized 'B' Company into a Support Group and Assault Group. Basera gave young Salick permission to renew the attack and wished him good luck.

After the wounded had been evacuated, Salick ordered the Support Group to commence an engagement of the enemy positions. Smoke, mixed with high explosive mortar bombs, from three 2-inch light mortars and rifle grenades began to rain down on the enemy's defences. In addition, devastating automatic fire of nine LMGs and two MMGs raked the enemy. At the appropriate time Salick gave the signal, and the

Assault Group rose to their feet and launched another determined assault on the enemy. Salick could not resist the urge to be with his men and he was seen leading the charge. Seeing young Salick, the men cheered wildly. Their battle cries floated above the din of machine-gin fire, as they charged the stunned Pakistan Army troops in defence.

The attackers were surprised to see the blood-soaked figure of Naik Nar Singh leading an assault which silenced an enemy LMG post that had been holding up the right flank of the assault. Nar Singh had been wounded at the beginning of the assault and left behind to be given first aid with other wounded soldiers. After dispatching the Pakistan Army LMG crew, Nar Singh staggered forward and engaged some more enemy trenches, till he was killed by a burst of enemy fire. Seeing Salick's brave assault and Nar Singh's conspicuous gallantry,[2] nothing could stop the men of 'B' Company. After nearly six hours of bitter fighting, Salick's men captured 'Master' and put the surviving enemy to flight. Basera ordered Salick to fire 'red over green' Verey lights that depicted the 'success signal'.

It was a major victory. The intensity of fighting can be judged by the losses the enemy had suffered. Dead bodies of 30 enemy personnel of 15 Punjab Regiment (Pakistan Army) lay on the smoke-filled battlefield. Although the enemy sub-unit had put up a brave fight, it had been dislodged by the gallant assaults of Salick and his men. During the attack, one MMG, five LMGs, four Sten guns, numerous rifles and large quantities of ammunition, including 3-inch mortar bombs, were captured. Nar Singh won a posthumous Maha Vir Chakra (MVC), Salick was decorated with Vir Chakra (VrC), while Basera was Mentioned in Dispatches.

Master of Unconventional Operations

At the time of Independence and the Partition of India, regiments were allotted to either Indian Army or Pakistan Army, based on the religious denomination of majority of their personnel. Officers were permitted to opt for either Army. Thus, Salick had recently been transferred to 4 Kumaon from the Baluch Regiment. In 4 Kumaon, this smart young

[2] At Ranikhet (Uttarakhand), a large flat ground is named Naik Nar Singh Ground after this brave NCO.

officer with a soft voice, piercing gaze and disarming smile, was an instant hit. The men loved it when he sat with them in their trenches and gave a patient hearing to their tales of woe and family problems. He had a joke for every occasion and made the troops smile, in even the most dangerous situations. He had an inimitable style of talking and smiling that endeared him to one and all. The officers and men, alike, recognized his quiet bravery and there was great jubilation in the unit when he won the coveted Vir Chakra at such a young age. There was little change in Salick's attitude after he had won the coveted award. Instead, he became more benevolent and understanding towards his men.

Salick was always closely linked to the mountains. He loved the mountains and invariably gave his best when he was among its folds. When the unit returned from a United Nations assignment in Gaza in 1961, it was stationed in Ranikhet, home of the Kumaon Regiment.[3] At the time, differences were brewing with the Chinese over the Himalayan border issue. Salick and 'D' Company were launched to take up defences at Munsiyari (Shialekh) on the India–Tibet border. They were the first Indian servicemen to patrol this desolate portion of the border. While at Shialekh, Salick developed a close understanding with the local inhabitants and even recruited two Bhutia lads named Gaje Singh and Inder Singh[4] in 'D' Company. Later, in 1963 he led a long-range patrol over difficult and forbidding high-altitude terrain, along the Ceasefire Line in the Tangdhar Sector of J&K. This close reconnaissance of the area allowed Salick to use it as an unconventional approach, for the move of 4 Kumaon to Jura Bridge (in Bugina Bulge, Pakistan Occupied Kashmir [POK], J&K), during the India–Pakistan War of 1965.

Salick possessed a unique and fertile mind and he formulated and executed the most audacious plans for unconventional operations. Plans for the commando type of operations were conceived by him with almost childlike simplicity and they invariably turned out to be stunning successes. The Jura Bridge Operation in 1965 is a case in point. His tenure as Commander of the 'Commando Wing' at Mhow (Madhya Pradesh) and the hugely successful operations by Mukti Bahini guerrillas in

---

[3] 4 Kumaon became the first unit of Indian Army to receive President's Colours from President Rajendra Prasad in 1961, at Ranikhet.

[4] Inder Singh was a Section Commander with Commando Platoon, when he was killed in the severe fighting during 'Road-block Action' behind enemy lines in East Pakistan (present-day Bangladesh) during the 1971 War.

East Pakistan (now Bangladesh) in 1971, amply demonstrate his unique aptitude for unconventional operations. Salick is undoubtedly among the few officers in our Army who have practically used unconventional operations to their advantage in battle. He received Ati Vishisht Seva Medal (AVSM) for masterminding Mukti Bahini guerrilla operations during the 1971 War in East Pakistan. Captain Satyevir Yadav (later Lieutenant General and Colonel of Kumaon and Naga Regiments and Kumaon Scouts) served with Salick during these operations.

It was among the mountains that Salick fell in love. He met Marie, the charming daughter of the couple who ran West View Hotel in Ranikhet and it was love at first sight. Their meeting was followed by a whirlwind courtship and a fairy-tale wedding. It is doubtful whether Marie could ever tame the swashbuckling young officer of Kumaon Regiment, who had fought so gallantly in J&K operations and proudly wore the saffron and black ribbon of Vir Chakra on his chest.

Arthur Salick's Finest Moments as a Soldier – 1965 War

Arthur Salick's finest moments as a soldier were probably during the time when he commanded 4 Kumaon during the India–Pakistan War of 1965. Major P. N. Kathpalia (later Lieutenant General and Colonel of Kumaon and Naga Regiments and Kumaon Scouts) was 2IC to Salick during the India–Pakistan War of 1965.

The operations conducted by 4 Kumaon under Salick are indeed remarkable operations launched against Pakistani infiltrators—the determined attack on Pt 9018 (named 'Kumaon Hill' after its capture) and finally the battalion-sized commando operation behind enemy lines that led to the destruction of Jura Bridge. The capture of Bugina Bulge, in POK bears the hallmark stamp of Salick's unique style in battle.

On 11 October 1965, the enemy launched determined counter-attacks to dislodge 4 Kumaon from a position called 'Ring Contour', adjacent to Jura Bridge. Salick had to be physically removed to a safer place, just in time before the enemy captured the Tactical HQ, which was located in a Gujjar's huts. Salick's sleeping bag, dark glasses and a map-case were lost to the enemy. The map-case contained a sheet of paper on which the rough plan for Jura Bridge Operation was written in Salick's barely legible scrawl. Later, the paper was produced in the

United Nations (UN) General Assembly, New York by Pakistan. General K. S. Thimayya, DSO was then the UN Commander in Cyprus. He acquired a copy of the 'operational plan' and sent it back to 4 Kumaon with a simple noting that said, 'Good plan – workable!'[5]

> *As the enemy counter-attacked 'Ring Contour', Salick was seen standing in the open with Subedar Major Lachham Singh. Bullets whizzed through the air and smacked into the ground around them. They stopped the soldiers who were falling back under pressure of the enemy counter-attacks and formed a new defensive line and temporarily halted the enemy. The Pakistanis had already captured a number of forward positions and were rapidly increasing their numbers from across Kishenganga River. Salick realized that the situation would be disastrous if the enemy was not repelled immediately. However, there were no reserves available and time was at a premium.*

A MI-4 helicopter hovers before descending to deliver fresh rations to 4 Kumaon which was infiltrating to destroy the vital bridge over Kishenganga River, at Jura.

[5] This was to be General K. S. Thimayya's last communication with the unit. He sadly died in harness in Cyprus, in December 1965. After he died, a postage stamp featuring Thimayya was issued by the Government of Cyprus. Today a main road is named in Cyprus after the remarkable general from India.

That is when Salick's soldierly instincts came to the fore. Without a moment's hesitation, Salick took a bold and historic decision. He told the Intelligence Officer (IO), Captain (later Colonel and CO 4 Kumaon) Narendra Singh to immediately launch a counter-attack with signallers, tradesmen, the lightly wounded and any other personnel who were fit enough to attack. It was a timely decision. Salick had to be physically restrained from joining the attack. However, Lachham Singh joined the IO and his rag-tag bunch of attackers. 'Ring Contour' was recaptured after very bitter fighting.

A lot of blood was shed that day as more than 100 dead bodies, both in olive green and khaki uniforms lay on the bullet-swept battlefield. The counter-attack had been a resounding success, and the enemy was pushed across the Kishenganga River.

Despite the great victory, Salick was deeply saddened by the heavy casualties 4 Kumaon had taken. He was inconsolable at the loss of the gallant Subedar Nand Kishore (Senior JCO, 'A' Company), Subedar Sardar Singh, Captain Karunakaran (Artillery Observer), 2nd Lieutenant D. K. Gupte (Engineer Officer) and many others who had been killed. Salick passed orders for the evacuation of Major Y. S. Bisht, who had been badly wounded by a burst of enemy Browning Machine Gun fire (five bullets had hit him in the chest and one bullet had pierced his neck), and many other seriously wounded personnel.

Later, Jura Bridge was destroyed in a unique manner. To avoid further casualties, Salick planned to destroy the bridge from a distance, with the fire of a 106 mm recoilless (RCL) gun. Kathpalia arranged for the RCL gun from 1 Para through his colleague, Major (later Lieutenant General and Governor) Ranjit Singh Dayal, MVC. The RCL gun was moved from Hajipir Pass to Tangdhar by road.

Thereafter, the heavy gun and its ammunition were hefted by soldiers over the high mountains, to the bank of Kishenganga River. Here, the heavy RCL gun was lashed to some sturdy pine trees as it could not be depressed low enough to effectively engage the bridge while remaining affixed on its mount.

In this manner, the RCL gun boomed and engaged Jura Bridge again and again. The seventh RCL shell destroyed the wires that held up the suspension bridge and it came crashing down into the swirling waters of the river below. As the shells exploded, enemy soldiers in khaki uniforms were seen getting out of their bunkers around the entrance of Jura Bridge and fleeing in utter panic. With the destruction of Jura Bridge, the operation was deemed to have been concluded successfully.

Support for his Men

After the Jura Operation, Salick went to the HQ at Tangdhar to submit citations for gallantry awards. He was told by the Brigade Commander to reduce the number of citations. It was a shock for Salick, but he did not relent. He insisted that since he had witnessed the actions himself, all the men he had recommended richly deserved the gallantry awards. He was told that 4 Kumaon had performed incredibly well during the War. Thus, the higher authorities wanted Salick to be recommended for the award of MVC. But, if Salick refused to reduce the number of citations, he would not be recommended for the high award. Salick was outraged at the humiliating suggestion. Officers who were present in the office, testify that Salick stood straight and said in a level voice, 'If my men are not recommended for the gallantry awards they so richly deserve, Sir, I definitely do not deserve an award.' Saying this, he placed the citations on the table, saluted smartly and left the Brigade Commander's office.

Replica of Jura Bridge mounted on fired case of 7th RCL shell that destroyed the bridge.

It is well known that Salick did not receive a gallantry award, despite the stellar role he had played in the remarkable operations. However, he stood firmly by his men and refused to bask in personal glory, at their expense. This was one of Salick's finest moments as a soldier of Kumaon Regiment and Indian Army. It is a strong lesson of the courage of conviction, selfless behaviour and high values that are needed while soldiering with troops. Salick has shown the way for others to follow.

Tribute to the 'Green Hackle'

Salick later commanded an Infantry Brigade in J&K and hung up his boots after serving with the National Cadet Corps in Ahmedabad, Gujarat. Today, Brigadier Nasim Arthur Salick, AVSM, VrC is no longer with us, but his deeds continue to inspire generations of Kumaonis and others, both on the battlefield and in our daily lives.

It is a matter of great pride that he was a part of the Kumaon Regiment (4 Kumaon), when it fought in the 1947–48 War and 1965 War in Kashmir. He later served the Indian Army in East Pakistan (now Bangladesh) during the 1971 War. He will always be remembered as the soft spoken, simple and unassuming gentleman of Kumaon Regiment. His name will live on forever as a brave soldier of the Indian Army. Salick was loved by his troops and in turn, he proudly wore the 'green hackle'. Soldiers who don the 'green hackle', can be proud that the hackle of Kumaon Regiment once also adorned the head-gear of a superhero called Nasim Arthur Salick.

Brig. N. A. Salick, AVSM, VrC at 4 Kumaon during Bicentenary – 1988.

Ambush at Khatir Nar

With capture of the towering 'Master' feature, 4 Kumaon had completed its allotted task to clear Qazinag Range. The enemy tried repeatedly to recapture 'Master' and gain a foothold on the ridgeline. Each time the enemy was driven off with casualties. The enemy then resorted to shelling the captured positions with 3.7-inch howitzers and caused some harassment. On 6 June 1948, a patrol from 'A' Company clashed with the enemy in Khatir Nar area. The enemy suffered three soldiers killed and five wounded, while the patrol lost one OR killed.

During this period two companies of 2 Dogra had been placed under command the Battalion and they held picquets to the north of 'Pandu'. Because of the repeated counterattacks by the enemy to recapture the picquets held by the companies of 2 Dogra, on 19 June 1948, Lieutenant Colonel M. M. Khanna decided to visit the Dogra companies and take along a captured MMG to strengthen their defences. Unwittingly, a Battalion HQ signaller transmitted the information of CO's visit in clear, without the use of codes. It was later known that the wireless message was intercepted by the enemy, who prepared to ambush the CO's party. The CO's party left 'Pandu' at about 10 a.m. and proceeded along a route that was frequented by patrols of 2 Dogra. Because of the intercepted wireless message, the enemy had organized a well-planned ambush at Khatir Nar (a picturesque valley with a bubbling stream). A company of Pakistan Army troops laid the ambush and deployed automatic weapons and mortars to cover the killing ground. At approximately 12.30 p.m., CO's party reached the stream and they were mowed down by deadly bursts of automatic fire. Khanna was repeatedly shot through the chest and the Bren-gunner with the patrol was killed while he was taking up a firing position. No. 2 of the Bren-gun detachment briefly handled the weapon but he was also killed on the spot.

Sepoy Jodh Singh found himself stranded in the open with the enemy's automatic bursts hitting the ground around him. Though the enemy's fire had killed both Bren-gunners on the same spot, Jodh Singh rapidly rolled over and took hold of the abandoned LMG. He fired all ammunition that remained in the magazine at the enemy soldiers who were now approaching the wounded CO and other members of the Indian patrol who were lying wounded in the killing ground. Jodh Singh's accurate fire killed four enemy soldiers and another six were wounded. While he was firing the LMG, Jodh Singh was hit by a burst of fire in the face and leg. Having run out of ammunition and bleeding profusely, he left the Bren gun and began to crawl to the MMG that was lying nearby. In the process he was overwhelmed by the enemy and killed. Believing the patrol to have been wiped out, the enemy picked up the unattended MMG and made a quick getaway. The CO's party of 15 personnel had lost one JCO and 12 OR killed while the seriously wounded CO and one wounded jawan were both presumed to be dead.

A Kashmiri villager named Jumma Mohammad had been grazing his goats near the gushing waters of Khatir Nar, when he was startled by the loud sounds of heavy firing. Initially he lay down in fear with his animals, but his inquisitiveness soon got the better of him and he cautiously approached the ambush site. He was aghast to see dead bodies strewn all over the narrow valley. The painful moans of two wounded personnel soon attracted his attention. He overcame his fears and approached the two wounded men. Khanna was in great pain and barely coherent while the other casualty was unconscious. One by one, Jumma Mohammad carefully carried the wounded men and hid them in a nearby mud hut made by gujjars for their cattle. With difficulty, Khanna asked Jumma Mohammad to quickly go to the nearest Indian Army picquet and get help. Thus, at great personal risk, Jumma Muhammad went through the enemy dominated area to get help for the two wounded men.

On getting to the picquet he narrated the tragic situation to surprised Indian Army soldiers and then guided a relief column to the ambush site. Jumma Mohammad had been gone for over an hour and this was the most difficult time for the badly wounded CO. With the other

Jumma Mohammad, VrC, meets Gen. K.S. Thimayya, DSO and Col. (later Lt. Gen.) M.M. Khanna

wounded OR in an unconscious condition, Khanna did not know whether the Kashmiri civilian would return with help, or quietly disappear to his village. He was losing blood rapidly from the chest wound and he did not know if he would survive. Also, Khanna was worried about the enemy returning to the ambush position. It was a great relief when Jumma Mohammad returned with the 2 Dogra patrol. On improvised stretchers, the two wounded men were quickly evacuated to the picquet of 2 Dogra and from there they were taken to Baramullah and then to the bigger hospital at Srinagar.

On that day Jumma Mohammad showed great bravery and determination, when he could have easily departed and proceeded for personal safety to his village. Because of his efforts the severely wounded CO and OR were both saved. The Government of India recognized the gallant actions of Sepoy Jodh Singh and Jumma Mohammad by awarding them both Vir Chakra. Jumma Mohammad thus became the first Indian civilian to receive the coveted gallantry award of Vir Chakra.

Unique Patrol to Aksai Chin

Soon after the Chinese Revolution of 1949, India under Prime Minister Jawaharlal Nehru unilaterally withdrew Indian claims in Tibet. The soldiers of China's People's Liberation Army (PLA) entered Lhasa. With India out of the way, the Chinese made immediate plans to consolidate Tibet with mainland China, as they had already done for Sinkiang (Xinjiang). With the 'Great Game' assuming importance to keep an expanding Russia in check, all along the British had maintained a strong hold on independent Tibet.

Thus, it was decided by the Chinese government to improve their road communications on a war footing. The Chinese had rightly assessed the easiest way to consolidate and unify their recently acquired, vast empire was to construct a network of roads. Thus, the road construction began almost immediately after the arrival of the first lot of young Chinese soldiers in Lhasa. High priority was given to the construction of outlying roads, like the Chamdo–Lhasa Road, Qinghai–Lhasa Road and the Sinkiang–Tibet Road (also known as Aksai Chin Road). The last-named road was to serve a dual purpose, as it would link the newly assimilated Sinkiang Province on China's western border with its restive Uygur Muslim populations. The first surveys for this vital road were conducted at the end of 1951, and construction began in real earnest in 1952.

India had been running a consulate in Lhasa, and this had continued even after its independence from Britain in 1947. Very strategically, the consulate had earlier been set up by the British-India government. The British government in India had worked hard towards keeping Tibet as an independent country, a 'buffer state' between India and China. At no place was India's' northern border touching Chinas' southern border; thus, there were relatively few chances of any misunderstandings that could lead to a border war. At the time, India was Britain's largest, principal colony. However, the Indian Consulate in Lhasa was closed down when India withdrew its Tibetan claim in 1949.

Erstwhile Indian consulate building in Lhasa, Tibet

Closure of Indian Consulate at Kashgar and Trade Office at Shiquanhe (Gartok)

If the Government of India had been ready to read beyond China's rhetoric and to disbelieve Chinese Prime Minister Zhou-en-Lai's hollow assurances of friendship, it may have seen the emergence of more ominous signs of potential conflict. One of these was the Chinese demand for closure of the Indian consulate at Kashgar that had been functioning for a considerable period of time. The Indian side accepted the Chinese demand and promptly closed down the consulate at Kashgar. Here again, as in several other cases, the Indian Prime Minister Jawaharlal Nehru justified Chinese talk of 'revolutionary changes' taking place in their country, without taking any retaliatory measures or even lodging a formal com-

The consulate at Kashgar, Sinkiang (China), was closed down voluntarily by India

plaint. Closing down of the Indian consulate at Kashgar on Nehru's orders has rightly been called an 'original sin', as with the closure of this consulate, India's interests in Central Asia were lost for all times to come. Today, with the advantage of hindsight, it is abundantly clear that the Chinese side had planned their sinister actions very well, to once and for all time remove India's influence in Central Asia.

All along, the Chinese were aware the proposed strategic Sinkiang–Tibet Road would cut across Indian territory of the Aksai Chin plateau in Ladakh. Therefore, they also wanted the Indian Trade Agent based at Shiquanhe out of the way at the earliest, as otherwise their intrusive road-building activity would have alerted the Indian side. Although, construction of this road by the Chinese was known to the Government of India long before it was officially made public, sadly there was no protest by India.

Different incidents which occurred in the early fifties should have awakened the Government of India and distracted it from succumbing to the Chinese euphoric chant of 'Hindi-Chini Bhai-Bhai'. Sadly, this did not happen and instead of alarming the Indian side, the disturbing reports probably reinforced the determination of India to bolster a stance of friendship with China. Thus, the Chinese went ahead with their plans to oust any Indian presence that could monitor activity on

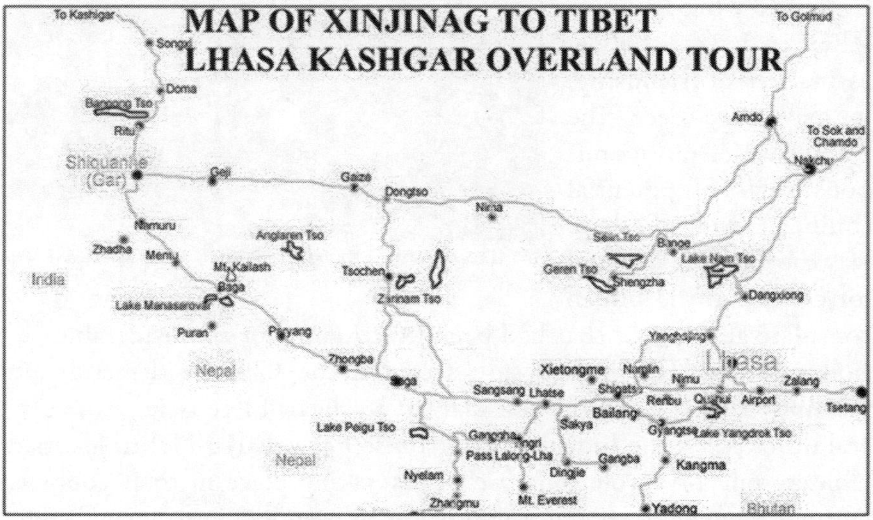

A Chinese map (of 1950) showing their planned new roads

the Chinese road that illegally passed through the Indian territory of Aksai Chin. There was repeated harassment of the Indian Trade Agent posted at Shiquanhe (Gartok), in Western Tibet. Initially, India's Ministry of External Affairs reacted sharply and got the Prime Minister to write to his counterpart in China about the needless harassment of the Indian Trade Agent, but there was no follow-up action. The Chinese conveniently looked the other way and forgot about the matter, as it suited them the best to outwardly ignore this issue.

The harassment of the Indian Trade Agent was without doubt linked to the construction work that had already commenced on the Sinkiang–Tibet Road. Shiquanhe, located midway between Lhasa and Kashgar is the last small town before the highway enters the Indian territory of Aksai Chin plateau, from the Lhasa side. The presence of Indian officials at Shiquanhe was a big embarrassment for the Chinese. Thus, they urgently wanted the Indian Trade Office to be closed down. It appears that despite being briefed in detail by Ministry of External Affairs officials about these ominous negative signs, Nehru still believed in the elusive and pseudo-Chinese goodwill. He did not want to 'rock the boat' and impair his supposedly burgeoning image as a 'world leader of diplomacy'. His advisors like V. K. Krishna Menon, Raksha Mantri (Defence Mijnister) and Bhola Nath Mullik, Director Intelligence Bureau (DIB), went along with the flawed approach and took no actions to exercise caution against the Chinese road construction activities or to expose their nefarious designs.

India's Trade Office at Shiquanhe; the office was vacated by India and handed over to China in 1957

With regard to the so called 'revolutionary changes' taking place in China, Nehru had declared in the Parliament:

> *... some major changes have taken place there [Kashgar]. As a result of those changes, which have nothing to do with India at the moment ... our Consul went there – I speak from memory – probably in 1948, maybe even later, in 1949. But when these revolutionary changes took place over*

there, it is perfectly true that the Chinese Government told us that they intended to treat Sinkiang as a closed area. They told that to other Governments too. Well, nothing happened and our Consul remained there. But because of those changes and because of many factors – among them being what had happened in Kashmir – the trade ceased ... Kashgar is important to us as a trade route. The trade went over the Karakoram, passed through Ladakh and Leh on to Kashmir. Various factors, including developments in Kashmir led to the stoppage of that trade ... The overall result of this was, our Consul remained there for some time, till recently ... but there is now no work to be done. So, we advised him to come away and he did come away.

India had been trading with Central Asia and more particularly Kasha and Yarkand areas for ages via the Karakoram Pass. Just because 'revolutionary changes' had occurred in China, quite incredibly the Government of India, quietly accepted the Chinese version and closed its trade with Sinkiang as a mere fait accompli. Since the winter of 1948, India had physically controlled the Zoji-La Pass as well as Ladakh, having driven out the Pakistani invaders from most of the areas. At that time, the Karakoram Pass was still open to the caravans, which came and went as usual between Central Asia and India.

According to the DIB, the Indian Trade Agent in Shiquanhe had reported about Chinese construction of a road from Sinkiang to Lhasa in July and September 1955 and also in August 1957. Some authors have also mentioned about construction of the Aksai Chin Road and that it was known during the mid-fifties to both the Ministries of Defence and External Affairs. In his book *The Saga of Ladakh*, Major General Jagjit Singh mentions that in 1956, the Indian Military Attaché (MA) in Beijing, Brigadier S. S. Malik, received information that China had started building a highway through Indian territory of the Aksai Chin. Malik reported the matter to Army HQs in New Delhi and a similar report was sent by the Indian Embassy to the Ministry of External Affairs. In a recently published book, *1962: The War That Wasn't*, author Shiv Kunal Verma writes about Chinese activity in Indian territory and makes a mention of two patrols that were sent to confirm reports of road construction by the Chinese through the Aksai Chin plateau. One of these patrols was led by Lieutenant Colonel R. S. Basera, an

Lt. Col. R.S. Basera

officer of the Kumaon Regiment, who had commanded 1st Kumaon Rifles (now 3 Kumaon [Rifles]) in Tangdhar (J&K). Five months later, in a special report to Delhi, the MA drew attention to the construction of the strategic highway that passed through Indian territory of Aksai Chin. On 6 October 1957, the Sinkiang–Tibet Road was formally opened after a brief ceremony in Shiquanhe. 12 trucks proceeded on a trial run from Yarkand and reached Shiquanhe. In January 1958, the China News Agency reported that the Sinkiang–Tibet highway had been opened two months earlier and the road was being fully utilized.

Another interesting account about how the Indian Army already knew in 1955 that the Chinese were building a road across Indian territory of Aksai Chin, has recently been published in the UK. In 1955, Sydney Wignall, a British mountaineer went on an expedition inside Tibet with the express knowledge of Indian Military Intelligence authorities. The Indian Army Chief, General K. S. Thimayya, DSO, had seriously suspected for some time that the Chinese were building a road on Indian territory and wanted this startling information to be quickly confirmed. Thus, Wignall was asked to get proof of the illegal construction activities. Wignall confirmed the Chinese road construction, but unfortunately, he was apprehended by the Chinese Army, interrogated and kept as a prisoner for several weeks. He was later released in the midst of winter on a high-altitude snow bound Pass. The Chinese had apparently hoped Wignall would perish in the strong blizzards that ravaged the area, and never find his way back to India. But after an incredible journey, Wignall managed to reach India and was able to report about the road to the Indian Army authorities, who in turn informed Thimayya, Menon and Nehru.

Opening of Sinkiang–Tibet Road (Aksai Chin Road)

On 6 October 1957, a Chinese newspaper *Kuang-ming Jih-pao* reported:

> *The Sinkiang–Tibet Road – the highest highway in the world – has been completed. During the past few days, a number of trucks running on the highway on a trial basis have arrived in Ko-ta-k'e in Tibet from Yehch'eng in Sinkiang. The Sinkiang–Tibet Highway is 1,179 km long, of which 915 km are more than 4,000 metres above sea level – 130 km of it is over 5,000 metres above sea level, with the highest point being 5,500 metres. Thirty ('Liberation' model and Chissu 150) heavy-duty trucks, fully loaded with road builders, maintenance equipment and fuel, running on the highway on a trial basis, headed for Ko-ta-k'e from Yehch'eng. In addition, two trucks fully loaded with Hami melons, apples and pomegranates, all native products of Sinkiang, headed in the same direction. These fruits were gifts brought specially by the road builders of Sinkiang for the people of various nationalities.*

It appears that one reason the news of the Chinese road through Indian territory came to the Indian public late was that for a few years New Delhi must have had doubts on how to react to this astounding report. In 1957, when the Indian Ambassador to China and his military attaché had been invited to a special function to celebrate the opening of this road, they politely refused. They had refused to fall into the cleverly laid Chinese trap. By their expected presence at the inauguration of the highway, the Chinese side must have expected the Indian dignitaries to unknowingly give the stamp of approval to the Aksai Chin Road (Sinkiang–Tibet Road) and its controversial alignment that passed through Ladakh. Sadly, for the Chinese, the Indian officials did not attend the controversial function.

It took another year for the Nehru government to officially complain to Beijing about the Chinese built road that intruded through Indian territory of Ladakh. An 'Informal Note' was given by the Foreign Secretary to the Chinese Ambassador on 18 October 1958. New Delhi had finally decided to take some action. He wrote, 'The attention of the Government of India has recently been drawn to the fact that a motor road has been constructed by the Government of the People's Republic of China across the eastern part of the Ladakh region of the Jammu and Kashmir State, which is part of India'. In the Note, the Indian government referred to the treaty signed by Jammu and Kashmir State (including Ladakh) ruler Gulab Singh. The Note concluded that it was a matter of 'surprise and regret' that the Chinese government had built a road through 'indisputably Indian territory without first obtaining the permission of the Government of India and without even informing the Government of India'. In conclusion, the Note stated: '... the Government of India are anxious to settle these petty frontier disputes so that the friendly relations between the two countries may not suffer. The Government of India would therefore be glad for an early reply from the Chinese Government.' Ironically, the 'petty frontier disputes' are still not solved till today and the issues are likely to have become even more

The Sinkiang–Tibet (Aksai Chin) Highway

'knotty' with time.

The Aksai Chin Road enters Indian territory just east of Sariah Jilgnang, runs north-west to Amtogar and to the western bank of the Amtogar lake, runs north-west through Yangpa, Khitai Dawan and Haji Langer, which are all indisputably in Indian territory. Near the Amtogar Lake several branch tracks have also been made motorable by the Chinese. The India–China boundary in the Ladakh sector as in others is traditionally well known and follows well marked geographical features. The territory which the road traverses has been part of the Ladakh region of India for centuries and the old established frontiers have been accepted by the Chinese in the treaty of 1842, as the International Boundary.

At the end of the letter, another pressing issue was raised. For some time, an Indian patrol had been reported to be 'missing'. Delhi wanted to know if the Chinese had seen 'an Indian party consisting of three Military Officers and four soldiers together with one guide, one porter, six pony owners and thirty-four ponies ... out on a normal patrol in this area near Shinglung in Indian territory'. Indeed, the patrol had been seen and captured by the Chinese border guards on Indian soil. Beijing had admitted immediately that they were in their custody, but according to the local Chinese commanders the Indian jawans had trespassed on Chinese side of the frontier at the time of their arrest. This was the first of a long series of incidents. Hundreds of letters and notes would be exchanged on the subject. It is quite clear that the Indian Army and Government of India, urgently wanted confirmation of the Chinese activities in Aksai Chin area. Thus, it was decided to send patrols on an urgent and difficult mission to Aksai Chin and ascertain facts of the intrusive road construction and trespassing by Chinese, on ground.

A Daring Patrol to Aksai Chin

With increasing focus on Chinese road building activity through Indian territory, in early 1957 an Indian Army officer was selected to lead a special patrol to this very remote part of north-east Ladakh. The patrol was to physically confirm reports of the Chinese intrusion and their ongoing road-building activities through Indian territory. The officer selected for this difficult mission was Lieutenant Colonel R. S. Basera[1] of

---

[1] R. S. Basera was commissioned in 19 Hyderabad Regiment in 1944 and dispatched to 10/19 Hyderabad Regiment (Regimental Centre) at Agra. After initial liaison, he proceeded to 8/19 Hyderabad Regiment in Arakan (Burma). His CO was Lt Col K. S. Thimayya and he fought in the epic and vicious Battle of Kangaw, in which the unit defeated the Japanese, won Battle Honour 'Kangaw' and the CO won a DSO. For his gallantry during the battle Basera was Mentioned-in-Dispatches. At the end of the War in 1945, it was decided to disband 8/19 Hyderabad Regiment (as was the norm for all 'war raised' units). However, the unit's battle honours, history and all ranks were merged with 4/19 Hyderabad Regiment (after the War dubbed as 4 Kumaon) as that unit was grossly under strength after crippling losses during battles in Malaya, Singapore and years in wretched Japanese POW camps. In 1947, Basera proceeded to Jammu and Kashmir with 4 Kumaon and fought against the tribal raiders from Pakistan. As 2IC of 4 Kumaon, he participated in the capture of 'Master' feature with Lt (later Brig.) N. A. Salick and

Kumaon Regiment. Basera was a tough soldier who had recently completed the command of his battalion (1st Kumaon Rifles). His clandestine mission was to be tough, exciting and unique, as he had to proceed undercover to the vast plateau of Aksai Chin and confirm incoming reports that stated the Chinese were constructing a motorable road from Kashgar (Sinkiang) to Lhasa (Tibet). This road supposedly passed through the northern part of the vast, barren and high-altitude swathe of Indian territory called Aksai Chin. Interestingly, Basera was to proceed on the mission disguised as a yak herder. He was accompanied by Havildar Diwan Singh of the Engineers. Both Army personnel were to move in the company of three genuine yak herders and their large, shaggy beasts.

Basera received his briefings at headquarters in Srinagar and Leh. During these briefings he was told about the mission in detail. He was also told that the patrol must exercise extreme caution and not repeat the case of the British mountaineer Wignall, who had been apprehended by the Chinese while he was surveying the Aksai Chin Road from the Tibetan side.

The Intelligence personnel who conducted the briefings in Srinagar, had stressed on the need to maintain utmost secrecy for this vitally important mission. The two Army personnel were strictly told not to carry any tell-tale documents or other items that could disclose their identities, if they were ever caught and bodily searched by the Chinese during the patrol. They were also told that the mission was of national importance and it would be physically and mentally exhausting and quite tough. During the mission they would move on foot from Leh, along with three trusted Ladakhi graziers and their yaks. They were to travel as light as possible and their rations and other essential loads would be carried both in their backpacks and on the yaks. They were explicitly told that even after they had returned from the mission, they were never to tell their family and friends where they had been or ever recount any details of their secret mission.

'B' Company, 4 Kumaon. Later, in 1953 he commanded 3 Kumaon (Rifles) at Tangdhar. After his command, in 1957 Basera was personally selected by his erstwhile CO, General K. S. Thimayya, DSO, to lead the special patrol to Aksai Chin and check for construction of the highway from Sinkiang to Tibet, through the Indian territory of Aksai Chin plateau in Ladakh.

Basera was shown a large map and enlargement of the Ladakh–Tibet area and asked to memorize the route they were to follow. He was not permitted to make any notes, and even asked to destroy any notes he may have made earlier. On the map they were shown the route to be followed from Leh to Aksai Chin and back. After setting out from Leh, they were to move in the north-easterly direction for about 250–300 km, till they reached the expected location of the new road built by the Chinese through Aksai Chin. Initially, they would pass over difficult, undulating terrain, till they crossed the Karakoram Range and Shyok River. After passing the Ladakhi settlement at Tangtse, they would move into the barren, high-altitude plateau of Aksai Chin. The Intelligence officers had warned Basera that they would have to carefully conserve their water supply during the mission as potable water was scarce in the area, especially on the desolate Aksai Chin plateau.

The men and animals would have to survive on the water they carried in goatskin containers, which were to be filled at Leh and carried on the yaks. There were some large drinking water sources on the way, before they entered Aksai Chin, such as Pangong Tso Lake and the Shyok and Chang Chenmo rivers. Here, the containers could be refilled. He was also told of small freshwater sources that existed in the eastern part of Aksai Chin plateau. These distant and small water sources could be used in case of a grave emergency. It would entail some deviation from their route, but the water sources would save human and animal lives, if such a need were to arise.

After the briefings at Leh, they met with the three scruffy-looking yak graziers who were to accompany them. The three Ladakhis included two short, tough, middle-aged men and a bright young man named Nawang. The young man knew a smattering of Hindustani, and was to act as the interpreter. The yak herders spoke only Ladakhi dialect and had been employed by the Army authorities in Leh. The herders were said to be trustworthy but they emitted a peculiar smell that was a heady mix of the sharp, all pervading smell of rancid yak butter, their unwashed clothes and the slovenly yaks themselves. Basera and Diwan dreaded the fact that very soon they too could smell like their companions!

As a prerequisite to their proceeding on the mission, Basera and Diwan Singh were glad to be permitted to stop shaving. They soon grew a stubble of hair on their faces. Both the Army personnel removed their olive-green Army uniforms, jerseys and jackets. They donned sets of well-used and shaggy clothes that were similar to the ones worn by the three yak herders. After adjusting the unwieldy headgear made of skins and sheep's fur, both Basera and Diwan looked very similar to the yak herders whom they were to accompany on the patrol. The headgear had large 'ear flaps' that hung down the sides of their faces. These leather flaps with fur on the inside, could be buttoned below the chin to ward off the icy, cold winds that whistled down from the Karakoram Range. The buttoned-down flaps were an effective covering that protected their faces from the cold winds and also hid their identities. This was a nice covering, if the need should ever arise to hide their identities from a Chinese patrol.

The Army authorities in Leh gave the yak herders rations to be carried for five individuals, for a month's duration of the patrol. The rations were simple and comprised of rice, dal, tea leaves, salt, jaggery, milk powder and a few condiments. The rations were packed in containers that were tied in two bundles and carried as a body load on the first yak. The second yak carried the bedding bundle of quilts, rough fur-skins and cooking utensils. The third yak carried two goatskin tents (one was a small tent and the other one was much larger), the wooden poles and some containers made of skins with potable water for the men and animals. The smaller tent was for use of the Colonel, while the other four men were to sleep together in the larger tent. In addition to their loads, the yaks also carried sheaves of dried grass that would cushion the loads and serve as the animal's food during the long trek.

The three Ladakhis had cooked some large rotis that could be eaten during the next morning and afternoon (as breakfast and lunch) with some salt and pickles, and washed down with hot tea. The yak herders would put rancid and foul-smelling butter in their tea, while Basera and Diwan would drink their tea with regular milk powder, and sweetened with jaggery. This was to be the routine for meals for the next month or so, while they were on the mission to Aksai Chin. Food would be cooked only once a day, when they halted and set up their tents in the evening. When, the evening meal was cooked, rotas would be made for the next day as well. These large rotis would be carried for their breakfast and lunch on the following day. In the evening, they would have the luxury of eating hot rice and maybe some lentils (*dal*).

Onwards to Aksai Chin

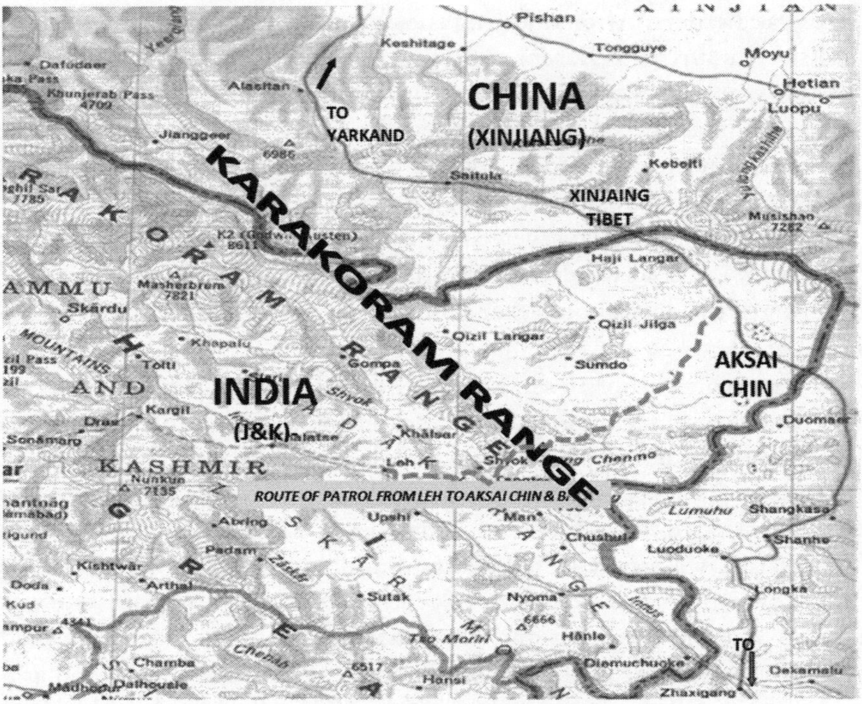

Map showing the route taken by Lt Col R. S. Basera's patrol
from Leh to the Sinkiang–Lhasa Highway and back.

Early the next morning, before sunrise the strange patrol of five individuals and three shaggy yaks, moved out of the sleeping town of Leh. Three staff officers, accompanied by a few jawans had come to see off the patrol. They shook hands with Basera and Diwan Singh and wished them good luck for their adventurous trek. The officer and non-commissioned officer (NCO) strode into the dark and cold March morning, closely following the lumbering yaks and three sombre Ladakhi yak herders. The patrol trudged along at a steady pace set by the slow moving, sturdy beasts. Soon the sun came up and its strong rays warmed the five men as they plodded along the rugged landscape. Barren mountains rose sharply on either side. After moving along in this manner for about three hours, the patrol halted and huddled in a circle. The yaks sat around the men and effectively blocked out the sharp and cold breeze that had begun to whip around them. With difficulty a small fire was lit and the men and yaks protected it from the breeze. Soon, hot tea was brewing and rotis were warmed on the blazing fire. The men looked about them at the vast expanse of treeless terrain that was of varying shades of grey and brown hues, as they ate the large rotis and pickles and sipped the hot tea.

Soon the yaks were plodding along again, followed by the three yak herders and two Army personnel. After covering about fifteen more kilometres, the patrol halted in the treeless expanse and pitched their tents against some large boulders that would protect them from the cold wind that blew strongly, every night from the north. Every day the patrol would cover about 25 km. Then they halted for the night, well before it had become dark. They would then cook the night's meal and rotis for the next day. The herders pitched the tents, fed and watered the yaks, and then had their evening meal before settling in for the night.

On the third morning after leaving Leh, they were going about their morning chores – preparing tea on a small wood fire and putting down the tents – when they were startled to hear the rising thunder of horse hooves beating on the hard ground. Stopping whatever they were doing, the patrol members stood by the yaks and were fascinated to see a cloud of dust rising above a herd of Tibetan wild asses or kiangs, as they galloped across the vast, treeless plain. The herd of wild asses seemed to be heading towards the soaring heights of the Karakoram Range that could be seen in the far distance. The short and stocky animals had a coat of rough fur that kept the bitter cold at bay. After another three days they neared the small village of Tangtse. The hamlet comprised of a few houses with stone walls that were plastered with mud, and had roofs made of flat pieces of shale stones. These houses were located in the flat gap between the lofty Karakoram Range to the north and deep-blue-green waters of the vast Pangong Tso Lake. Because of the security of their mission, they stopped for the night well before they reached Tangtse village. On the next day, they moved fast and avoided meeting any of the few old people and children that could be seen on the outskirts of the hamlet.

The motley patrol crossed the fast-flowing waters of the Shyok River over a rudimentary wood and stone bridge. It took a fair amount of coaxing to get the yaks to step on the bridge. Once they were firmly on the bridge, they crossed over to the other side in a tearing hurry. Once they were all across the river, the patrol halted and permitted the yaks to drink to their fill from the gushing waters of the river. The men also drank as much as they could and the nearly empty water containers were all filled to the very top. Thereafter, the march was resumed. All members of the patrol were upbeat, even the animals seemed to have gained a great deal of renewed energy. Shortly after this crossing, they came across the Chang Chenmo rivulet. It was a much smaller drift and hardly contained any flowing water. The patrol could not find a bridge to go across this stream. They splashed through the shallow, ankle deep water and went over to the other bank. They were happy that after crossing the Chang Chenmo, they were finally entering Aksai Chin plateau and thus getting closer to their goal. They would now have to be extremely cautious, and keep a sharp look out for the road that the Chinese were supposedly building and watch out for armed Chinese patrols that could be lurking in the area.

The Aksai Chin was a vast and desolate expanse of flat territory that was devoid of any form of vegetation, including grass. Nehru had correctly stated before the Indian Parliament, '... it is an area where not even a blade of grass grows ...'. Because of their deep, instinctive sense, even the yaks were fearful of the area and had to be literally beaten from behind with a stick and pulled forward, to enter Aksai Chin. However, after all their exertions the patrol was soon plodding along the gravelly, flat soil of the Aksai Chin plateau. From a distance, the patrol was visible as eight large dots moving forward on the vast plain that formed an unending grey backdrop. As they proceeded towards the north-east direction, the distant shapes of the imposing and snow-clad Kun Lun Mountains became increasingly clearer. To the left side and beyond was the mighty Karakoram Range, bounding the forbidding, flat expanse of Taklamakan Desert.

They kept proceeding over the flat and rocky surface of Aksai Chin for three more days, always cautious about suddenly coming upon the Chinese road-builders and the newly constructed road! On the evening of the second day after entering Aksai Chin, Nawang shook Basera's shoulder and pointed towards a distant, dark line that stretched across the horizon. They promptly halted and had their first look at the still distant road—the ultimate goal for which they had travelled such a long distance over the forbidding terrain. They had soon pitched their tents and the hot rice and dal was soon sending out inviting smells, as they sat by the dancing flames of the small fire. Basera got everyone together and went over the actions that they would take when they had physically reached the road. Surprisingly, after they had settled in for the night there was very little small talk, quite dissimilar to other evenings. They were all lost in their deep thoughts, and even the otherwise talkative Nawang, who normally had a host of questions on just about everything, was very silent.

The next morning, they completed their chores early and set off towards the distant road. The otherwise sluggish yaks too seemed to move forward with renewed energy, matching the sudden spring in the step of their handlers! Around midday, when they stopped to eat their rotis, they were near the raised road and could see it quite clearly. The road had a gravel surface that still had to be tarred. There were no vehicles moving on the road and neither could any Chinese workers be seen in the area. The patrol halted just next to edge of the road and the yaks huddled down and began to chew cud. Diwan Singh quickly got busy with taking measurements of the road and even picked up some of the gravel to examine later.

The Chinese highway as it cuts across Aksai Chin plateau in Indian territory; the snow-clad Kun Lun Mountains can be seen in the far distance.

Basera checked the road in detail, and he and Diwan Singh even walked over to the areas on either side of the road for a good distance. He picked up a piece of gravel from the Aksai Chin Road and put it into his pocket. For 'good luck' he told an interested Diwan Singh who wanted to know why Basera had picked up the piece of gravel. They pitched their tents next to a large heap of gravel that had possibly been left over from the time the road was being constructed.

During the early hours of the morning, they were woken from their slumber by the roaring sound of a convoy of three heavy-duty trucks (Chissu 150) that thundered past them on the gravel road. The trucks were coming from Kashgar and heading towards Lhasa. This was the only activity they had seen on the road and they all came out of the tents and watched the amber coloured tail lights, as the trucks roared down the straight section of road towards Lhasa. They hurriedly loaded the yaks and began their long return journey to Leh. They were lost in their thoughts as they trudged behind the yaks. Their mission had been successfully completed and now Basera was in a hurry to tell the authorities in Leh and Delhi about the road the Chinese had built through Indian territory.

During the return journey they seemed to be travelling at a faster pace, than on their way to the road. The terrain was known and they were no longer overly cautious about being discovered and caught by the Chinese. Even the sluggish yaks seemed to know they were returning home and moved at a faster pace. A few large vultures lazily circled over them, high up in the clear, blue sky, and seemed to move along with them. The days passed quickly and soon the patrol spotted habitation and the built-up areas of Leh. As usual, Narang was most talkative on the return journey and he even evinced a keen interest in Basera's wristwatch. At Leh they met the Military Intelligence officers, who asked them a lot of questions about the road in particular and also the Aksai Chin plateau.

At Leh, Basera and Diwan Singh had a sad parting with the three yak herders. They had become good friends during their month-long trek. Basera gave Nawang his wristwatch, and the simple yak herder's joy was unimaginable. Basera and Diwan Singh had a long session with the Intelligence officers, where they were verbally debriefed about their long trek. They were asked to describe the Chinese-built road in its minutest of detail. Basera also wrote a detailed account of their trek and the road they had seen. The Intelligence officers got busy on the telephone, informing their superiors about the safe return of the patrol and the vital information they had brought back. Their reports must have sounded alarm bells, as the Intelligence officers returned and told Basera and Diwan Singh that they were to proceed immediately to Delhi, where they would be interrogated by higher officials. There seemed to be a pressing need for them to be at Delhi, as they were given a Jeep to convey them to Srinagar and on to the rail-head at Pathankot.

Debriefing in Delhi

After the long journey from Leh to Delhi, Basera and Diwan Singh were happy to be received at the Delhi Railway Station and taken to Army HQs at the imposing South Block building. Here, they were debriefed by officers from Military Intelligence and reminded about the need for utmost secrecy concerning their mission to Aksai Chin. There were detailed debriefing sessions concerning the mission and of the Aksai Chin road, in particular. At the end of the day, they were told by a lieutenant colonel from MI that their report would be sent to Raksha Mantri V. K. Krishna Menon, who would then discuss it with Prime Minister Nehru, in presence of the DMI (Director of Military Intelligence). The lieutenant colonel congratulated Basera for the fine work done by the patrol.

V. K. Krishna Menon with Jawaharlal Nehru.

The next day, the officer from MI told them that the Prime Minister had been apprised of their patrol report on the previous day. However, DMI had been told that he must be very sure about location of the road in question and that it had been constructed through Indian territory, before any further action could be taken in regard to the matter of 'intrusion'. The Raksha Mantri had asked DMI if the area through which the road passed had been confirmed on a map by the patrol. The DMI told him the patrol had not carried a map for security reasons. The Prime Minister agreed with what the Raksha Mantri was saying and told hm that no more such patrols were to be sent to Aksai Chin till the matter had been thoroughly investigated. He had added that such patrols could easily vitiate the good relations that existed between two friendly neighbours – India and China.

(Author's Note – Ever since the daring mission was executed in 1957, details of the patrol have been shrouded in secrecy. However, the author managed to obtain some details of the mission from the son of late Lieutenant Colonel R. S. Basera (named Lieutenant Colonel A. S. Basera [Retd]), who had found a paper with hand-drawn sketches and some details of the patrol, written by his late father and hidden away in a box for the benefit of posterity. This chapter has been crafted from this paper, while using other available historical facts of the time.)

Operations 1970–1974

My father, IC-60, Brigadier Balbir Singh, MC, was from Kumaon Regiment (4 Kumaon), and therefore, while in Indian Military Academy (IMA), Dehra Dun, it was natural that I, Cadet Jasbir Singh exercised my 'parental claim' option and was commissioned in my father's Battalion, on 20 December 1970 at the age of 19½ years. I was a tall, strapping, athletic lad – a happy-go-lucky young teenager – glad to be stepping into the complex adult world.

2 Lt. Jasbir Singh as 'Commando Platoon Commander' during operations in East Pakistan – November 1971.

After being commissioned at IMA, I spent a few days with my parents and then took a train to join 4 Kumaon in the north-east of India. After a three-day-long journey, I alighted at the World War II (Burma Campaign) railway station of Manipur Road (later called Dimapur), and joined my Battalion in Chazuba, Chakhesang area of Nagaland. The unit was conducting intensive, counter-insurgency operations against Naga rebels in thick, tropical jungles that covered the steep slopes in the area.

In those days news broadcasts were bringing in ominous tidings on another front in the country. I used to listen in on the transistor radio and was aware of the magnitude of exodus to India by hapless Bengali refugees and the volatile situation that was developing in East Pakistan. We, in of the unit knew of the deteriorating situation and were aware that it could lead to war with Pakistan. I took in the rumblings within East Pakistan as it came in the news and had heard of Sheikh Mujibur Rehman and a vicious Pakistani general named Lieutenant General Tikka Khan, who had unleashed a reign of terror in the territory. However, my main concern at that time was to successfully fight the Naga rebels who were in their camps and hideouts in the deep jungles. Also, Major B. K. Sharma, Adjutant, had ordered that I was to ensure I did not get killed in these jungle operations, as there was a lot more important work to do in my life! This advice of the Adjutant had left me quite confused, but as a second lieutenant I was used to intelligently nodding his head, although I mostly never understood many of the 'words of profound wisdom' that were often showered down by the senior officers.

I was posted to 'D' Company, No. 10 Platoon, which was located at Sathazumi, about 20 km from the Battalion Headquarters (Bn HQ) which was located at Chazuba. The company was commanded by a firebrand named Major D. K. Dhawan, Sena Medal (SM), who had won his gallantry award during the Jura Bridge Operation in the 1965 War. The other young officer in the company was 2nd Lieutenant Virendra Singh. We were soon involved in serious operations against the self-styled Naga Army in the deep jungles, where I was quite successful and had acquired a 'price' on my head.

Operations in India's North-East – 1965–1971

After its impressive performance in the India–Pakistan War, 1965, 4 Kumaon had spent the next four years at Jammu and Kapurthala military stations. Manpower shortages were made up with drafts of new recruits from Kumaon Regimental Centre, Ranikhet and training exercises were conducted. Lieutenant Colonel (later Brigadier) K. Lakhpat Singh handed over command of the Battalion to Lieutenant Colonel (later Colonel) Lakha Singh. It was soon time for the unit to leave the peaceful environs of Kapurthala and move to a field area in eastern India. In November 1969, 4 Kumaon received orders to move to Nagaland, after conducting training at the Counter-Insurgency and Jungle Warfare School (CIJWS), Vairengte, in the Mizo Hills. Lieutenant General P. S. Bhagat, VC, Corps Commander, bid farewell to the Battalion at Kapurthala Railway Station, on 10 November 1969.

At Patna railway station, Colonel N. K. Sinha (ex-CO) received the special train and wished the troops good luck for the impending operations in Nagaland. At Vairengte, the Battalion excelled in training for counter-insurgency operations and it was inducted to Nagaland on 31 December 1969. The Battalion relieved 31 Rajputana Rifles (Raj Rif) at Chazuba in Chakhesang Area of Nagaland. 4 Kumaon's Area of Responsibility (AOR) lay in hilly terrain that was covered with thick, tropical jungles. Posts were located on hill tops, near Naga villages. Battalion HQ and Support Company were deployed at Chazuba and other were located at Mile 22 ('A' Company), Dihoma ('B' Company), Thevopisimi ('C' Company) and Sathazumi ('D' Company).

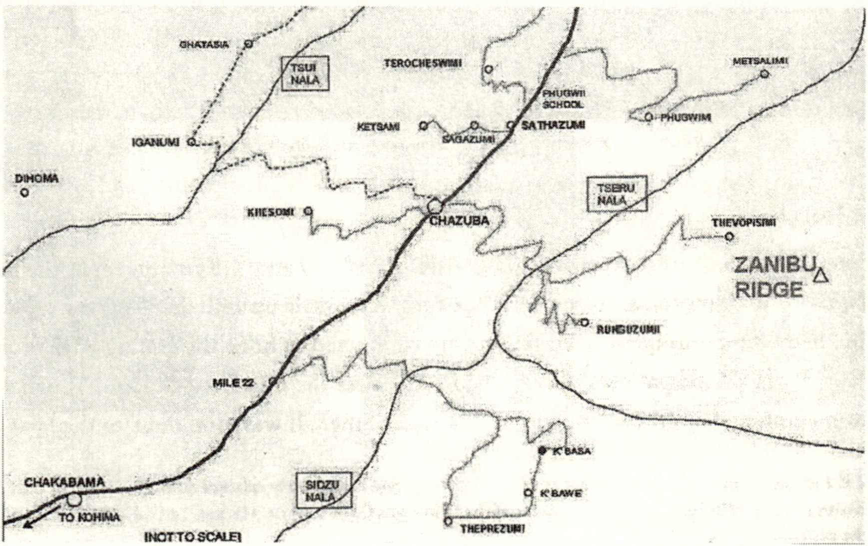

Map showing Battalion's AOR

A section of Nagas were hostile to the Indian government, and they were fighting for an independent Nagaland. These Naga hostiles were taking orders from the illegal Revolutionary Government of Nagaland (NFG), headed by an underground leader named Zashie Huerre. They were mainly armed with weapons and ammunition captured from the security forces (SF) during ambushes. The hostiles also possessed older weapons that had been left behind by invading Japanese forces during World War II. In addition to these two categories of weapons and ammunition, modern weapons were also acquired from China during the 1960s and early 1970s. The modern weapons and ammunition were painstakingly carried over the high mountain ranges by Naga gangs, who returned to India after military training in China. The self-styled Lieutenant Colonel Thuingaleng Muivah (later a well-known political leader) led Naga hostile gangs to China and returned after obtaining military training and arms. Rebel soldiers who had been trained in China, formed the backbone of the self-styled Naga Army units. The returning gangs carried back modern weapons and ammunition from China. The Naga soldiers who went to China were a hardy lot, as it was a difficult trek across the high Himalayas.

The rebels were provided with information, sustenance and recruits by local villagers. At the time of 4 Kumaon's induction in Nagaland, the Sema Area was relatively peaceful after the surrender of self-styled General Mowu Angami and his troops of the Revolutionary Government of Nagaland (RGN). However, NFG troops were active in the Chakhesang Area. They staged bold ambushes and raids on SF patrols and posts and then withdrew into deep, jungle sanctuaries on Zanibu and Khumnaboto ridges, when they were pursued by the SF.

Troops quickly familiarized themselves with the terrain, adapted to their new role and commenced operations against the insurgents. A couple of suitable men in each company were taught Chakhesang and Sema dialects. Operations by SF included search and destroy missions, cordon and search of villages, patrolling, ambushes and raids on Naga hostile camps and hideouts. SF posts were keenly observed by informers of Naga insurgents and whenever a SF patrol left the post, the information was quickly passed to the rebels. Thus, it was during the night or in bad weather conditions that 'hunter-killer patrols' would silently slip out of the posts and operate in the jungles for many days. The patrol would lay ambushes and search the deep jungles for rebels and their camps. After a few days in the jungle the patrol would emerge at an unspecified location on the main road and radio their position to the HQ. A vehicle convoy would arrive with replenishments and the patrol would then emerge from their hiding places near the road. The troops would replenish their rations, radio-set batteries and ammunition. Mail from home was eagerly awaited and the letters would be put away, later to be read over and over again. Some personnel would exchange their tattered uniforms and jungle boots for fresh ones before slipping back into the jungles. Operations with hunter-killer patrols were difficult and called for extreme mental and physical toughness.

Informally, these operations were called 'jungle bashing' and young officers (YOs) were generally detailed to lead these patrols. During the operations, insurgent camps and hideouts were destroyed and a number of Naga hostiles were captured. It was a difficult life for innocent Naga villagers often caught between the grindstones of rebel Naga Army and Indian Army operations. On the night of 17/18 March 1970, 'A' Company under Major Y. S. Bisht with a patrol from Battalion HQ under the Adjutant, Major V. K. Madra recovered a large haul of weapons. The captured weapons included an LMG, a Sten gun and seven rifles which were hidden in the thatched roofs of 'kheti huts'. It was an excellent beginning for the unit in the counter-insurgency environment.

Theprezumi Encounter

On 10 July 1970, 2nd Lieutenant M. P. S. Khati led a patrol of 'A' Company to Theprezumi village. On reaching the outskirts of the village, the patrol ran into a group of about ten armed Naga hostiles, who were wearing Indian Army uniforms and moving in a military formation. A sharp encounter followed and one hostile was wounded, while the others escaped. There were no casualties to own troops. An analysis of the encounter revealed that the hostiles had managed to get away because the patrol had delayed opening fire on them. The patrol had been deceived because the hostiles were craftily dressed in Indian Army uniforms. It was a bitter lesson for the troops. A similar situation had arisen nearly 56 years earlier, during World War I in East Africa. At that time, German troops had succeeded in attacking the Uganda Railway Line guarded by the Battalion, when they had approached the railway dressed in British uniforms!

The so-called, 14 Battalion, Naga Army operated in Chazuba area and it was led by the self-styled Lieutenant Colonel Hochoveyi, a dreaded hostile. During early 1971, a large gang of armed insurgents had reportedly entered Nagaland after being trained and equipped in China. Reports were frequently received about the presence of a gang of hostiles who had returned after training in China, in 4 Kumaon's AOR.

Khesomi Encounter

On 2 April 1971, an ex-Naga Army soldier reported the presence of a large body of hostiles in the areas around Khesomi village. It was decided to launch an operation and neutralize the hostiles with 'D' Company led by Major D. K. Dhawan, SM and a 'Adhoc' Company from Chazuba under 2nd Lieutenant Virendra Singh. 'D' Company was to search Khesomi ridge and raid the camp while 'Adhoc' Company deployed 'stops' around 'Khesomi Bowl'.

The operation was given code-name of 'Thimayya March 3' and troops were launched at 2 a.m. on 3 April from Chazuba. At daybreak, 'D' Company was moving down the narrow ridge to Khesomi village when the scouts suddenly halted. They had spotted a large group of hostiles camping in paddy fields on the neighbouring ridge. Wisps of smoke rose into the sky from their cooking fires. The hostiles too, spotted the descending troops and began to move off towards Khesomi village. A small group of hostiles were left in the camp and they began to fire at 'D' Company and cover the move of the escaping hostiles. 'D' Company took up a chase through the thick undergrowth. Again, the company came under hostile fire and the troops were forced to go to the ground. The hostiles managed to break contact in the thick jungle.

The 'Adhoc' Company had deployed three 'stop' positions, of a platoon each, to block the likely escape routes. When the fleeing hostiles found their path was blocked by the 'stops' they opened fire on Virendra Singh's group. The officer scrambled up an escarpment and fearlessly engaged the hostiles, who desperately tried to break out of the trap by bringing down heavy automatic fire.

Undeterred by the heavy firing, the YO hoisted an LMG to his hip and fired quick bursts at the fleeting rebels. He shot dead self-styled Lieutenant Sukhayi and wounded self-styled Sergeant Major Sevetso in the heel of his left foot. The wounded rebel was captured as he collapsed on the ground. Firing broke out across 'Khesomi Bowl' as other 'stops' also engaged the fleeing hostiles. It was later confirmed that four hostiles had succumbed to their wounds during the firefight. One LMG with a filled magazine, a Thompson Sub Machine Gun (.45-inch calibre), ammunition and equipment were captured. Virendra Singh was awarded COAS Commendation for his gallant action.

Ambush Near Runguzumi Village

After the encounter at Khesomi, pressure was stepped up on the rebels. Their camps were raided and a large number of hostiles were apprehended. At 7 a.m. on 21 May 1971, a patrol from Battalion HQ apprehended a self-styled Lance Corporal from Chazuba Town. During his spot interrogation, he disclosed the presence of three hostiles in Runguzumi village. He said the hostile party was in Runguzumi to collect rations for their camp on Zanibu Ridge. As a patrol of 'C' Company under Captain H. C. Sah was operating in the area a radio message was flashed, asking Sah to lay an ambush outside Runguzumi village.

At 10.25 a.m., the opportunity ambush had just been established when three hostiles approached from the village. The hostiles were challenged to halt. The alert hostiles opened fire and tried to escape. The ambush party returned the fire and one hostile was wounded and captured as he fell to the ground. Another hostile promptly raised his arms and surrendered. The third one leapt into a ravine and escaped. The patrol captured one rifle, four hand grenades, ammunition and some documents from the two hostiles. Sah was awarded COAS Commendation for the successful ambush. The action near Runguzumi is a fine example of good spot interrogation, quick reactions and sound battle drills.

During operations in the jungles, at times freak radio transmissions would be heard on the AN PRC-25 radio-set. The radio signals being received appeared to be from US Army troops operating in Cambodia (now Kampuchea). Once, while searching the higher reaches of Zanibu, US troops could be heard desperately asking for helicopter gunships and artillery support. They were locked in combat and had suffered heavy casualties.

Terocheswimi Encounter

Rain lashed the bamboo walls of huts at Sathazumi Post and made a deafening sound on the corrugated iron sheets of the roof. At intervals, violent gusts of wind and rain buffeted the post, jarring the foundation of the huts. It was the night of 9 June 1971 and Major D. K. (Dick) Dhawan, Virendra Singh and I – both young 2nd Lieutenants then – were huddled next to a red-hot, wood burning stove or bukhari in the Company Commander's hut. I poured another round of drinks as Dhawan and Virendra discussed the merits of 'canned sardines' as snacks or *chhota khana*.

The Company Commander told the officers that frequent reports were being received from local informers about a concentration of Naga hostiles in the area of Ketsami and Terocheswimi villages. After receiving these reports, Dhawan had left the area undisturbed and not sent any patrols to Ketsami, Terocheswimi or Sathazu Nasa villages. It was expected the hostiles would gain confidence and remain oblivious that SF knew of their presence in the area. It was deduced that the rebels were gradually getting more confident as their patrols had begun to visit Sathazu Nasa, Ketsami, Terocheswimi and Phugwi School during day. Informers had reported the rebel force in the area consisted of more than 60 armed men, commanded by Hochoveyi. Choveyi, as he was commonly known, had reportedly moved to Sathazumi area from Theprezumi. The general area of the rebel concentration was under 'D' Company of 14 Battalion Naga Army, commanded by the self-styled Captain Therelu of Zulhami village.

Dhawan told us that we would hit the hostile force early next morning. While we ate a hot meal, he briefed us on his map. The plan was for Virendra to move with No. 12 Platoon to Terocheswimi while I took No. 10 Platoon to Ketsami village and laid ambushes. It had been appreciated by Dhawan that rebels would be spending nights in the comfort of the villages because of inclement weather conditions and lack of interest by the SF. It was expected that the rebels would leave the comfortable shelter of villages during the early hours of each morning, and move to hideouts in the jungles. Both the patrols were to silently move around the villages and lay ambushes along paths that led down to the terraced fields and jungles. Orders for the impending operation were passed to Subedar Narain Singh, Senior JCO and Company Havildar Major (CHM). It was well after midnight when the officers retired to catch a few hours of sleep before the operation. The officers slept fitfully while the heavy rain beat down on the tin roofs. Before they knew it, Sepoy Bahadur (Muggoo) Singh was waking them with glasses of steaming hot tea. It was dark and silent outside and the rain had stopped. The hot tea was sweet and had a strong taste of milk powder. However, it was welcome and refreshing. The pre-dawn hour was chilly as the officers laced up their jungle boots, strapped on anklets and slung loaded carbines on their shoulders. The cold breeze hit them as they made their way to 'convoy ground', a few levels below their *basha*. The ground was wet and there were puddles of rainwater on the track.

Virendra and I walked down the rough steps leading to the 'convoy ground' where the troops were assembled. There was some misunderstanding regarding the destination of the platoons. On enquiry, the CHM told us that Dhawan had ordered a change of plan and No. 10 Platoon was to proceed to Terocheswimi while No. 12 Platoon would proceed to Ketsami village. We inspected our platoons and spoke to the men. As the cold breeze whistled through the trees, I set about inspecting the weapons of No. 10 Platoon. The noisy cocking of self-loading rifles (SLR) was completed and safety catches were clicked to the 'safe' mode. '*Kalika Mata ki Jai – ki Jai – ki Jai*' rang out thrice as the men shouted the battle cry. At 3.30 a.m., both patrols silently left Sathazumi Post in a single file formation. The jungle boots made little noise and No. 12 Platoon led the way till the football ground, located below the post. Here, the platoons parted ways and No. 12 Platoon disappeared in the darkness towards Ketsami village while No. 10 Platoon moved to the Shooting Range and PWD Rest House.

Directly behind the leading 'scouts' of my platoon, No. 10 was Lance Naik Bhawan Singh—I closely followed. The patrol crossed the PWD Rest House and descended to Phugwi School. The school lay in darkness and there was complete silence. The troops swiftly moved along the commonly used path to Terocheswimi village. The night's rain had made the track slippery and the men had to tread carefully. The damp leaves and pine needles muffled the patrols' footfalls and there was no sound. The only sounds heard were the occasional thud of a heavy footfall or deep metallic sound of a weapon gently striking against ammunition-filled magazines. Soon, the dark silhouettes of huts of Terocheswimi village were visible. The troops were again cautioned with hand signals, not to make any sounds as they passed the sleeping village. Because of the steeply sloping ground, the patrol had to stay close to the village huts. The overpowering smell of cow-dung, cattle and pigs was heavy in the morning air. Suddenly, a dog growled and some more dogs began to bark loudly. Thankfully, no humans stirred in the village and the patrol successfully reached the track below Terocheswimi.

As the first rays of warm sunlight were starting to shine through the silver oak trees, we halted about 150 m below Terocheswimi village, near some large 'prayer stones'.[1] As per plan, the patrol quickly occupied an ambush position facing the village and the troops began to visually scan the area. It was not the ideal ambush position as the troops were located on lower ground and they would have to engage hostiles coming down from the village, which was located on higher ground. Meanwhile, Virendra, who was laying an ambush below the neighbouring Ketsami village saw a fascinating sight. In a *pani kheti*[2] about 1,000 m below my ambush, a large group of armed and uniformed Naga hostiles were being briefed by a thick-set man who had a red blanket draped over his shoulders. After being briefed, the hostiles inspected their weapons and began to move stealthily up the ridge in a staggered file formation. Virendra watched in horror as he realized the hostiles were moving to strike at the rear end of my ambush below Terocheswimi. He could barely warn us with a brief transmission on the VM2-5A radio-set, when the communications snapped abruptly.

The VM2-5A was an unreliable radio-set and Sepoy Ganga Dutt, radio operator, tried unsuccessfully to re-establish communications with Virendra. When Virendra realized that the communications could not be established, he aborted his ambush and moved with his men on the run towards the Terocheswimi ambush. Virendra's move entailed a descent of about 1,500 m into a nullah followed by a steep climb to Terocheswimi. At my end, the brief radio transmission stirred us into action and my men were quickly alerted about the threat from the rear. An LMG group and some riflemen were re-deployed to face the slope away from the village.

Just after the interrupted radio transmission there was loud rustling

---

[1] These large sized stones, normally 4–6 feet high, are embedded in the ground at the entrance of most Naga villages. They are called prayer stones and believed to bring good luck to the village.

[2] *Pani kheti* are terraced fields used for cultivation of paddy crop. The crop is irrigated with water, that flows along water-channels dug from a nearby stream or rivulet.

of bushes near the prayer stones. The Platoon Havildar emerged from the bushes tightly holding a Naga hostile who had been surreptitiously moving in the undergrowth, parallel to the track on which the ambush was sited. I quickly conducted an interrogation of the stubborn rebel in elementary Chakhesang dialect. The captured individual was a Naga Army soldier named Abhi, who had been sent through the bushes to check the track for Indian Army soldiers and provide a warning to the rebel force. I had just knelt near the prayer stones when seven or eight Naga hostiles crashed through the undergrowth and sprayed the patrol with heavy automatic fire.

Firing from his 9 mm carbine, 2 Lt. Jasbir Singh charges at Naga hostiles who are assaulting his ambush position

Without a second thought, I swung around to face the assaulting hostiles. I loudly shouted 'Charge', and leapt at the assaulting rebels. The automatic bursts fired by the attackers narrowly missed me and ricocheted off nearby rocks and prayer stones. Bullets thudded into the trunk of a large pine tree to my right as I counter-charged and sprayed the rebels with a complete magazine of carbine fire. I killed one hostile (the self-styled Lance Corporal Vephuyi) and wounded two others. The spontaneous charge took me into the midst of the totally bewildered hostiles. I had run out of ammunition, and so reversed my carbine and smashed the butt onto the nearest hostile's skull. I incapacitated him but damaged the weapon's butt by the unorthodox manner of its usage.

Events suddenly seemed to be moving very fast, indeed. I threw down my empty carbine and picked up the dead hostile's weapon, a 7.62 mm Chinese Siminov rifle. With this semi-automatic rifle, I began to fire at the stunned hostiles around me. When the hostiles had suddenly emerged, Lance Naik Bhawan Singh had taken aim to fire a burst. Providentially, he did not pull the trigger as he saw me in the gun-sights.

The hostiles were not expecting such a violent reaction and they broke and fled. A hot chase took place with I and one of my platoon jawans rushing after the rebels as they crashed downhill through the undergrowth. Leaping from boulder to boulder and running frantically downhill all of us must have descended about 1,000 m. After losing sight of the rebels, we stopped at a break in the bushes. I could see some hostiles about 50 m below desperately splashing across a water-filled paddy field. Thinking they had outrun us, the hostiles were panting for breath and some had their hands on their hips. I steadied himself against a tree-trunk, took careful aim and fired rapidly with the captured Siminov rifle. Sounds of gunfire echoed across the silent valley and one hostile pitched head first into the water and lay still. Another hostile clutched his thigh and sank slowly into the paddy field. The other hostiles desperately leapt over the edge of the *pani kheti* and disappeared downhill.

I fired a few random shots in the direction of the fleeing rebels and then quickly descended to the *pani kheti*. After the gunshots the silence was more pronounced and the acrid smell of gun-smoke filled the air. A barking deer coughed in the distance, startled by the sudden firing. The wounded hostile was sitting on a small embankment and whimpering softly. His thigh wound was bandaged with a 'first field dressing' to stop the flow of blood. After his wrists had been securely bound with line-bedding, I gave the hostile a drink of water from my water bottle and questioned him in Chakhesang. The wide-eyed prisoner stared at me with a stunned expression—he was too shocked to speak.

Urgent shouts were heard from above and some troops led by Naib Subedar Nain Singh came running down to the *pani kheti*. The soldiers were positioned in the undergrowth beyond the paddy fields, for protection. A stout bamboo was cut from the jungle, and the dead hostile was slung under it by his wrists and boots. Carrying the packs, rifles and dead hostile we slowly climbed back to the encounter site. As to the wounded hostile, we helped him up the steep foot-track.

The bold and aggressive action had brought us resounding success. Two Naga hostiles (including Vephuyi, who had been trained in China) were killed, two hostiles captured and six hostiles had been wounded (including the self-styled Captain Therelhu, 'D' Company Commander, 14 Battalion, Naga Army).

Virendra Singh and his patrol heard the firing when they were down in the nullah. They lengthened their stride and arrived at the scene of the encounter after the steep climb. Radio transmissions were made to Dhawan and Major V. K. Madra, Adjutant, informing them of the successful encounter. Dhawan rushed to the encounter site at Terocheswimi. Both the platoons carefully searched the area and recovered another magazine and a few packets of ammunition. Some terrified villagers of Terocheswimi gingerly arrived at the encounter site. They were taken around and briefed on the details of the action. This was to provide them with reassurance of SF protection at all times. Hostiles had been pestering the villagers for rations, recruits and information of Indian Army moves. Thus, the villagers required to be reassured. The dead bodies were handed over to Gaon Buras (GBs) or the village headmen for burial. 'D' Company had successfully appreciated the insurgent designs, struck them hard and scattered their concentration. The encounter at Terocheswimi stands out as a major success[3] in counter-insurgency operations.

Ambush of Vehicle Convoy

After being repeatedly mauled, the hostiles were desperate to take revenge. On 20 July 1971, a vehicle convoy under Major Narendra

---

[3] After the action at Terocheswimi village, captured documents revealed that Naga hostiles had put a price on my head. In sheer desperation they wanted me 'dead or alive'. The rebels' action revealed their insecurity and goaded the SF to undertake some more successful actions.

Singh, was ambushed between Chazuba and Mile 22 Post. The windscreen of a 'one-tonne truck' that was moving as part of the convoy was riddled with ten bullets.[4] The Convoy Protection Party under Naib Subedar Hans Raj was quick to react. Under hostile fire the troops jumped down from the moving vehicles and assaulted the ambush. The hostiles rose from their positions and fled. The fleeing hostiles were engaged with 2-inch mortar fire and they suffered casualties. Hans Raj was awarded COAS Commendation for his role in countering the ambush.

Raid on Thevopisimi Post

In August 1971, the hostiles under Hochoveyi decided to raid an isolated post of the unit. Thevopisimi Post was singled out for punishment as it was on a limb and not linked with a motor road. The move to Thevopisimi involved a hard trek from Chazuba along a steep and narrow foot-track that crossed the fast-flowing Tseru Nala and steeply climbed about 2,000 feet (about 610 m) to Thevopisimi. The Thevopisimi Post had been held by 'C' Company (less a platoon) and it was a vulnerable location at the best of times. When the Battalion commenced a process of thinning-out its posts for move to Dimapur and East Pakistan, Thevopisimi Post was reduced to platoon strength and it became an ideal target to be raided. From its intelligence network the unit learned of the rebel's intention to raid Thevopisimi Post. Thus, to counter their plan, Thevopisimi Post was reinforced during the night of 29 August and Captain B. S. Jodha, Officer Commanding (OC) 'C' Company was prepared for the raid when the hostiles struck at 4 a.m. on 30 August.

The thatched huts (sleeping quarters) and latrines of Thevopisimi Post were raked with LMG and rifle fire followed by some well-aimed 2-inch mortar bombs. Unknown to the hostiles, Jodha and his men were no longer in the huts. Expecting the raid, the troops were manning the trenches and they immediately returned the fire. Jodha ordered the men to keep up the engagement of hostiles while he led a platoon from the post and assaulted from a flank. During the spirited assault Lance Naik Lachhman Singh was shot in the leg. He limped forward and shot dead one hostile. The other hostiles fled with their lives, leaving behind two

---

[4] Later, the vehicle accompanied the unit to East Pakistan. Before the 1971 War, troops of other units often examined the bullet holes in the windscreen with surprise and in awe.

dead bodies, weapons and equipment. It was later confirmed that five hostiles were wounded during the unsuccessful raid. Jodha was awarded SM for gallantry during the operation and Lachhman Singh received a COAS Commendation.

Operations Behind Enemy Lines During War in 1971

On 9 September 1971 the Battalion, along with two other infantry battalions of 81 Mountain Brigade, was ordered to hand over their posts in Chakhesang Area of Nagaland and move down to Dimapur. Since soldiers of the Battalion had been deployed on distant posts, their concentration was a welcome opportunity to meet one another. For the next month they trained hard and exercised in crossing of water obstacles, patrolling, operations behind enemy lines, assault on enemy defences and field firing. This training was carried out around Dimapur.

During the early hours of 17 October 1971, the unit steamed out of Dimapur. The YOs were young, impetuous and having great fun! It was an exciting time, and as their seniors often told them, they, were lucky as war with Pakistan seemed imminent and soon, they would get some real battle experience!

On 19 October, onwards from Badarpur the unit proceeded in two trains due to the weak section of the railway track and a constant threat of enemy sniping and destruction of the railway track by enemy saboteurs. The railway line passed close to the border with East Pakistan. As expected, the first train was fired at by enemy snipers. However, no serious damage was caused and on 20 October the Battalion arrived at Sonakhira, and unloaded its stores. They were deployed in 'Bagichara' Tea Estate, with a rifle company each at Churaibari ('B' Company) and Patharkandi ('D' Company). The enemy's sniping on the train had perhaps primed our minds towards war and I realized that soldiering was all about carefully facing enemy's bullets, and then giving it back to the enemy, in full measure – as good as one got! However, there was so much more that I had yet to learn.

During the entire month of October 1971, the Battalion remained at Sonakhira, conducting intensive training and preparations were made for offensive operations. It was nearly the same kind of training the men had done at Dimapur. Quite frankly, as a subaltern, I really did not understand what was going on. We were kept busy with training and yet more training! In my view, after the jungle operations we had been through in Nagaland, we were a jolly good fighting outfit and the CO was unjustly wasting valuable time by training for what was already known! But these 'stupid 2 Lt. ideas were best kept to oneself', as the Senior Subaltern would often seriously tell us. With the advantage of hindsight, I would now say that we could have trained for the entire year and even then we would not have been prepared for what lay ahead—the mighty apocalypse that was fast approaching.

I received ordered from Major B. K. Sharma (Adjutant) to form a Commando Platoon, with a section of troops each from 'B', 'C' and 'D' Rifle Companies, that is with Kumaoni troops. I conducted special training for the Commando Platoon by ensuring that these troops were able to conduct clandestine operations, deep behind enemy lines. I got a few sagacious tips from battle-seasoned company commanders and went about training the Commando Platoon with great zest, and instilled a sense of bonhomie and camaraderie among the commandos.

We soon received orders to move from Sonakhira to 'Assembly Area' at Kailashahar. During this move I shared the cab of an Isuzu lorry with Captain B. S. Jodha, Intelligence Officer, who had recently won a coveted SM for defeating a Naga raid on my isolated post at Thevopisimi. He mentioned that we were indeed lucky to be going into battle, as till then we had been listening to our seniors about their experiences. For a while I was quiet and thought about the exciting times that lay ahead of us. But I also heaved a sigh as I realized that I would be 'lucky' if I lived to recount my personal war experiences to wide-eyed junior officers during cold, winter evenings, before a crackling fire—in the same way my seniors had told wide-eyed youngsters about the operations in Kashmir, during the India–Pakistan War, 1965.

Reconnaissance of Pakistan Army defences opposite Kailashahar, was carried out by a patrol of YOs and Specialist Platoon Commanders. The patrols were launched from 'Kailashahar Pocket'. This was a small salient of East Pakistan territory that had been captured in March 1971, by Mukti Bahini guerrillas. The 'Kailashahar Pocket' had a Mukti Bahini Check-Post, located in the primary school. Atop the tin roof of the school building, fluttered a curious looking green flag with a jagged piece of yellow cloth stitched on it. As the enemy was extremely sensitive to Indian Army movements, all our reconnaissance tasks were done with troops dressed in civilian clothes.

The Bengali boys of Mukti Bahini, all of them about my age, were a highly motivated and spirited lot. They were enthusiastic about getting to grips with Pakistan Army troops. They were taught how to launch clandestine operations and handle heavy calibre weapons. Soon, our Commando Platoon had integrated themselves into an effective team. On 25 Nov, a reconnaissance patrol comprising of YOs and Specialist Platoon Commanders had a narrow escape, when they were engaged by accurate Browning Machine Gun (BMG) fire from the enemy Border Out-Post (BOP) at Chatlapur. The patrol had halted in a ripening paddy field near the International Border (IB), to consume haversack lunch. The enemy had spotted them and there were sharp cracks over our heads as distant enemy rifle bullets snapped overhead. A young Bengali boy, named Mian Makbuddin was sharing haversack lunch of *puri–alu*, when the enemy opened automatic BMG fire. Quite sensibly, Makbuddin had dropped the *puri–alu* and dived head first into the paddy field. On being fired at, we, in the patrol burst into spontaneous laughter. In utter horror, the boy looked up and saw us Indians sitting calmly on the edge of the paddy field and laughing loudly, while machine gun bullets cracked over their heads. They were more concerned with saving their lunch packets, than to worry about bullets that had luckily not hit them in the head! On looking at us rolling in mirth, with haversack lunch packets in our hands, young Makbuddin must have thought all Indian soldiers were totally mad! Ours was a strange reaction, on being under enemy fire for the first time. Maybe it was the release of pent-up nervous tension. After repeatedly hearing fascinating accounts of 4 Kumaon's operations in 1947–48 and the 1965 war with Pakistan, we were indeed excited as the real thing was happening. At the time it had appeared unreal and maybe even humorous!

Since we were within range of their artillery guns, I called up the Adjutant on radio and informed him that we had come under fire from the Pakistani BOP, at Chatlapur. I gave him the map coordinates and went back to eating my lunch. Soon there was heavy shelling of the enemy's BOP with 75/24 mm field artillery guns, located deep within Indian territory.

As the first artillery shell exploded, the Pakistanis immediately stopped firing from the BOP. Through my binoculars, I watched in fascination as some of the shells fell directly on the Pakistani Post, shattering their roofs. However, many of the shells fired by the 'pea shooter' guns exploded harmlessly in Manu River, well short of the enemy post. The exploding shells sent tall plumes of water into the clear blue sky. We had no idea how to give artillery fire corrections or how to guide artillery fire. So, with a wry look at the enemy post we simply gathered the patrol and headed back to base. No one told us whether the patrol was successful, and nor did we ever ask anyone about the results of the patrolling.

On arrival at Assembly Area, Senior Company Commander Major 'Dick' Dhawan, SM, told officers and JCOs that the town of Shamshernagar was the unit's objective. There was much excitement and maps were opened and perused. The day was spent in making preparations for offensive operations and men were briefed about their tasks. Combat loads, mostly ammunition, food and water, were redistributed and 'improvised assault charges' were prepared by Pioneer Platoon personnel and issued to Rifle Platoons. These assault charges were meant for destruction of enemy bunkers and other fortifications in Shamshernagar.

Morale was high and the troops were eager to lock horns with the enemy. On 28 November 1971, General Officer Commanding (GOC) of the Infantry Division, Major General K. V. Krishna Rao, visited the Battalion and gave them a stirring talk on the eve of battle. All personnel were seated on canvas tarpaulin sheets and they listened intently, as the GOC reminded them of the unit's long combat history. He said the Battalion was well prepared for the allotted offensive task, adding the unit had been on active operations in jungles of Nagaland for nearly two years and could not have been better prepared to tackle the allotted task of capturing Shamshernagar. He reminded the men that 4 Kumaon had won the 'Best Battalion Trophy' for outstanding combat operations against Naga hostiles, out of the other 22 infantry battalions of the Division. At the end of his speech, the GOC light-heartedly remarked, 'Since your objective is the town of Shamshernagar and name of your Subedar Major is Shamsher Singh, I am certain your Paltan will be awarded Battle Honour of Shamshernagar'. Perhaps it was a prophecy and troops cheered wildly and cries of '*Bajrang Bali ki Jai*' and '*Kalika Mata ki Jai*' rent the air.

After dark, the soldiers hefted their heavy packs onto their backs and the Battalion moved off around the sleeping town of Kailashahar. The columns silently snaked their way to 'Forward Assembly Area', like heavily laden ghosts. A few stray dogs barked in the sleeping town as columns of troops silently passed through the narrow lanes. By first light of 29 November, the unit was deployed among low hillocks adjoining Shamshernagar. It was a prosperous 'tea town', with a large tea factory, and an airport linked by regular flights.

Street fighting is an infantry man's nightmare in a built-up area. Thus, intelligence reports were gathered by Captain Jodha and compiled with those received from the higher HQs. The reports indicated the enemy had made elaborate preparations to ward off an attack on Shamshernagar. They had made extensive use of obstacles and landmines to strengthen the defences, and created a network of concrete bunkers with the outer perimeter being guarded by several rows of bamboo 'panji stakes'.

Automatic weapons had been sighted on roof-tops, in sandbagged enclosures, and they had overlapping fields of fire. Even I – the youngest subaltern in 4 Kumaon – was aware that a formidable battle awaited them. The CO went off to confer with the Brigade Commander and he returned by lunchtime on 29 November. Then, he called the officers and JCOs to brief us on the overall Brigade Attack Plan. He told us Shamshernagar was to be captured in two phases. In Phase 1, on 30 November, 10 Mahar would capture Chatlapur BOP, while 3 Punjab simultaneously captured an intermediate enemy position called No. 9 Tila Complex. Along with these two attacks, 'D' Company under Dhawan was to move forward and establish a firm base for the attack on Shamshernagar. Lastly, their Battalion was to infiltrate 'A' Company Group under Maj. Y. S. Bisht (including Commando Platoon, section each of 3-inch mortars, 57 mm RCL rifles and 7.62 mm MMGs) behind enemy lines and establish a road-block on the road from Shamshernagar to Munshi Bazar.

The road-block was meant to isolate Shamshernagar and prevent its defences from being reinforced. In Phase 2, the remainder of the Battalion was to capture Shamshernagar, which had regular Pakistan Army troops deployed at PIA complex, area school, railway station, tea factory, airfield, bridge over Manu River and the Katarkona township.

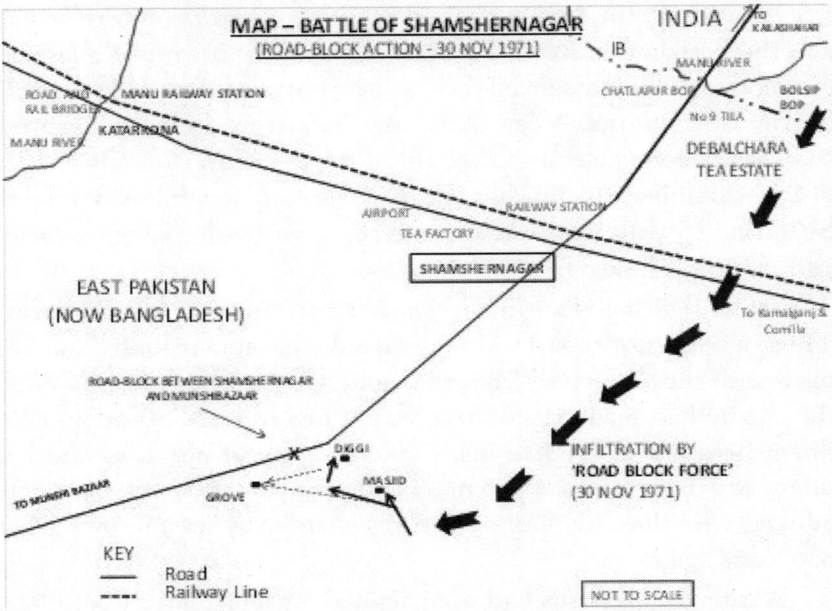

Map of road-block action, Battle of Shamshernagar, 30 November 1971

During the briefing, specific tasks were given to the companies. Broadly, 'A' Company Group under Bisht, of which Commando Platoon was a part, was to infiltrate that very night and establish the road-block. 'D' Company under Dhawan was to occupy a position at Debalchara Tea Estate and hold it as 'firm base' for the attack on Shamshernagar. Remainder of the Battalion was to build up on this 'firm base' and attack Shamshernagar. The road-block force would be armed with two 3-inch mortars, two 57 mm RCL rifles and two 7.62 mm MMGs. The road-block force was to have some 'Fighting Porters' from Pioneer Corps for the carriage of 3-inch mortar, MMG and 57 mm RCL ammunition. It was to also have one section of Mukti Bahini guerrillas under a smart, young officer named Lt Waki.

The Infiltration

The road-block force moved from FAA on foot, at about 4 p.m. on 29 November and reached a Border Security Force (BSF) picket named

Bolsip, located on the IB. The CO, 2 IC, Adjutant and Subedar Major were waiting at Bolsip, when the road-block force arrived on foot after travelling across cross country in the dark. The CO and his party shook hands with all personnel and some last-minute details were coordinated. At 7 p.m., the heavily laden troops silently crossed the IB and began to infiltrate behind the enemy lines.

Tea bushes on the East Pakistan side of the IB were tall and dense, as they had not been pruned for a long while. The column inched forward into the dark night, struggling through the bushes and bypassing known enemy positions along the way. While they were inching forward, one of the soldiers accidentally activated a trip-flare. The flare hissed loudly and emitted a blinding, white light from its fiercely burning phosphorous tube. Troops immediately hit the ground, crawled rapidly to whatever cover they could find and lay very still. Almost immediately there were nervous shouts from a nearby enemy picket that was located on a raised mound. A long LMG burst was fired from the picket, but the bullets snapped well above their heads. Someone, probably a Pakistan Army JCO, yelled choicest abuses at his men in chaste Punjabi, ordering them to stop firing. 'Cease your firing immediately, you no good wretches. It must have been a dog that tripped the flare!' he screamed. He was possibly annoyed that his sleep had been disturbed. Soon, the firing stopped, but the infiltrators remained motionless for more than half an hour. Then very cautiously they resumed their march. It had been an unnerving, yet exciting experience.

By around 3 a.m., the road-block force had occupied a low knoll which dominated the Shamsher Nagar–Kamalganj–Comilla Highway. While Major Y. S. Bisht was reporting the position of his troops to Adjutant on the radio-set, the troops rested their heavy loads on the barrels of their weapons, with the butt placed on the ground for support. I, along with 2nd Lieutenant M. P. S. Khati quickly deployed some sentries and occupied an ambush position. The lights of passing Pakistani military vehicles could be seen at regular intervals on the road below us. Surprisingly, some of the soldiers had even drifted off into a deep slumber that was accompanied by loud snores. I was quite surprised to see these men, who seemed quite unconcerned that they were behind enemy lines on a dangerous mission! After a while, Bisht passed orders for troops to wait for gaps between passing enemy vehicles and then swiftly dash across the highway, in twos and threes! Once the executive orders had been passed to cross the road, the sleeping soldiers were quietly awakened. Quite unabashed, they promptly rose to their feet and looked sharp as ever. There were a few abrupt disruptions while crossing the road, when lights of an unexpected vehicle were seen rapidly approaching. However, by 4 a.m., the road had been safely crossed and the leading scouts neared a rail bridge on the Sylhet–Comilla rail line, that ran parallel to the highway. There was an armed sentry at either end of the bridge, while some more enemy soldiers were sleeping in a nearby tent.

We approached the rail bridge silently and unseen, through the heavy winter mist. The leading elements of 'A' Company quickly overpowered both the surprised sentries at the ends of the rail bridge. The enemy troops within the tent were roused from their sleep under warm blankets, and swiftly taken prisoner. After they had pulled on their boots, their wrists were bound and the befuddled prisoners were sent to the rear of the infiltrating column. No one remembers what was their subsequent fate for as events unfolded rapidly during the coming day and we were embroiled in heavy action. At about 6 a.m. on 30 November, the column had safely crossed the railway embankment and we had neared the road-block site. Pink hues of approaching dawn heralded a new day that was to be filled with intense combat action. It would be a day during which many soldiers would be killed on both sides. Many others would bear their wounds for decades to come. It was to be a day of reckoning, and packed with action. It would be a day to be remembered for many years to come. Indian Army, Mukti Bahini and Pakistan Army soldiers would perform extraordinary feats of courage and valour. As daylight increased, the raised alignment of the road running from Shamshernagar to Munshibazaar became visible, about a kilometre from where the column had halted. After surveying the area through his binoculars, Bisht ordered the road-block to be established.

Commando Platoon, with Lt Waki's Mukti Bahini section and No. 2 Platoon led by Subedar Bhura Singh, were ordered to advance through the fields of golden, ripening paddy and occupy Areas 'Masjid' and 'Diggi' respectively. They were to face in the direction of Shamshernagar and dominate the road. In the meanwhile, 'A' Company HQ, No. 1 Platoon and No. 3 Platoon, directly under Major Y. S. Bisht, OC 'A' Company, were to take up positions at Area 'Grove' and cover the road, facing in the direction of Munshibazaar. The two 3-inch mortars and MMGs were to deploy in Area 'Grove'. Bisht summoned all the Platoon Commanders and briefed them on each platoon's task, on establishing the road-block. While the Platoon Commanders were being briefed, troops sank to the ground and rested their weary feet. Some industrious men even undid their packs and extracted the haversack breakfast packets and consumed the packed puri–sabzi with great relish. After the short halt, Platoon Commanders moved back to their troops and ordered them to move to their allotted positions.

Both 'Masjid' and 'Diggi' were located on raised ground and they effectively dominated the fields of ripening paddy. When Commando Platoon and No. 2 Platoon reached within about 200 m of their objectives, they were pinned down by volleys of automatic fire from the enemy. We hugged the ground in the dry paddy fields, but there was no cover from the enemy's firing. So, we started advancing towards 'Masjid', at a run. Just then, an enemy BMG began to engage us from a bush, adjacent to 'Masjid'. I glanced back and saw the awesome sight of my brave commandos rise to their feet, under withering enemy fire and follow me. Half way to 'Masjid', I yelled for the 57 mm RCL rifle to be brought forward. With bullets clipping over our heads, Havildar Mohan Singh and another jawan crawled through the ripening paddy crop, with the RCL gun and its ammunition. I pointed to the enemy BMG that was firing at us and Mohan Singh took aim and fired the RCL gun with a loud back-blast. But the round went wide of its intended target and hit the 'Masjid'. I shouted instructions at my small band of men and we continued to engage the 'Masjid' area with rifle and LMG fire. In the meanwhile, Mohan Singh took aim deliberately and fired once again.

The second RCL round scored a direct hit on the enemy BMG in its gun pit. Enemy soldiers were seen running away from the BMG gun pit. As they ran, we cut them down by accurate bursts of LMG fire. Immediately, I formed my troops in a staggered assault line and moved forward, with weapons held at our hips. I ordered the troops to fire at will and immediately shots rang out from the SLRs and LMGs of the assaulting commandos. In the meanwhile, No. 2 Platoon had also risen from the paddy fields and begun their assault on Diggi Area. Suddenly, bursts of enemy automatic fire swept No. 2 Platoon. Subedar Bhura Singh, the Platoon Commander was hit by a bullet and also thrown to

The first RCL shell's hit and LMG bullet marks are visible on the wall. The second RCL shell destroyed the enemy BMG, located under a bush, adjacent to the 'Masjid' (shown by arrow).

the ground. On seeing the JCO and his 2 IC go down, the platoon too went to ground and the assault on 'Diggi' petered out. Realizing the unwanted situation that had been created, Bhura Singh staggered onto his feet and loudly shouted 'Charge', in a hoarse voice. As the determined attackers were assaulting into the hail of fire, the enemy panicked, abandoned their positions and fled. During the assault, No. 2 Platoon Commander had been shot through the shoulder and his three Section Commanders were either killed or wounded. Though heavy casualties had been suffered, both platoons managed to secure foot-holds on their respective objectives at Diggi and Masjid. Here, both No. 2 Platoon and Commando Platoon held on doggedly.

Both 3-inch mortar tubes had been deployed at 'Grove', and they began to rapidly engage the enemy. All hell seemed to have suddenly broken loose, and there was firing all around them. With loud bangs, high explosive (HE) mortar bombs began to explode around 'Diggi' and Masjid' and their MMG fire also swept the area. Most of the enemy troops got up and ran back, but a few brave Pakistani soldiers stood steadfast and faced the attackers with courage. After a fierce close quarter fight with these enemy defenders, Commando Platoon and No. 2 Platoon captured 'Masjid' and two bunkers of 'Diggi'. Enemy firing continued unabated from the other two bunkers across the short, stretch of water between the bunkers. Havildar Hari Shankar, of No. 2 Platoon

Area Diggi: Enemy bunkers, marked with dotted circles can be seen below the trees. No. 2 Platoon charged across the paddy fields and captured three bunkers under the tree on the left. The paddy fields were swept with grazing, machine gun fire that caused numerous casualties on the attackers.

had led his men from the front and fought the enemy at 'Diggi', with raw courage. In the fighting he was killed by a burst of fire in the chest.

No. 2 Platoon uses the body of Hav. Hari Shankar (lying dead in the foreground) as protection while fighting to capture 'Diggi'

Heavy fire was being received from enemy in bunkers across the Diggi's water. Hari Shankar's son was born after his father was killed at 'Diggi'. He followed his father's footsteps and today serves with honour in 'A' Company of 4 Kumaon. In 1997, he asked me if had possessed a photograph of his father, whom he had never seen! Since a photograph of Hari Shankar was not available, I had an oil painting made of the NCO lying dead, with soldiers taking cover and fighting from behind his dead body.

Subsequent Actions

The main road from Munshi Bazar to Shamshernagar had come under the effective domination of road-block force. By 9 a.m., 'A' Company Group had suffered 19 casualties—six were dead and 13 personnel had been wounded. Enemy parties had begun to work their way around the flanks of the road-block force, in an effort to surround and remove the serious threat. Just then, an enemy convoy carrying troops was seen hurtling along the road and heading to Shamshernagar. The convoy was led by an olive green coloured 'Kaiser' jeep,[5] followed by two lorries that were loaded with troops. The lorries were probably carrying reinforcements to boost the enemy's strength in Shamshernagar Area. Alerted by sounds of firing, the enemy vehicles attempted to physically smash through the road-block position. With excited shouts, our men of No. 2 Platoon and Commando Platoon began to engage the vehicles, with all their weapons. Quite unbelievably, a high-explosive (HE) bomb fired from a 2-inch mortar with Commando Platoon exploded in the leading lorry, loaded with troops.

The leading lorry careened off the road and caught fire. The direct hit of the 2-inch mortar HE bomb on the moving lorry was a pure stroke of good luck and the men cheered wildly. The lorry crackled and burned in a road-side ditch, sending up plumes of thick, black smoke. There were a number of explosions as ammunition in the lorry detonated due to the flames. The explosions caused serious casualties and a number of enemy soldiers were flung off the enflamed lorry.

---

[5] The Kaiser jeep was captured from Pakistan Army defences at Shamshernagar. The jeep was used by 4 Kumaon for the duration of the war and returned to Bangladesh authorities when the unit returned to India, in end of December 1971.

The second lorry skidded to a halt and enemy soldiers jumped off and took up firing positions on the road's side. From Area 'Grove' our MMGs fired long bursts into the enemy troops as they were jumping from the lorries. The MMG fire caused many more casualties, and enemy dead bodies could be seen piling on the road. The enemy troops who had taken up positions below the embankment, were seen firing at the positions. We engaged them with 2-inch and 3-inch mortar HE bombs. While the lorry burned, the Kaiser jeep ran the gauntlet and sped off towards Shamshernagar, presumably leaving the enemy leaderless. Despite this, the few enemy soldiers alive must have rallied around their JCOs, for they started to crawl forward towards us using natural cover, behind the paddy crop. There was great expectation, when artillery fire was called from guns located in India by Captain A. P. S. Dhanoa, Field Ordering Officer (FOO) with 'A' Company. Soon, distant explosions were heard as the in-coming shells fell almost 1,800–2000 m short of the enemy positions, and exploded harmlessly towards India. Since the Indian Army artillery guns had been firing at maximum range, a frightening reality dawned on Dhanoa. He realized that the battlefront was beyond the range of the artillery guns that were firing from India. He quickly realized our awful predicament and informed us that we should not expect any fire support from India! The lack of artillery support from India must have put the Company Commander Major Bisht, in a quandary, as the enemy was just beginning to surround Area 'Grove'.

Remains of the troop-carrying enemy lorry, destroyed at road-block on Road Munshibazaar–Shamshernagar

On seeing the troops break contact and begin to crawl back from 'Masjid' and 'Diggi', the enemy soldiers charged yelling 'Ya Ali' and firing with all their weapons. They made all efforts to close in for the kill, but were kept away by accurate MMG and 3-inch mortar fire directed from Area 'Grove'. With full knowledge that his actions would invite certain death, a young sepoy named Bishram Singh of No. 2 Platoon, on his own initiative did not break contact but kept engaging the enemy from his position at 'Diggi'. Lying prone behind his LMG, Bishram began to fire long bursts to cover the retreat of his colleagues. While he was blazing away with the LMG, he was struck by enemy bullets in the left shoulder and left arm. Despite his wounds, this brave jawan kept the enemy at bay, till he was certain that both the platoons had occupied their new positions at 'Grove'. Then, the sounds of Bishram's LMG gradually died out. His stomach had been ripped open by a well-aimed burst of enemy BMG fire, and it is hoped that this hero died instantly. Sepoy Bishram Singh knew he could not escape a fatal end, when he had volunteered to stay behind and cover the move of his comrades. It was an exceptional act of supreme courage. He knowingly gave up his life to allow his comrades to withdraw to Area 'Grove'. The withdrawal orders for Commando Platoon and No. 2 Platoon were implemented with difficulty, as we had to first break contact and then crawl rapidly back for nearly 800 m, through flat fields of ripening paddy. There was no cover at all, but they received accurate, supporting fire from the MMGs and 3-inch mortars at 'Grove'. However, despite the supporting fire it was with great difficulty they managed to crawl and reach Area 'Grove' as enemy machine gun and rifle bullets snapped viciously overhead.

Enemy Counter-Attacks and Mortar Fire

All day long the position at 'Grove' was subjected to enemy fire from 120 mm mortars located at Shamshernagar Airfield. The enemy also brought reinforcements from Maulvi Bazar–Munshi Bazar to launch determined counter-attacks from that direction. Due to their accurate fire from several quarters and lack of cover, the enemy suffered heavily during these counter-attacks and withdrew towards Munshi Bazar, to regroup. They had been fighting for many hours and the men had almost run out of ammunition. To conserve the precious ammunition, Major Bisht had ordered the LMGs to engage the enemy with only 'single round' fire. In addition, all troops were given instructions to engage the enemy at closest range, so they were sure of hitting the targets. The remnants of No. 2 Platoon were by now under my command, along with my own Commando Platoon. Remnants of the valiant Mukti Bahini section under Lt Waki, and what was left of the Pioneers, also came under my command. Lt Waki and his band of guerrillas, as also the Pioneers, had fought shoulder to shoulder with us, equalling their zest and grit. They all silently suffered the depredations of war that all were being subjected to since morning. The Mukti Bahini guerrillas were different to the Kumaoni troops, but in the heat of battle they all had developed an uncanny camaraderie, and become brothers-in-arms.

Area 'Grove' with craters made by exploding 120 mm mortar bombs
Area 'Masjid' can be seen (white rectangle at middle-right) from where we had crawled to 'Grove'

We doggedly held their position, even though the enemy had completely surrounded the 'Grove'. There were many casualties due to the enemy's mortar attack. I too was wounded, with multiple injuries on both legs, by shell fragments. But I crawled about from a gun position to another, to get a firsthand appreciation of the situation and cheer up my men. I recollect Sepoy (NA) Muni Lal Mahato fearlessly moving about Area 'Grove' and administering morphine and life-saving first-aid. A number of lives were saved by Mahato's selfless devotion.

Around midday, one Indian, fixed wing Air Observation Post (Air OP) aircraft came and circled about lazily in the sky, above the road-block position. The enemy stopped the mortar bombardment, perhaps to prevent the discovery of their mortar positions by the Air OP aircraft. For a while, they stopped paying attention to the road-block and turned their ire against the aircraft, engaging it with intense small arms automatic fire. However, they soon gave up the futile effort as no damage was being inflicted on the small aircraft. We used this respite from mortar fire to regroup themselves and to tend the wounded. After a while the aircraft turned and went out of sight towards India, possibly to refuel. As soon as the aircraft departed, the enemy started to pound the 'Grove' once again. However, like an albatross, the aircraft soon reappeared. The enemy mortars fell silent once again. We prayed for the aircraft to stay longer above us in the sky, but after a while it went away once again, and we were back at the receiving end of being pounded with the mortar barrage.

At about 4 p.m., the enemy subjected the position to a concentrated mortar bombardment. About 300 bombs of 120 mm mortar exploded on 'Grove'. The bombardment left the position pock-marked with deep, smoking craters. Radio sets were destroyed and with that went the communications within 'A' Company as well as with the Brigade HQ in India. The vicious bombardment was followed by another fanatical counter-attack. Fortunately for us, the Brigade swiftly moved one 5.5-inch medium artillery gun well forward to support the action. This single medium artillery gun started to engage the enemy positions rapidly, but in a random manner. Though the shelling did not do the enemy much harm, the shattering explosions of heavy 5.5-inch shells helped to augment our morale, and we felt confident that we had not been abandoned behind enemy lines and left to our own fate! The enemy continued to rain mortar bombs on Area 'Grove', while the medium artillery shells exploded in the paddy fields with earth-shattering bangs.

Suddenly, two mortar bombs whooshed down and exploded near me in rapid succession. I was hit by shrapnel and flung onto his back by force of the explosion. There was heavy dust in the air and my ears were ringing as I struggled to get back on my feet. I felt a sharp pain at the back of my head, right wrist, elbow and right leg. Looking down, I saw blood was beginning to seep through my shirt sleeve as well as the leg of my trousers, with drops of blood dripping from my head. Realizing that I had been wounded, I looked around and spotted Sepoy (NA) Muni Lal Mahato. I beckoned to Mahato and asked him to speedily bandage my wounds before the next salvo of bombs slammed into the position. As I was getting myself bandaged, the enemy launched another counter-attack. Some of the attackers nearly broke into the defended position. I pushed Mahato aside and staggered to the edge of 'Grove'.

Savage hand-to hand fighting was taking place and the enemy counter-attack seemed to be faltering. At one time, I distinctly remember running out of ammunition. So, I quickly reversed my 9 mm carbine and viciously swung it around. The weapon's butt slammed down hard onto the face of the nearest enemy attacker. The butt struck with a loud crunching sound and the enemy attacker's helmet went flying. He emitted a loud wail and fell to the ground. The commando next to him fired a short burst of 9 mm bullets into the falling enemy soldier. As the bullets thudded into the enemy soldier, he shuddered and collapsed in a heap. On seeing the enemy assault closing-in with the position, even the wounded men had grabbed their weapons and begun to fire at the attackers. In this heavy fighting, Lance Havildar Man Singh (MMG Section Commander), Havildar Mohan Singh (RCL Section Commander) and nine OR were killed.

The ferocity of the enemy attack was such that within minutes, 2nd Lieutenant M. P. S. Khati and nine ORs were also wounded. Subedar Bhura Singh, No. 2 Platoon Commander, a tall and physically tough JCO, was wounded for the second time that day. Despite these setbacks, the enemy was hurled back and they rapidly moved into distant hedgerows that were beyond the range of aimed MMG fire. Having observed the repeated enemy counter-attacks that were being launched on Commando Platoon and No. 2 Platoon, Major Bisht, accompanied by Sepoy Basant Singh (radio operator), dashed through the heavy mortar fire and came to the Commando Platoon position at the forward edge of 'Grove'. Bisht and I had a brief discussion, and his words of encouragement swept me with great reassurance and a new determination to fight and win. Then, he and his radio operator dashed all the way back to the Company HQ, again through the intense firing. It was leadership at its finest!

Lance Naik Inder Singh (ex 'D' Company), a Section Commander of Commando Platoon was standing beside me and directing the fire of his section, when a mortar bomb exploded near me. Inder Singh was hurled about ten feet into the air and landed on me. I noticed that a piece of shrapnel had pierced Inder's gullet and he was desperately gasping for air. A spurt of blood would gush out with every breath he took. I tried unsuccessfully to block the flow of blood with thumb, as more mortar bombs exploded all around. Inder sucked in a long, rasping breath and slumped in my arms. His eyes were fixed, and had a desperate look, with the eyeballs beginning to glaze over. His lips had turned bloodless and I knew immediately that Inder Singh had died in my arms. With mortar bombs exploding around us and enemy assaulting 'Grove', I realized I had to be with the men along the defensive perimeter. I quickly handed over Inder's dead body to Sepoy Ram Singh (Burmia), who was standing next to me, and charged to the perimeter suddenly beset with uncontrolled anger. Not held back by my bleeding wounds, I dropped my SAF carbine and grabbed hold of a LMG. I placed the weapon on his hip and sprayed the attackers with long bursts of automatic fire. All the time I was yelling and cursing, very volubly at the enemy. This perhaps had a salutary effect on my platoon, for they too increased their firing and started shouting and cursing very loudly. We brought down intense fire on the enemy and halted the assault. Above the din of exploding mortar bombs and small arms fire, Havildar Man Singh could be heard goading his MMG detachments to keep engaging the attackers.

The 120 mm HE mortar bombs were raining down on 'Grove' and exploding with loud bangs. Through the dust haze, I saw Sepoy Gokal Nand jump about in pain and shock. His left arm had been severed above the elbow by mortar bomb shrapnel and he was rapidly losing blood from the flailing stump. I wrestled the crazed sepoy to the ground, ripped off his lanyard and wound it tightly around the stump to stop the bleeding. Luckily, a lull in the incoming mortar permitted me to carefully set the wounded soldier down in a bomb crater. Quite suddenly, I felt dizzy from loss of blood, so I sat down with a forward LMG detachment and took some sips of water from a soldier's water bottle. Not giving up the fight, the enemy remained at a safe distance and continued to fire at the road-block position. After the day's fighting, it was a great relief when the shadows lengthened and sun began to set. Area 'Grove' was pock-marked with craters, where enemy's 120 mm (HE) mortar bombs had exploded during the intense bombardment (around 300 bombs had exploded on 'Grove' in about half an hour).

Naik Venugopal, the Artillery Radio Operator, managed to repair one of the radio sets and patch into the Brigade Radio Net. The Brigade Major (Major Pandit), I was told later, had passed instructions to Major Bisht, over the Artillery Radio Net, to return to India and rejoin the Battalion. Having successfully completed the task of preventing the induction of reinforcements that could have impeded the capture of Shamshernagar, 'A' Company Group was ordered to fight its way out of the enemy's encirclement and undertake the arduous trek to India, with its wounded personnel, MMGs and RCLs.

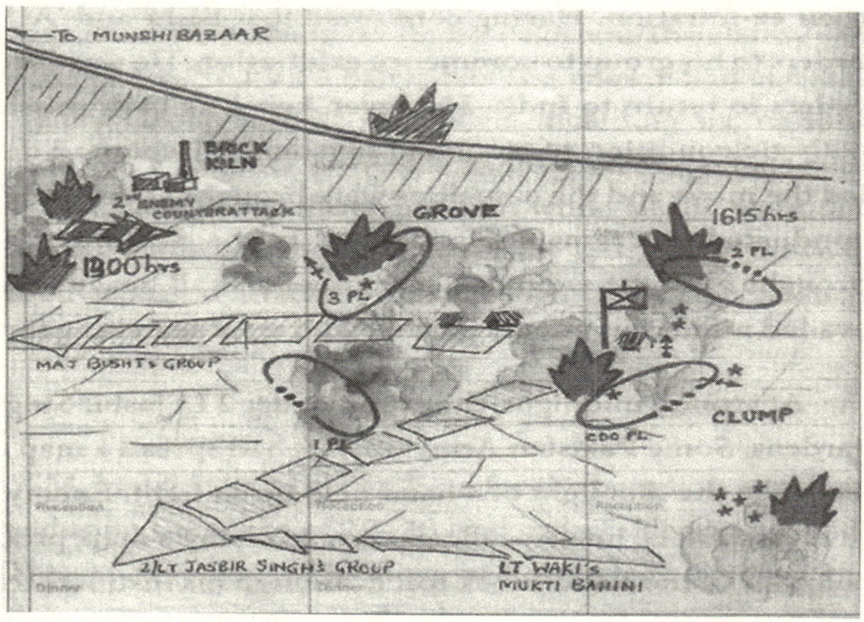

Fighting around Area 'Grove'

Just as Major Bisht had passed orders for the move, a fierce enemy counter-attack drove a wedge between the Commando Platoon and most of 'A' Company Group. To find a safer ground, I moved the troops with me to a large bamboo clump, towards the railway line. During this move from 'Grove', we continued firing and had to occasionally take 'lying position' behind the small embankments that bounded the paddy fields. The movement was very slow since there were a large number of wounded men with the group. Due to the increasing darkness, we managed to evade the enemy. But, in the process, I lost touch with Major Bisht and the 'A' Company Group. Soon darkness had completely surrounded us, except for the occasional para flare that the enemy kept firing to locate us. They were quite unsuccessful in their attempts. As there was no communication with Major Bisht, I was in a quandary about my next move, and quite unsure of what I was to do. Despite my gross combat inexperience as a raw 2nd Lieutenant, the military training and fine values I had imbibed since my schooling at the Rastriya Indian Military College, Dehradun, did not allow me to leave the road-block position, without specific orders from Major Bisht.

In desperation, I asked the wizened old Senior JCO (SJCO) of 'A' Company, Subedar Sultan Singh what I should do in the difficult situation. Strangely, the SJCO just shrugged his shoulders and said, 'You are now in command. Do as you please.' As a subaltern it was perhaps the first time the thought came to me that I could be in 'command'. That the lives of so many good men, the fair name of the unit, victory in war, the image of my country, could all be on my young and inexperienced hands!

I called Lt Waki, the only other officer with me, though he was from Mukti Bahini and ordered him to take four men with him to reconnoitre a rendezvous with Major Bisht if possible, and bring back orders regarding their move back to India. The enemy continued to fire at us, rather blindly though, and we continued to return the fire. Waki and his four Mukti Bahini men ran off towards the 'Grove'. Waki returned in half an hour and reported that he had seen large numbers of the enemy soldiers swarming over 'Grove', but there was no trace of either Major Bisht or 'A' Company. When the enemy saw his party and began to fire at them, Lt Waki had quickly moved back to look for me and my men.

Having confirmed that Major Bisht and remainder of 'A' Company had left 'Grove', I gave orders to my men to commence the exfiltration to India. They had fought for the entire day, a large number of them were wounded and there was little fight left in most of the men. I looked around himself and only saw the wounded men and an enemy aggressively searching our previous position at the Grove.

We slipped into the dark, overgrown and forbidding tea gardens. It was fascinating to see lesser wounded soldiers helping along the more seriously wounded casualties, without any orders from me. Thankfully, the stars were out in the dark sky, and the bright starlight helped us to navigate through the tea gardens. On their way we often mistook distant trees and bushes for the enemy, till we came close enough to discern what it really was. On many occasions we did actually encounter enemy search parties. At such times, we silently went to the ground, tightly covering the mouth of the groaning wounded and tried to blend with the tea bushes. We did not fire any weapons even though the enemy did so, at random to provoke us to fire back and reveal our position. It was a remarkable night move, as often we were crawling on our stomachs and dragging the wounded as well as heavy weapons along with us. It was all the more difficult because most of us had been wounded during the day's fighting.

At around midnight, we came upon a large enemy party in the dark, tea gardens and adopted lying position. A Pakistan Army officer had spread a map on the bonnet of a jeep, and was bending over it in the dim light of a hand-held torchlight. Three others, probably JCOs, stood around him. Many enemy soldiers were also standing in the shadows, around the vehicle. In the darkness we could make out there were two more vehicles parked nearby. The enemy officer was studying a map, and probably trying to assess the escape route that had been taken by the columns of our road-block force. Though my basic instincts told me to spray the enemy with automatic fire, I realized that would be a great folly. We went to ground and once again muffled the groans of the badly wounded and totally exhausted men. After a while, the Pakistanis got back into their vehicles and roared off in the opposite direction.

The return journey was torturously slow and the wounded kept moaning in pain. Slowly the darkness was dispelled and the eastern sky began to light up. I was surprised how soon the night had ended. While leading the column, just before dawn I came upon a stone pillar. In the darkness, I ran my fingers over the pillar. There were deep inscriptions that read 'EAST PAKISTAN'. On the other side of the pillar, the inscriptions read 'INDIA' followed by 'BP' and a certain number. To my great relief I realized it was a 'Border Pillar' on the IB. Great joy and relief spread through the column. The men quickly crossed to the Indian side and sank to the ground, to rest. When they had started their infiltration, the previous evening, the road-block force had crossed IB near Bolsip BOP, quite close to the spot, where they had now entered India. With some difficulty I got the weary men back on their feet. The relief of having reached India was overpowering and they moved forward with a brisk step and at a much quicker pace.

After a short distance, we came across a field telephone cable running along the ground. We followed the cable and approached the BSF post at Bolsip. The surprised BSF sentries opened fire on our party, mistaking them to be an enemy patrol. After we shouted identifications, the firing stopped. Fortunately, there were no further casualties by the friendly fire.

The BSF post was very hospitable and made us as comfortable as they could, including the customary cup of tea for all of us. Using the field telephone at the post, I informed Major Pandit (16 Cavalry), the Brigade Major (BM), about our return to India. I was asked details of the road-block action and the whereabouts of Major Bisht's group. I asked for an ambulance, and informed the BM that almost everyone with me, including myself, was wounded. Promptly, vehicles were sent to Bolsip BOP and wounded personnel were admitted to the ADS.

On 1 December, the 'road-block' action figured in a news bulletin on Radio Pakistan. They claimed that a rogue Battalion of Indian Army had penetrated deep to the south-west of Shamshernagar and that a Pakistani Brigade had annihilated the Indian Battalion with loss of 40 Pakistani lives. They, however, did not say how many Pakistan Army soldiers were wounded. The Radio Pakistan broadcast made our CO smile, though our situation at the time was grim. In the road-block operation, 'A' Company lost 21 men and 32 were wounded. The operation helped 4 Kumaon and the Brigade to capture Shamshernagar with lesser casualties, and move on with the Brigade to Munshibazaar, Maulvibazaar and Sylhet. Like a ripe fruit, the enemy's defences at the crust were strong and fighting was fierce. But, as they advanced inwards, it became much easier as the enemy generally fled rearwards. Pakistan Army units and formations only put up a fierce fight where they were surrounded and could not readily flee.

A week later, Commando Platoon was again with 'A' Company and leading 4 Kumaon advance from Shamshernagar to Maulvi Bazar. On the way, they stopped at the road-block site, where they had been fighting a week earlier. Here, I described the battle to Major General K. V. Krishna Rao, GOC, 8 Mountain Division. The dead bodies of 15 comrades, who had been killed during the fierce fighting, were recovered from the paddy fields where they lay as they had fallen. Sepoy Bishram Singh's body was found at 'Diggi' with deep gashes in the stomach, caused by bursts of automatic fire. His LMG had been removed by the enemy. The dead bodies were collected from road-block site by Subedar Major Shamsher Singh, taken to Kailashahar and cremated with military honours. Bishram Singh was later awarded a posthumous SM for his gallant act.

2 Lt Jasbir Singh, Commando Platoon commander (extreme left with back to camera) explains 'road-block' action to Maj. Gen. K. V. Krishna Rao, GOC 8 Mountain Division, during 4 Kumaon's advance from Shamshernagar to Maulvi Bazaar, on 6 December 1971
Maj. Y. S. Bisht is standing on extreme right, with back to camera

Back to Nagaland After 1971 War

In 1971, a large number of infantry battalions were conducting counter-insurgency operations in Nagaland. It is a matter of pride that 4 Kumaon had been awarded the 'Best Battalion' trophy for operational achievements and successes during the operations. On 28 December 1971, 4 Kumaon was back in Nagaland after an outstanding victory in the 1971 War. The troops returned with heads held high and chests filled with pride, after the gallant actions they had fought in East Pakistan (now Bangladesh). After a short halt at Dimapur the unit was back in its old 'hunting grounds' in Chazuba area. While the Battalion had been away from Nagaland the hostiles had consolidated and boosted their strength through forced recruitment. In addition, they had liquidated many carefully cultivated informers and nearly crippled the unit's fine intelligence network. While most Indian Army units had a well-deserved respite after the war, 4 Kumaon was busy dominating the AOR and regaining initiative. A 'ceasefire' with NFG was in place and the Naga hostiles avoided direct confrontation with SF patrols.

Counter Ambush at Theprezumi

On 4 February 1972, I led a patrol of 'A' Company from Mile 22 Post to Theprezumi village for area familiarization and to invite the GBs for Kangaw Day celebrations. As the patrol descended into Sidzu River valley, it must have been observed by Naga hostiles from Kalazu Bawemi (K'Bawe) and Kalazu Basami (K'Basa) villages, which were on high ground across the river. The hostiles had planned to break the 'ceasefire' with an ambush of SF. They occupied a prepared ambush position on the outskirts of Theprezumi village. The morning air was heavy with moisture and swirling mist, as the patrol sloshed through the cold, knee-deep water of Sidzu River. After crossing the river, we searched some abandoned 'kheti huts' and then began the steep climb to Theprezumi village.

I was moving behind the leading scout. As the scout and patrol leader entered a deep and dark pine grove that straddled the track, the morning calm was shattered by long bursts of LMG and rifle fire. The sounds of automatic fire reverberated across the silent, hill slopes. Caught under grazing fire, I swung into action and shouted at my men to follow me as I led the assault on the ambush party. Firing my carbine from the hip, I led a determined charge as the hail of bullets thudded into surrounding pine trees. Assaulting up-hill, we reached the dominating ambush position. At the top I found himself face-to-face with the self-styled Lieutenant Pusatso, the rebel ambush commander. Having emptied his carbine magazine, I drew my .38-inch calibre personal revolver and rapidly fired five shots at the rebel officer. Simultaneously, I slammed my boot into Pusatso's stomach and snatched his rifle. Bullets from the rebel ambush snapped in the air around me as I fired repeatedly from my revolver and shot Pusatso dead.

Unnerved by the ferocious counter ambush, the rebels rose to their feet and fled into the surrounding jungles. At that time, Major P. S. Pathak was with a patrol on the neighbouring ridge. Hearing the sounds of heavy firing, his patrol rushed to the ambush site. A search of the area revealed another .303 rifle and some abandoned ammunition clips. For conspicuous bravery while assaulting the hostile ambush, I was decorated with the SM.

With this ambush, the 'ceasefire' was broken and the rebels were given little respite. Their camps were raided and burned and they were forced to keep moving in the rain-soaked jungles, not knowing when the SF would launch a raid. Conditions were tough for both the rebels and SF. Patrols hacked their way through the thick jungles as they searched for the rebels. Other SF personnel braved the pouring rains and lay still in ambush positions. It was torturous to lie in ambush and see leeches crawl up an arm or leg and not be able ward them off. Villages were cordoned and searched for suspects as 4 Kumaon choked off the supply lines of food and recruits. Having had enough of the hardships and counter-terror, Naga hostiles began to surrender in large numbers. While these operations were in progress, Lieutenant Colonel Lakha Singh, VSM, received his posting orders and handed over command of the unit to Lieutenant Colonel (later Major General) D. P. S. Raghuvanshi, who had been Adjutant during the 1965 War.

Capture of Naga Hostiles

On 22 February 1972, an informer told Captain Satyevir Yadav, Adjutant, about the presence of a Naga officer in a shop in Chazuba Town. Yadav immediately mustered a small special patrol of six men, including me from the Battalion HQ at Sathazumi. The patrol rushed to Chazuba Town in two Jonga vehicles. Before reaching the town, the patrol dismounted and stealthily approached the suspected shop. A loose cordon was laid, while Captain Yadav and I rushed into the shop with loaded carbines on the hip. In the lightening swoop, the self-styled

Lieutenant Shorveyi was nabbed by Yadav as he tried to escape from the rear door of the shop. With hands bound behind his back, Shorveyi was lifted into one of the Jongas and driven up the steep road to Chazuba Post. Yadav showed courage and daring while capturing the Naga officer.

Back at Sathazumi Post, I had struck up a close friendship with nephew of the village pastor. One day while I was in the village, the young lad came up to me and tugged at my hand. He told me in Chakhesang that two hostiles were in the village to collect rations. The hostiles were in a large hut adjoining the home of Yashai, the *dobhashi* (interpreter). The surprised hostiles were easily captured from the hut, where they had sat down for a meal of rice and hot pork curry. The young lad had helped to rid the village of its unwanted guests.

Raid on Camp near Ghatasia Village

'B' Company was located at Ghatasia in low-lying Sema area. A trusted informer told the Company Commander, Captain R. S. Sandhu, VrC about the presence of a large Naga camp in the area. The information was conveyed to Battalion HQ and numerous patrols were sent to areas around Ghatasia to confirm the reports. When the information was confirmed, an operation was immediately launched to raid the camp. 'C' and 'D' Companies marched 24 km from Chazuba via Iganumi and they concentrated at Ghatasia, on 15 June 1972. During early hours of 17 June, the large rebel camp (comprising of 35 huts) was raided by 'D' Company while 'B' and 'C' Companies established blocking positions or 'stops'. As the 'raiding party' under my command neared the camp, there was a heavy exchange of fire. Bursts of automatic fire hit the trees and leaves floated down on the us. The troops took up kneeling and lying positions behind the trees and returned fire. The fierce firing by rebels died down and the camp was assaulted. We entered the camp and saw cooking fires burning near the huts. The unattended fires cast weird shadows and presented an eerie sight. Military equipment lay scattered on the ground and it appeared the rebels had been surprised by the dawn raid. The hostiles had fled downhill in panic and crossed a stream that flowed below the camp. 'D' Company accompanied by a tracker dog (a black Labrador) took up the chase. Cleverly, the fleeing hostiles had crossed and re-crossed the fast-flowing stream to ensure their scent was not picked up by the tracker dog. Nonetheless, the troops pressed on after the hostiles, their wet foot-prints were clearly visible on the narrow foot-track, up the steep slope to Hebolimi village. Soon, the sun was up and temperature rose sharply in the tall grass owing to the stifling humidity. Undeterred by the torturous climb of more than 2,000 feet (about 610 m) in sweltering heat, the relentless chase continued. I led the column and was followed by the tracker dog, dog handler and the two jawans. The others followed at a distance. Knowing they could not shake off their pursuers, the hostiles took up positions in a small jungle clearing below Hebolimi village and waited in ambush.

We had barely crossed a small crest when the Labrador gave a low, warning bark. On hearing the bark, the pursuers halted momentarily. Almost simultaneously the hostiles opened automatic fire from the jungle clearing. As the heavy sounds of close-range firing echoed across Sidzu River valley, I and the three men with me dived behind some boulders. The dog handler pulled the Labrador in with him as bullets smacked onto the rocks and ricocheted downhill with a whirring and whining sound. The rest of my men were stretched along the steep track and would take time to reach the jungle clearing. So, I made a signal to the two jawans and charged the hostiles, loudly shouting the war cry. The jawans too rose and charged across the jungle clearing, shouting loudly and firing their weapons from the hip. Bullets were smacking into the ground around us, but they did not waver. Captain Sandhu and others who were still at the hostile camp, could clearly see us charge the rebels, high above them on the track to Hebolimi.

The tired hostiles did not wait for us to reach them, and scattered into the jungle. At the rebel position, I found two dead bodies, one Chinese semi-automatic rifle and two .303 rifles. Blood trails indicated that some more casualties had taken place. It was later confirmed that five hostiles had been wounded. One of the wounded hostiles had ripped off a bunch of leaves as he ran and pressed them against his bullet wound to stop the flow of blood. The bunch of bloodied leaves was found on the track about 100 m from the encounter site. The Labrador was confused and it dashed behind the fleeing hostiles for a short distance before returning to the dog handler. The Army dog had saved the day and deserves rich praise. Once again, the hostiles were on the run and demoralized after the series of successful actions.

Recovery of Arms Dump and Capture of 'Tatar'

On 12 November 1972, a special patrol from 'B' Company captured a Naga officer who led them to an arms dump near Iganumi village. Five rifles were recovered from the arms cache. It was a setback for the rebels and raised the morale of 'B' Company, who were located a long way from the unit. The company was linked to Chazuba by a winding, dirt road and all essential commodities were carried by jeep convoys or columns of mules.

For a while, 'B' Company had been following the movements of a high-ranked Naga hostile named Shihapu Sema, who held the post of 'Tatar', or a 'Member of Parliament'. Finally, on 2 June, after painstaking efforts the location of this hostile was identified. Leading a small patrol, Sandhu raided the camouflaged hideout and skilfully captured the ranking hostile. The lightening raid was a culmination of many months of diligent efforts by Captain Sandhu.

Encounter on Zanibu Ridge

On 9 February 1973, I led a patrol of 'C' Company to search the jungles around 'Water-Point', which is located between K'Basa and K'Bawe villages. As no Naga hostiles had been found, we moved to the deep jungles of Zanibu Ridge and laid a night ambush. It was dark by the time the ambush position was occupied by the patrol. Ambushes in the jungle were tough operations, especially at night. It was easier for 'hunter-killer patrols', which would lurk around a hostile infested area and the patrol leader would pick the right spot for a 'night ambush'. When a patrol approached the proposed ambush site, it would halt and adopt fire positions to ward off any rebels who arrived while the ambush was being deployed. The patrol leader would take a couple of men to reconnoitre the ambush site and decide on the 'killing ground' and location of various parties. The ambush positions would then be occupied with stealth and in a phased manner. The patrol leader would go to the 'killing ground' to quickly check the area for unguarded escape routes and to see that none of the parties were visible. This was a crucial time, as the ambush would be compromised if hostiles arrived while the patrol leader was at the 'killing ground'.

After the troops had taken up their positions with cocked weapons, would start the long wait to spring the ambush. Once the ambush had been occupied, troops would lie prone with their fingers on the triggers. There would neither be any sound nor movement. Accidental firing could take place if an individual dozed off and depressed the trigger. Such fatal errors were most dreaded, as the sound of a gunshot would alert the hostiles. At night, an ambush was a bit easier as minor movements were permissible. However, nights in an ambush were always long and time dragged on endlessly. The troops had developed an uncanny knack of 'switching off' the mind while they remained physically alert. The faraway, twinkling lights of Kohima would mock the soldiers and the minds would wander awhile, envying lucky people who were snug in cosy homes. Occasionally, a soldier would softly cough or clear his throat, much to the annoyance of his neighbour or a nearby NCO. The mind could play tricks and troops would see lurking shadows move about in the dark. At such times a 'buddy' provided silent reassurance with a touch of the arm, a gentle nod or low whisper.

The nights were cold and a breeze generally hissed through the trees bringing in occasional showers of cold rain. The troops had been lying very still in the ambush with wooden butts of weapons pressed against their cheeks, as they peered into the inky darkness. Rain trickled down their faces and dampened their clothes. As their noses ran with the cold, the soldiers could only blink their tired eyes and wait for either the morning light or for the rebels to arrive. After a long and harrowing night, first light seemed the most wonderful thing in the world. As the dark trees and countryside became visible, troops were amazed to see the areas they had occupied in the dark of the previous night. The individual positions were quickly readjusted and there was a heightened alert as the rebels were known to commence their movements around 'first light'.

With approaching dawn, the temperature fell rapidly and the troops shivered uncontrollably. I had to order the men to remove fingers from trigger guards of their weapons, so that there was no accidental firing by involuntary movements caused by the cold. Within an hour it was dawn and warm rays of the sun were shining through the trees and bathed the forest in soft morning light. After the cramped and cold night, I rose to my feet and signalled the troops to terminate the ambush and move out of their positions. The men rose like ghosts and stretched their tired limbs in the warm sunlight. Sentries were posted around the ambush position and the welcome smells of wood-smoke and brewing tea filled the air. The men cleared their weapons and talked to one another in muted voices. Low coughs and soft laughter rang out, as some incorrigible fellows cut jokes and made others laugh. After a glass of hot tea and haversack breakfast, the patrol members checked the arms, ammunition and equipment and moved slowly up a grassy slope.

At about 9 a.m. the leading scout froze on seeing a uniformed Naga hostile on the adjacent spur about 200 m away. The patrol quickly went to ground and observed the hostile through the blades of tall grass. A sentry was seen standing near the uniformed hostile with his back to the patrol. The sentry had a SLR slung over his left shoulder and he was scanning the 'Quarry' ridge with a binocular. I, along with the LMG gunner crawled forward through the high grass and reached about 100 m from the rebel sentry. I rose onto my knees, parted the grass and took careful aim with my SLR. I had the rebel fully covered in the sights but had to lower my weapon and stalk closer through the tall grass. There were three more armed hostiles moving through the elephant grass in a loose formation. I decided to exchange the SLR for a LMG, then stood up and engaged the rebels with automatic bursts of fire. The hostiles began to run as a hail of bullets hit the ground around their feet. Mud flew into the air and one hostile was hit in the head. He spun around and fell on the ground, and lay still. The others dashed for cover with bullets kicking up dust around their feet. From the jungle above, their colleagues engaged the patrol with bursts of fire from two AK-47 rifles. The second LMG with the patrol opened fire and I took up the 2-inch mortar and fired two HE bombs. The sounds of LMG fire were loud in the silent jungle followed by hollow bangs of exploding mortar bombs. I hand-signalled to the patrol to rise and charge towards the hostiles, who fled in different directions.

Near the body of the rebel, we recovered two .303 rifles and a number of charger clips loaded with .303 ammunition. The firing soon died down as the hostiles escaped towards 'Water-Point'. For the rest of the day, we searched the thick jungle, but could not find the rebels or any deserted weapons. The search was difficult as we were carrying the dead hostile, slung on a stout bamboo and the captured rifles. With dusk approaching, the we called off the search and proceeded to Runguzumi village for the night. The exhausted troops relished the hot meal cooked at Runguzumi and were happy that the encounter had been a success.

Chazuba Raid

At the end of July 1973, information was regularly being received about a concentration of hostiles near Chazuba. The hostiles were reported to be collecting for a high-level meeting which would be followed by a daring strike on the SF. To maintain secrecy, the hostiles frequently shifted their hideouts. It was reported that a hideout was to be established near Chazuba for the important meeting. Early in the morning on 4 August 1973, a daring informer named Choneyi came to Battalion HQ at Chazuba and informed Major B. K. Sharma, Adjutant that the location of the meeting had been finalized. He agreed to guide a patrol to the hideout where the meeting was to take place. Although, Choneyi could not tell the exact location of the hideout, he told Adjutant that the hostiles were lurking near Chazuba village. He added that the hostiles were well-armed and extremely alert. They had a web of sentries and informers and moved out of their hideouts at the slightest suspicion.

Lieutenant Colonel D. P. S. Raghuvanshi, CO decided that immediate action was required to tackle the hostiles. Since the move of a large body of troops would give away surprise, I was to lead a small party with 2nd Lieutenant (later Lieutenant Colonel) D. B. Thapa, Subedar Joga Singh, Subedar Adjutant and 20 OR. The team was quickly mustered and briefed by Major Sharma. At about 9.30 a.m., the 'raiding party' moved out of Chazuba Post in a convoy of a couple of vehicles.

Choneyi accompanied the party disguised as a jawan. Draped in a rain-cape and with an olive-green cap on his head, Choneyi huddled between two soldiers in the open, one-ton truck. A short distance from Chazuba, the convoy halted and troops silently got off the vehicles. It had rained during the previous night and the wet leaves allowed the patrol to move soundlessly. Choneyi led the troops down into the jungle a couple of times. Each time they went down the track, the informer felt he was near the hideout and warned me. In anticipation of combat the patrol readied itself, only to be told that the hideout could not be located. After the empty-handed patrol had been led back to the track a couple of times, I began to doubt Choneyi's credibility. But the informer appeared to be confident and asked for patience. The repeated nods of the head, contorted facial expressions and open palms would have provoked laughter at another time.

Unfazed by the false starts, Choneyi led the patrol down yet another slope with thick undergrowth and trees. After descending about 50 m, he sank soundlessly to the ground, motioned downhill and pointed to his ear. We dropped quietly to the ground too and listened intently. Above the constant twittering of jungle insects, low human voices could be heard. The voices were floating up through the undergrowth from the suspected hideout. Choneyi, jabbed a finger towards the sound of voices and repeatedly nodded his head towards me to confirm the location of hideout and meeting in progress. To maintain surprise, I adopted an unorthodox approach. With hand signals I conveyed to Thapa that Joga Singh and he would raid the hostiles' hideout. Under Thapa the patrol was to move down to Tseru Nala, that thundered about 200 m below and lay ambushes for hostiles who tried to flee. Choneyi was scared and nervous, so he was sent back to the vehicles with two soldiers. Before descending to the hideout, Joga and I cocked our SLRs with loud clickety-clack sounds. Joga murmured a silent prayer and piously touched me on the shoulder for good luck. He nodded his head and gestured that I should commence my descent to the hideout.

Shutting out my fears, I tightly gripped the SLR and began to descend to the hideout. The jungle was quiet and every little sound seemed to be amplified. The carefully parted the undergrowth and moved down slowly on his hands and bent knees. I was followed by the wizened JCO, who covered my move with his SLR. After descending a short distance, we saw a hostile sentry and froze. The sentry was a few metres away from us and was leaning against a large tree with his weapon slung on the left shoulder. The hostile sentry had his back towards us and was observing the slopes across Tseru Nala. Shielding his eyes with a hand, the sentry was standing very still against the tree. With bated breath, we cautiously bypassed the sentry and crawled down the slope.

The voices from below had become louder though the hideout could still not be seen because of the thick foliage. I could sense that the hideout was close by and the conference was in progress. It seemed too good to be true, as such tactical situations were rare. Soon, I realized we could crawl no further, and I signalled to Joga Singh that we were going to assault the hideout. I slipped the SLR's safety catch to 'R' position, rose to my feet and crashed through the undergrowth towards the unseen hideout. As I emerged from the undergrowth, I was surprised to see a thatched roof perched on a narrow ledge at the base of a sheer drop. Without hesitating, I leapt to the ledge. The frantic leap sent me sprawling near the hideout's entrance and my rifle fell to a side. My sudden arrival interrupted the meeting and there was a hushed silence. The rebels and I, in their hideout, stared at one another in amazement. Swiftly, I struggled to my feet and picked up the SLR. The hostiles swept up their arms, ran down a sloping track and jumped into the water-filled paddy fields below. I dropped to a kneeling position and engaged the fleeing rebels. A sharp encounter took place and bullets began to sting the air in all directions.

I followed the fleeing hostiles into the paddy field and gunned down the self-styled Captain Sashow Mao with a lucky shot through his eye and wounded some others. The dead body bobbed face down in the paddy field as other hostiles wildly splashed across the fields and jumped towards the fast-flowing Tseru Nala.

A fleeing hostile turned and fired an automatic burst towards me. Bullets hit the water around me and drenched me completely. I swung my SLR around and shot the hostile in the chest and face, killing him on the spot. There was complete bedlam and unseen hostile sentries opened fire on me from the hillside and lower edge of the paddy fields. Some Chinese hand grenades (stick grenades) were thrown towards me. I watched the grenades fly through the air but could not take evasive action as my feet were stuck fast in the water-filled field. The first grenade splashed into the water near my legs with a loud plop and failed to explode. Other grenades exploded in the water with muffled bangs and pieces of shrapnel whistled into the jungle. From above the ledge, Subedar Joga Singh's rifle barked repeatedly and he dropped a hostile who was about to shoot at me.

Rapidly, the hostiles faded away in the thick jungle. After the noisy encounter, there was a sudden silence and only the sounds of water rushing in Tseru Nala could be heard. The raid had been a stunning success. Three hostiles (a self-styled Captain, Corporal and Private) had been killed and a number of them were wounded. Three rifles, Chinese hand grenades, ammunition and some important documents were captured. 2nd Lieutenant Thapa and the patrol heard the firing and came up to the paddy fields. Once the firing had ceased, I called Battalion HQ on the radio-set and gave Major Sharma details of the raid.

The CO, Lieutenant Colonel Raghuvanshi, soon came to the hostile hideout and I took him around the encounter site and briefed him. Strewn papers and other remains of the interrupted rebel meeting were visible in the hideout. The dead bodies of the Naga hostiles killed in the raid floated in the paddy fields. Joga Singh was awarded SM for quick reactions and presence of mind in saving my life. I received COAS Commendation for my gallant conduct during the raid. After briefing the CO, I went up to the vehicles and complimented Choneyi for the timely information and his accurate guidance. But, Choneyi was frightened and shivered uncontrollably—probably due to the cold and also fear for his life.

Late in the evening while it was raining heavily, some bursts of fire were heard from Chazuba village. A patrol rushed to the village and found Choneyi lying dead outside his hut. His sobbing wife told the patrol that Choneyi had been sitting by the fire in the hut and playing with his small child. Armed Naga hostiles had barged in and asked Choneyi to step outside. Handing over the child to his wife, Choneyi went outside with the hostiles. The wife heard automatic bursts of fire and rushed out into the rain. She found Choneyi lying dead in a large rain puddle. The hostiles had slipped away into the dark jungle after the revenge killing! Thus, ended the saga of yet another brave Naga.

The unit's successes during operations in Nagaland, were as follows:

Hostiles killed	22
Hostiles wounded	23
Hostiles captured	601
Weapons captured	51

The Battalion won 12 gallantry awards during operations in Nagaland. 4 Kumaon was also proud winner of the 'Best Battalion' trophy of the Division for three consecutive years. 4 Kumaon had carried out relentless, offensive operations during the long, operational tenure in Nagaland. The unit was responsible for smashing the backbone of the underground movement in Chazuba area. Only one OR was wounded during the sustained operations. During the difficult tenure, the unit had won the hearts of local population with their professional and humane approach. In appreciation of its services the Government of Nagaland presented 4 Kumaon with a 'Silver Mithun' trophy and gave it a touching farewell at Dimapur.

The people of Chazuba area, Nagaland and soldiers of the unit suffered enormously during the years of fighting. There is finally peace in Nagaland and it is hoped that the tranquillity will continue to prevail, so that future generations can live in peace. All those who engaged in combat operations in the jungles since 1950s, will sincerely hope that angry sounds of gunfire never again echo in the beautiful hills and valleys of Nagaland. In January 1974, after an eventful tenure in Nagaland, the special train carrying 4 Kumaon steamed out of Dimapur for its next duty station at Jammu (fifth tenure in Jammu and Kashmir). In the distance, a lone dog could be seen running between the rail tracks with a steady lope, as the train picked up speed and chugged towards Lumding. The unit had been in continuous action for nearly four years (including the war in East Pakistan), and it was time for troops to enjoy a well-earned rest.

Field Area Visitor's Book

This story from my life goes back in time. It was 17 January 1965. I was on vacation in Kashmir from my school, the Rashtriya Indian Military College (RIMC) and was visiting the 4 Kumaon Officers' Mess at Trehgam, Kashmir, with my father Brigadier Balibir Singh, MC. Accompanied by my father and a Staff Officer, we had travelled from Srinagar to visit 4 Kumaon at Trehgam to visit his Battalion. Though on vacation, I was proudly dressed in my RIMC uniform—olive green (OG) coloured 'walking out' uniform. During most of the time we were at 4 Kumaon Officers' Mess, I was in a nearby bunker with YOs of the unit, a very spirited and jovial lot. And then, it was to lunch at the Officers' Mess, that we were summoned.

Before proceeding to 4 Kumaon on 17 January 1965

After lunch, and while the Visitor's Book was being signed by my father, Lieutenant Colonel N. A. Salick, VrC, CO ambled across, placed an arm on my shoulder and said with a disarming smile, 'Young man, I'll permit you to sign in our Visitors Book if you promise to join 4 Kumaon'. A wave of sheer happiness swept over me; indeed, I felt truly elated. I wanted to yell out that I would be honoured to join 4 Kumaon, but in the excitement all I could manage was a nervous nod of the head and a big, toothy, smile. Salick must have understood my confused emotions for he gently took hold of my shoulder and guided me to the table that held the Field Area Visitor's Book. Looking back, I must say that this encounter with CO, 4 Kumaon in Trehgam (1965), was responsible for my heightened interest in the operations of the Battalion during the coming War of 1965 and the book I was to later write about Salick and the unit's operations during that war with Pakistan, Roar of the Tiger.

Well, that was that. After the visit to the Officers' Mess, we drove back to Srinagar. I was quiet during the drive back – uncharacteristically so – and remained lost in my thoughts. Salick's words kept playing in his head—like a cracked 78 rpm gramophone record! Before I knew it, the vacations were over and I was back in school at Dehradun and busy with my studies. The India–Pakistan War of 1965 soon flared up and RIMC cadets had the pleasant task to listen to war news on a transistor radio and write about it every morning on one end of the class blackboard. I was delighted with the good news coming from Tithwal and Tangdhar, as I knew that 4 Kumaon was fighting in these sectors of Jammu and Kashmir. We even dug trenches behind our dormitory in anticipation of a Pakistani air raid. But to our great disappointment, there were no enemy air raids on Dehradun!

The following years swiftly flew by: I completed my studies during the five years at RIMC, trained at National Defence Academy (NDA), Khadakwasla for three years and at Indian Military Academy (IMA) for one year. Before I knew, it was 20 December 1970 and the day of the Passing-Out-Parade. As the Senior Under Officer (SUO) of Sinhgarh Company, I led the Gentlemen Cadets (GCs) marching smartly past the saluting base.

SUOs Achal Khullar, Virendra Singh and Jasbir Singh slow march into Chetwode Hall on the morning of 20 December 1970

We saluted the Chief Guest and formed up in a quadrangle for the Presentation Ceremony. After the Sword of Honour had been presented to SUO Swapan Bhadra, we listened to the Chief Guest's address. After that, we slow-marched in rows of three cadets and passed into Chetwode Hall. Once we were inside the hallowed building, we loosened up and congratulated one another as big smiles lit up our faces. Our training period was finally over! We returned our swords to the armoury or *kote* for the last time and walked joyously back to our Company lines. Soon it was evening and we were now in the pristine Chetwode Hall for our 'Pipping Ceremony', smartly dressed in 'blue patrols'. On entering the hallowed Chetwode Hall, I was overcome by a wave of nostalgia. Barely a few months back I had been slugging it out in the floodlit boxing ring in the heavy-weight finals bout with G. C. Mudenda from Nigeria. A heavy roar of cheers from the GCs had filled the hallowed building.

With my parents and sisters (L to R), at Chetwode Hall on night of 20 December 1970
I am wearing a star on my shoulder for the first time

At midnight, the lights were put out and our parents removed the piece of cloth covering our epaulettes, revealing a gleaming star on each shoulder. The lights came on and the IMA's Brass Band struck up a lively and deep throated rendition of the merry tune titled 'Congratulations'. I was very happy indeed as I had been posted to 4 Kumaon that was fighting rebel insurgents in Nagaland in the north-east of India, near the border with Burma. I left my parents side and walked across to congratulate my friends Pradeep Khanna, 'Mota' Madhok, D. K. Das and many of the others. There was laughter, excited chatter and great gaiety all around us. We would soon be beginning new lives as adults and officers of the Indian Army! What did the future hold?

After a short vacation at the family farm, I took a train to Lucknow and boarded the Assam Mail.[1] At Lucknow Railway Station I met my friend D. K. Das, a coursemate from RIMC, NDA, IMA (same Company) and now commissioned and posted to 12 Kumaon, striding rapidly towards me. He was smartly dressed in a starched, OG uniform bearing a solitary star. On his head he wore a khaki peaked cap with the Kumaon Lion crest. His formal attire, complete with a regimental baton tucked formally under his left armpit caused me to burst into a fit of laughter as I hugged and back-slapped him. Ours was a close friendship of nine long years, spanning time at RIMC, NDA and IMA, with warm letters exchanged during our holidays.[2] His unit was also located in the north-east of India and we happily travelled together on the Assam Mail. After two days of journey together, we parted company when I detrained at a small station named Manipur Road (now called Dimapur) and went to the Transit Camp.

On the next day, I boarded the convoy from Dimapur via Zubza to Kohima. At Kohima, I changed convoys at the TCP and boarded the 81 Brigade Convoy to Chakhabama. This was a smaller and faster moving convoy made up of one-tonne trucks and Jongas. I keenly observed the alert protection party from a Gorkha battalion, with great interest. As we drove along the winding hill road to Chakhabama, I noticed the thick jungles on sides of the road and imagined Naga rebels behind every tree! Soon we reached Chakhabama and from the TCP, I rang up the Rear Area of 4 Kumaon and announced my arrival to 2nd Lieutenant B. Singh who took the call. B. Singh was quite a well-known bounder from my Squadron in NDA. He was an officer of the Army Supply Corps on attachment with 4 Kumaon and was presently officiating as the unit's Officer Commanding, Rear at Chakhabama.

I was posted to 'D' Company which was located next to a large Naga village named Sathazumi. The Company Commander was Major D. K. 'Dick' Dhawan. He had won a Sena Medal (SM) for gallantry during the last war with Pakistan (in 1965). Dick would refer to his Sena Medal as the bloody gong! He had me posted to command No. 10 Platoon.

---

[1] In those days, at Barauni Junction the railway line narrowed to 'metre gauge' width and we had transfer to a smaller train. This smaller train was also called Assam Mail.

[2] D. K. Das was later killed by the direct hit of an exploding enemy artillery shell during the India–Pakistan War of 1971, in the 12 Kumaon attack on Akhaura, East Pakistan (Bangladesh)

The senior JCO named Subedar Narain Singh was a slim and wiry man who claimed to have fought in the Battle of Badgam as a 'Boy Company' recruit from Kumaon Regimental Centre (KRC) Ranikhet and served as *sahayak* to Major Somnath Sharma, PVC! Hearing Narain Singh's 'claim to fame' in his own words had left me totally impressed! Later I learnt that Narain Singh was ridiculed by the troops, whenever he mentioned his so-called association with Somnath Sharma. After a few days, we received a message from Major Bharat Singh, 2 IC, that I was required to come to Chazuba to attend our Battle Honour Day (Kangaw Day) celebrations on 7 February 1971. I was also told to be prepared with my speech that would be delivered by me during my dining-in party, on the next day at the Officers' Mess. 'Youngster, concentrate on your plate and take small helpings of food, despite whatever the 2 IC may tell you. If the goddamn chicken flies off your plate remember you are a dead man! Also, don't yap too much during the meal and keep your bloody speech short. Lastly, ensure you top your whiskey glass with a mix of soda and water. Topping the drink with only soda will make you take off like a bloody gas balloon! Also, make certain your turnout is perfect and your shoes are well polished and glittering', my Company Commander had seriously advised me before I left for Chazuba.[3]

Accordingly, my *sahayak* named Bahadur Singh (called Muggoo for short) prepared my clothes carefully for the functions at the Battalion HQ and left Sathazumi by a returning vehicle convoy. On reaching Chazuba, the Battalion HQ location, I met 2nd Lieutenant B. S. Jodha and 2nd Lieutenant M. P. S. Khati who had come for Kangaw Day Celebrations from 'C' Company at Thevopisimi and 'A' Company at Mile 22 Post. There was also that bounder B. Singh, who had come from Chakabama. We were all put up in a longish *basha* above the Officers' Mess.

On the next day (7 February 1971), after a nice and lazy breakfast in Officers' Mess, I went down to flat ground (Basketball Ground and 'Six-a-Side' Hockey Ground) where the Kangaw Day (Battle Honour Day) function was to be held. The celebrations comprised of a variety entertainment programme followed by a lunch *Barakhana*. It all went

[3] Maj. D. K. Dhawan, SM, would similarly advise me nine years later, when the unit was in Dehradun, and I was proceeding to the MES Inspection Bungalow to meet my future father-in-law for the very first time, to ask for his daughter's hand in marriage!

off beautifully well, except for a mischievous prank that had unfortunately backfired! Sepoy Lajja Ram of 'A' Company had dressed himself as an oversized white cock, by stripping off his clothes and pasting white cotton-wool all over his body, to resemble the white feathers of a cock. However, as he was flitting about the gathering and uttering ridiculous grunts to entertain 'A' Company, I saw a jawan rise from the crowd with a lighted match. He placed the lighted match at the back side of the crouching and jocularly gyrating Lajja Ram. The cotton wool had apparently been pasted onto Lajja Ram with some highly combustible glue, for all the cotton wool suddenly burst into bright flames. Lajja Ram let out a piercing yell, straightened up and fled from the ground. However, as he ran the burning cotton wool flared fiercely and Lajja Ram soon looked like an ever increasing and moving 'ball of fire'. I ran with great alacrity and with the help of other jawans we pinned down the yelling fireball and helped to douse the flames.

In the evening I went to the Officers' Mess for my dining-in party. The Officer' Mess was in a large *basha* which had been partitioned to form a largish anteroom and dining room, with a smaller at one end that was called the library. This room had some books placed in two steel cupboards along with a record player and some 33 rpm (long playing–LP), 45 rpm and 78 rpm (highly breakable Bakelite) records and the green coloured No. 5-A telephone set or leather cased No. 88 field telephone set. The telephone set was the Adjutant's (Major B. K. Sharma's and later Captain Satyevir Yadav's) exclusive domain! They would invariably be found speaking to the Company Commanders Majors Yeshwant Bisht, D. K. Dhawan, I. D. Khare, V. K. Madra and Captain B. S. Jodha at quaint sounding places such as 22 Post, Sathazumi, Dihoma, Awahumi and Thevopisimi. Later, when Major D. P. S. Raghuvanshi relieved Major K. Bharat Singh[4] as the 2 IC in June 1971, he would invariably be found here forever ready to play the LP record of songs by his favourite singer Begum Akthar (referred by him as Akhtari Bai).

Legendary Mess Waiters Sher Singh and Laccham Singh[5] served

---

[4] He was the son of Brigadier Aapji Randhir Singh, an old officer of the Battalion who had the singular honour of winning the Gold Medal and five sports Blues during his training period at Royal Military Academy, Sandhurst, UK.

[5] The third Mess Waiter named Pillay was away on ERE posting.

the officers in the unit and kept the Officers' Mess in a 'tip-top condition' with the silver trophies always shinning bright. They had a great amount of compassion for the junior officers, and would actually act as their surrogate mothers and feed them up when they returned from jungle operations!

In the evening I dressed up, rehearsed my speech and went down to the Officers' Mess. All the officers were already present in the anteroom. As I entered the Mess, the unit pipe band struck up a racy tune. Lieutenant Colonel Lakha Singh, CO, stepped forward, twirled his moustaches, gave a laugh[6] shook my hand and whispered 'welcome'. Then the waiting YOs took over the situation and plied me with an unending supply of whisky! This was followed each time by the omnipresent waiter Lachham Singh putting forward a silver-plated tray containing small jugs of soda and water. The YOs energetically continued their act all evening under the watchful gaze of Sher Singh. This continued till the smartly dressed Mess Havildar brusquely strode up to CO, halted noisily and announced in a loud voice, '*Shriman, bhojan taiyyar hai!*' At that, one of the YOs who had his back to CO announced in a stage whisper, '*Toh, hum bhi taiyyar hain!*'

We took our seats at the table. I was seated at the dining table wedged between the CO and 2IC. While walking to the table, I had been accosted by Sher Singh who asked me softly if I still remembered my speech after the rounds of drinks I had been made to consume? With a crafty smile I had nodded to silently assure him that all was well. Satisfied that I was fine, Sher Singh had disappeared into the kitchen to help carry the mugs of steaming hot soup to the table. The dinner went off well as there was little conversation and I ensured that I concentrated on the frugal bits of food I had placed on my dinner plate. Soon it was time for the CO to make a 'welcome speech'. He embarrassingly gave out some of my supposed virtues and wished me luck. I then had to take permission to 'say a few words' and quickly gave out the short speech I had prepared so well. After the speeches were over, the band played merrily while I was ushered to the small table with the small Field Area Visitor's Book by Major Bharat Singh and the Senior Subaltern. I sat down on the chair next to the table, glad that the Dinner Night was

[6] The CO was known to laugh in phases, that increased in volume!

nearly over.

On finding the book on the table before me looking familiar, my mind raced back six tumultuous years to my days in Kashmir in January 1965. I distinctly remembered my visit to 4 Kumaon Officers' Mess in Trehgam and the CO, Lieutenant Colonel N. A. Salick's words to me, followed by my signing in the Visitors' Book. I turned to the 2 IC and honestly told him that I had already signed in that particular book. On hearing my words, the 2 IC looked down at me with surprise. He shot off a nasty glance at the accompanying Senior Subaltern, to highlight the audacity of a youngster during the dining-in function.

'Sir, I have signed in this Visitor's Book earlier,' said I, to the disbelieving 2IC. Quite exasperated with me, Major Bharat said, 'Well, show me your signatures and be quick about it, youngster!' There was suddenly a heightened interest in the happenings that were taking place around the Visitors' Book table. Out of sheer curiosity Lieutenant Colonel Lakha Singh rose and faced the table. Watching the CO rise, all the other officers too rose from the dining table. Loudly CO asked 2 IC, 'What's happening there, Bharat?' Promptly came Major Bharat Singh's reply, 'This youngster is making a ridiculous statement that he has already signed the Visitors' Book.' Everyone drew closer, while I mumbled noisily and turned back the pages of the Visitor's Book searching for the particular date in January 1965. I clearly remembered having visited the unit during my vacations from RIMC in January 1965. It was before the War, and at that time the unit was located at Trehgam, Kashmir.

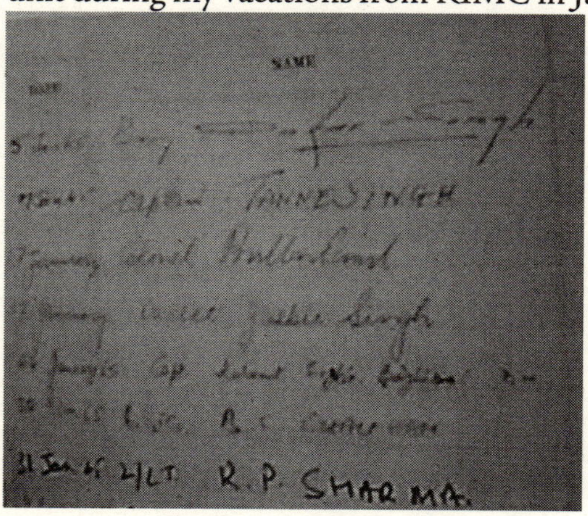

A page of 4 Kumaon Visitors' Book. The 4th name from the top is that of the author, Brig. Jasbir Singh

Suddenly, my face lit up as the desired page was before me and I could recognize my handwriting. 'Here it is Sir!' I tapped on the page a couple of times and looked up triumphantly at the 2IC. All the officers crowded around me to look down at the Visitor Book's page that I was furiously tapping. The hushed sounds of an incredulous 'How is it possible?' filled the air. I happily turned my chair around to face the gathering and narrated the long-forgotten events of that lunch in January 1965, and Salick's great words. After signing my name once again in the book I got up and sat on a chair in the anteroom. The pipe band continued to play happy music outside the and I am certain I saw Mess Waiter Sher Singh frown and shake his head in disdain as he folded a white serviette of *makhan zeen* procured for special Officers' Mess functions, all the way from Guwahati. Earlier having seen my antics around the Field Area Visitors' Book, Sher Singh vehemently shook his head and seemed to say, 'Oh these young officers of 4 Kumaon!